To my Mother & Father —
Sarina & Mardochée
with more love than
any pen can write —
Jacques M. Juven

AMERICAN PSYCHOANALYSIS: ORIGINS AND DEVELOPMENT

The Adolf Meyer Seminars

American Psychoanalysis: Origins and Development

The Adolf Meyer Seminars

Edited by

JACQUES M. QUEN, M.D.

*Clinical Professor of Psychiatry;
Associate Director, Section on the
History of Psychiatry and the Behavioral
Sciences*

and

ERIC T. CARLSON, M.D.

*Clinical Professor of Psychiatry;
Director, Section on the
History of Psychiatry and the Behavioral
Sciences*

New York Hospital - Cornell Medical Center

BRUNNER/MAZEL, *Publishers* • New York

Library of Congress Cataloging in Publication Data

Main entry under title:
American psychoanalysis, origins and development.

A series of seminars, named in honor of A. Meyer, held in 1975-1977 by the Section on the History of Psychiatry and the Behavioral Sciences, Dept. of Psychiatry, New York Hospital-Cornell Medical Center.

Includes bibliographical references and index.
1. Psychoanalysis—United States—History—Congresses. I. Quen, Jacques M.
II. Carlson, Eric T., 1922-   III. Meyer, Adolf, 1866-1950.   IV. New York Hospital-Cornell Medical Center, New York. Section on the History of Psychiatry and the Behavioral Sciences.

RC500.A48   150'.19'50973   78-7040
ISBN 0-87630-176-6

Published by
BRUNNER/MAZEL, INC.
19 Union Square, New York, New York 10003

MANUFACTURED IN THE UNITED STATES OF AMERICA

Introduction

THE SECTION on the History of Psychiatry and the Behavioral Sciences of the Department of Psychiatry of The New York Hospital-Cornell Medical Center was founded in 1958. Members of this Section soon became aware that there was a need for a regular meeting at which members and others having similar interests could present the results of their researches. These sessions have been held for nearly fifteen years and have developed into informal ongoing seminars at which a wide variety of people interested in the history of psychiatry can exchange ideas.

It was not until 1973, when a developmental grant was received from the Josiah Macy Jr. Foundation, that it became possible to launch another type of seminar, a formal series of meetings devoted to one topic. The title of the first series was The Allan McLane Hamilton Seminars, named for the first Professor of Psychiatry at Cornell University Medical College; the theme was "The Historical Development of the Mind-Body Problem."*

In selecting an appropriate topic for a new series of seminars, we felt that it should be pertinent to and explore a problem area of the field of psychiatry where an historical perspective might be useful. After some deliberation we chose the history of American psychoanalysis. A generation ago, psychoanalysis was at its peak; more recently its influence had

---

* Some of these papers will be included in a forthcoming book edited by Dr. Robert W. Rieber entitled *Body and Mind: Past, Present, and Future,* Academic Press, New York.

fallen into decline. We knew that the topic had been explored some time ago in a survey manner by Clarence P. Oberndorf and later in considerable depth by such scholars as John Burnham, Nathan Hale, and Arcangelo R. T. D'Amore. We were interested, however, in providing an overview of the topic and wanted our individual speakers to distill from their considerable knowledge of their given area.

It was an easy matter to decide to name the new series after Adolf Meyer, second professor of psychiatry at Cornell University Medical College (1904-1909). Meyer was undoubtedly one of the leading American psychiatrists in the first half of the twentieth century, achieving his mature fame and reputation while serving as Professor of Psychiatry at the Johns Hopkins University Medical School and the head of the Phipps Psychiatric Clinic. He was a man of great intellect and far-reaching curiosity, and became interested in psychoanalysis in its very early stages. This interest led him to become one of the founding members of the American Psychoanalytic Association in 1911, and he was still being honored as late as 1937 by being elected a charter member in the Washington Psychoanalytic Society. Although Meyer never had any analytic training and remained considerably sceptical about some aspects of psychoanalysis, he was impressed by what it could contribute to treatment, research, and knowledge in psychiatry. Meyer has sometimes been presented as being anti-psychoanalytic. This judgment is probably unwarranted. He never accepted analysis as a total answer and always retained the right to ask searching questions, but otherwise did much to support and encourage its development in the United States. In fact, he was responsible for blocking the 1919 move to eliminate the American Psychoanalytic Association by merging it with the American Psychopathological Association.

Perhaps more than that of any other science or clinical discipline, the history of psychoanalysis in America has been as much a product of social, interpersonal, and intraprofessional political forces as it has been a product of the state of knowledge of the art/science. The Adolf Meyer Seminar Series is an attempt to reevaluate that history from the perspectives of professional historians, psychiatrist-historians, and participants in the events that have become history. The authors represent not only different professional backgrounds but different "schools" of psychoanalysis as well. They may not agree on their understanding or interpretation of past or current events, but they all share a genuine concern for increased understanding of the historical forces that have led American psychoanalysis to its present uncertain status.

Hannah Decker, a former Research Fellow and then Clinical Instructor of the Section on the History of Psychiatry and the Behavioral Sciences, provides a reliable and authoritative perspective on the European culture in which psychoanalysis was conceived and nurtured; Barbara Sicherman presents an analysis of the American soil to which a shoot was transplanted; Dorothy Ross, a former Research Fellow of the Section, describes the often neglected contributions of two academic psychologists who played vital roles in this propagation; and John Burnham assesses the factors that exerted a major influence on its early decades in this country.

Samuel Atkin, Donald Burnham, and George Pollock present the histories of their respective institutes and societies, each different in origin, course, and philosophy—and each a major force in shaping the development of American Psychoanalysis.

Marianne Horney Eckardt provides a sensitive and perceptive analysis of the history of groups individuating out of the New York Psychoanalytic Institute and Society, contrasting the history of the "unorthodox" neo-Freudian groups (Karen Horney Institute, Psychoanalytic Division of New York Medical College, and the William Alanson White Institute) and the idiosyncratic (i.e., neither orthodox nor unorthodox) Columbia Psychoanalytic Clinic. Arcangelo D'Amore presents a broad overview of the last fifty years in the discipline, providing the more recent historical basis for the optimisms and the concerns about the present viability of psychoanalysis.

Roger Shapiro undertakes the herculean task of comparing three contemporary competing psychoanalytic approaches, those of the British Object Relations school, Erik Erikson, and Harry Stack Sullivan, in their relations to ego psychology. He does so with a unique and refreshing original focus on their important similarities, with their differences serving as indicators for later investigation. Finally, Earl Witenberg and Arnold Cooper, psychoanalytic educators from the two national psychoanalytic organizations, provide their views on the likely future of psychonaalysis. Here, too, the similarities appear to be far more significant than the differences.

All those who participated in the Adolf Meyer Seminar Series are agreed that history has much to teach us. Assuredly there is a great deal to be learned from the pages that follow. While it is our hope that psychoanalytic educators, students, and practitioners will make use of this material, we believe that it has importance, as well, for the broader audience of those who are concerned with understanding a significant determinant of the American culture in the twentieth century.

ACKNOWLEDGMENTS

We are indebted to the Josiah Macy Jr. Foundation for the support that made this series possible. When the developmental grant came to an end on June 30, 1976, the Department of Psychiatry provided support for the final lectures in the series. For this we are indebted to our Chairman, Dr. Robert Michels, and the Director of Education, Dr. Arnold Cooper. Thanks are particularly due to Ms. Marilyn Kerr for her cheerful, generous, and substantial contributions to the successful realization of the seminar series and this book.

JACQUES M. QUEN, M.D.
ERIC T. CARLSON, M.D.

Contents

AMERICAN PSYCHOANALYSIS: ORIGINS AND DEVELOPMENT

The Adolf Meyer Seminars

CHAPTER 1

Psychoanalysis and the Europeans

Hannah S. Decker, Ph.D.

IT WAS "CHARACTERISTIC" of the United States, Freud wrote in January 1914, that "from the beginning professors and superintendents of mental hospitals showed [an] interest in analysis." And that was "precisely [the] reason," he declared ungratefully, why America must not "be the scene of the decisive struggle over psycho-analysis." Rather the future development of his discovery should unfold in "the ancient centres of culture, where the greatest resistance has been displayed" (1).

Seven months later, the guns of August tolled ominously for the culture of Europe, though the official death knell did not sound for twenty years. Of course there was to be a renaissance after the Second World War. But by then it was clear that the decisive battles concerning psychoanalysis *would* take place in our country. Freud had long been aware that this would be the case, but his embitterment over the reality persisted until his death in 1939.

I am here today to investigate with you the course of psychoanalysis as it evolved from being predominantly European to being predominantly American. To understand this transition, I would like to ask and answer three major questions:

Presented October 2, 1975. Hannah S. Decker is Assistant Professor, Department of History, University of Houston, Hosuton, Texas.

1

1. What were the conditions of the European reaction to psychoanalysis?

2. To what extent did the American reaction share these conditions and how did it differ?

3. And what did European psychoanalysis give to American psychoanalysis, so that no matter what indigenous American influences there were and are, American psychoanalysis remains permanently affected by its European origins?

In January 1914 Freud spoke of the "resistance" to psychoanalysis. This was not the first nor was it to be the last time he stressed the hostility or rejection he and his ideas encountered in Europe. His accounts of the history of psychoanalysis and Ernest Jones' authoritative biography of Freud have enshrined numerous stories of Freud's "splendid isolation" and of the revulsion and enmity psychoanalysis evoked: Freud cut dead on the streets of Vienna; Freud rejected by his professional colleagues; Freud's works the victim of unintelligent or scurrilous reviews; Freud's colleagues fired from jobs or denied advancement; the findings of psychoanalysis heatedly denounced at medical meetings. These are the commonplaces of the early history of psychoanalysis as told mainly by Freud and Jones. But scholars since the publication of Jones' biography (and in some cases even before) have made some very important discoveries. The first is that although Freud was a radical innovator in psychology, psychoanalysis is a body of ideas for which the times were ready if one examines the preoccupations of avant-garde philosophical, literary, and artistic figures whose work was contemporaneous with Freud's. The second is that the perception of events by Freud and other early analysts was influenced by intellectual biases, emotional reactions, and unrealistic expectations which often affected their judgment of the initial response to psychoanalysis. The third is that Freud and other early analysts simply were not aware of the wide range of reactions to psychoanalysis and often did not know the extent to which psychoanalysis was acknowledged and welcomed (2).

Freud and Jones repeatedly stressed a trio of circumstances which they felt ultimately explained all reactions to psychoanalysis: Victorian sexual morality, anti-Semitism, and the neurotic resistances of critics whose fears had been aroused by Freud's theories. To be sure, all three factors were influential in the reception of psychoanalysis. There is no doubt that the middle classes were trained to consider any open display or acknowledgment of sexuality disgraceful. There was a great amount of unconscious sexual repression and of conscious suppression. Broaching the topic of sexuality aroused anxiety, guilt, shame, or disgust. Freud's first German pupil to open a medical practice in Berlin soon found that "it is the tendency of our time to conceal as much as possible anything to do with sex. Sordid or calculating motives are attributed to the person who dares to speak freely and openly about sexual life" (3).

Moreover, anti-Semitism in new racial dress was on the increase in Vienna after 1873 and in the rest of western Europe after 1890. This prejudice did retard the careers of some Jewish psychoanalysts. Karl Abraham's attempt to secure a university appointment without making a nominal Christian confession is a good case in point.

As for the critics' animosity attributable to their personal neuroses, evidence for that exists too. One of the early reviews of *Studies on Hysteria* was written by Adolf von Strümpell, the famous neurologist, whose textbook of medicine went into twenty-eight editions. The review was a lengthy, judicious, and often complimentary appraisal by a man who believed in the psychogenic nature of hysterical phenomena. But three consecutive sentences, each repeating a form of the verb "to penetrate" are indicative of the uneasiness that Freud's sexual theories aroused in Strümpell.

> This cathartic procedure demands, as the authors themselves emphasize, a penetrating investigation into the smallest details of the patients' private relationships and experiences. I do not know whether under all circumstances one should permit the most high-principled physician such a penetration into the most intimate private affairs. I find most questionable this penetration when it is a matter of sexual relations, and the authors repeatedly emphasize that it often concerns such things (4).

Another example of the influence of personal neurosis is the gradual change in the opinions of Herman Oppenheim, as equally famous a neurologist as Strümpell, who began by appreciating and ended by denouncing psychoanalysis. Oppenheim supposedly suffered from anxiety attacks and his wife was a hysteric (5).

Yet when all the sexual prejudice, anti-Semitism, and personal neurosis are added up they offer only a partial explanation of the reception of psychoanalysis in Europe. Psychoanalysis was not inimical to the

European spirit seventy-five years ago. Recognition of "subconscious" or "unconscious" elements in the mind formed an intrinsic part of the philosophy of Bergson, Croce, Dilthey, James, and Nietzsche. The stories, novels, and poetry of Hofmannsthal, Proust, Rilke, Schnitzler, and Zweig clearly displayed the complex and often unknown motivations that underlie most actions and thoughts. Impressionist musicians showed a decreased interest in the order and form that had previously characterized Western music in order to admit less disciplined tonal patterns. Debussy —and Strauss, too—wished to express the strong surges of feeling which continually broke the surface of "ordinary" life. So did the post-Impressionist painters who were impelled to use bolder and novel color combinations and to move away from representational art.

Additionally, at the turn of the century, psychoanalysis did not stand alone in its pursuit of sexual knowledge. Freud lived in an era in which several movements and individuals explicitly sought changes in sexual customs, though this was an endeavor that psychoanalysis only implicitly supported. Public attitudes about sexuality were being slowly changed as more and more sexual subjects were dealt with openly: the laws regarding homosexuality and sexual offenses; venereal diseases; illegitimacy; prostitution; contraception; sex education. Serious adult books on sexual life went through many editions. A tremendous debate raged in medical and lay periodicals before World War I over whether sex education for children was good or bad. More privately, among doctors and a good many patients, there was a great concern with contraception. The birth control movement had gathered momentum in the nineteenth century. Now that contraception was more highly regarded, the limited methods of achieving it were taxed to their utmost. Regular reliance on coitus interruptus and masturbation was regarded by many doctors, including Freud, as dangerous. Freud wrote pathetically to his friend Wilhelm Fliess, an otolaryngologist, begging Fliess to hurry up with his work on the periodicity of the female fertility cycle (6): the Freuds, after five children in six years, needed the information badly. The dilemma was great; the problem was becoming so widespread that it was soon to be discussed openly. In 1911 there was an international birth control conference in Dresden.

Freud's *Three Essays on the Theory of Sexuality* (1905) was original and profound, but it did not stand alone in its avowal of the importance of sexuality. One of the most telling indications that the concerns of psychoanalysis were a part of the European *Zeitgeist*, and not just Freud's

personal preoccupation, was the simultaneous appearance of Expressionist drama (c. 1912-1924). Some of Freud's famous case histories, particularly those of "Dora," the "Rat Man," and the "Wolf Man" could have
easily provided the core (plus a great many deatils) for the plays of the
Expressionists and their predecessors, Wedekind and Strindberg. Freud's
case histories, of course, were not meant to be judgmental; only rarely,
and then in other contexts, did Freud explicitly express his feelings about
the familial and social consequences of individual neuroses and about
the part played by social mores in producing the neuroses that shattered
individual lives. Only occasionally and tentatively did Freud ally himself
with reformers for a new sexual order.

In their dramas, the Expressionists described the same phenomena
which Freud had observed clinically. But the Expressionists were social
crusaders who directly attacked both the repression and hypocrisy of the
times. Expressionism savagely exposed the sham in the relations between all human beings, unambiguously depicting the resulting horrors.
No one and nothing was left out: parents and teachers ruined the lives
of children and students; wives destroyed the sanity of their husbands;
men and women, friend and friend were disloyal, capricious, vengeful.
The plays of Frank Wedekind (1864-1918) announced the movement well
before it had any coherence or definition. In 1891, Wedekind's *Spring's
Awakening* portrayed parental insensitivity to adolescent sexuality and
the abysmal failure of sex education. To the dramatist the result was
inevitable: suicide. Other of Wedekind's plays dealt with bizarre sado-
masochistic relationships; murder; murders that appeared as suicides;
prostitution; grotesque marital relationships. Rationality seemed to have
vanished, as brutal and horrible ideas were matter-of-factly expressed
by one character only to be quickly adopted by another. Human sexuality, in all its forms, was never hidden. In bourgeois society, Wedekind felt, people were always hiding their desires. In his plays, all the
characters acted on their desires.

The other precursor of Expressionist drama was August Strindberg
(1849-1912) whose *On the Road to Damascus* (1898-1901) stands out as
a sign of his revolt against the photographic Naturalism that was dominant at the end of the nineteenth century.

Expressionist drama began to blossom in the years immediately pre-
ceding World War I. The first "pure" representative of the genre is
probably R. J. Sorge's *The Beggar* of 1912. In place of the individual
persons of the Naturalists' drama, the Expressionists used human "types":

the father, the son, the woman, the mother, the beggar. The Expressionists' speech had a loosened form. Purely logical words—articles, conjunctions—were eliminated; strict grammar was ignored. Scenes followed upon one another in a dazzlingly quick array. Emotions were never controlled, but expressed vividly, sharply, ecstatically. The stage sets were not realistic but symbolic. Always the world of the father, with its hypocritical morality and order, was under attack. The recurrent father-son conflict was emphasized.

The independent but simultaneous appearance of Expressionism and psychoanalysis is significant. They stressed similar themes. Human sexuality was ubiquitous. People (unconsciously or consciously) felt one thing, but said or did another. In all of us there were savage, primitive forces. Deep, keenly felt emotions governed our acts. The son always tried to overthrow the father; the daughter always tried to replace her mother. Symbols were constantly employed in human expression, both while awake and in dreams. There was a "primary process," an irrational thought patterning that eschewed logical transitions and reasoned steps. Each human being shared a common psychic development: what was true for one "son" was true for all sons.

Clearly, in the broad cultural sense, Freud was not in "splendid isolation." It is true that psychoanalysis was not in the mainstream of late nineteenth and early twentieth century organically-oriented medicine and psychology, and Freud recognized that these fields did not share his outlook. He predicted with uncanny accuracy the reception that scientists and physicians—as opposed to lay intellectuals—would give his *Interpretation of Dreams*. "There can be no doubt," he wrote in the opening chapter,

> that the psychical achievement of dreams received readier and warmer recognition during the intellectual period which has now been left behind, when the human mind was dominated by philosophy and not by the exact natural sciences. . . . The introduction of the scientific mode of thought has brought along with it a reaction in the estimation of dreams. Medical writers in especial tend to regard psychical activity in dreams as trivial and valueless; while philosophers and non-professional observers—amateur psychologists — . . . have . . . retained a belief in the psychical value of dreams. Anyone who is inclined to take a low view of psychical functioning in dreams will naturally prefer to assign their source to somatic stimulation . . . (7).

But Freud did much by his own actions to isolate himself from potential followers. As early as 1899 he wrote to Fliess:

> I have given up my lectures this year in spite of numerous enrollments, and do not propose to resume them in the immediate future. I have the same horror of the uncritical adulation of the very young that I used to have for the hostility of their elders. Also the whole thing is not ripe yet—*novum prematur in annum!* Pupils *a la* Gattl [sic: he meant Felix Gattel] are to be had for the asking; as a rule they end by asking to become patients themselves (8).

Freud was a compelling speaker, lecturing clearly and logically without notes. When he did resume his lectures, he was very popular, though a contemporary observer recorded that Freud was reluctant to have personal contacts with his students. Moreover, students at the University of Vienna, unless they were simultaneously at work in the Psychiatric Clinic, needed Freud's permission to attend his lectures. This was an uncommon restriction among European professors (9).

A good example of Freud's idiosyncratic attitudes concerning publicizing his work occurred four months after the publication of *The Interpretation of Dreams*. Having learned from his friend Fliess that a leading intellectual periodical, the *Neue Rundschau,* had decided not to review the book, Freud rebelled against Fliess' suggestion that he write an article about it as an alternative to its being reviewed. He wrote Fliess that he had five reasons for not submitting such an article, the fifth obviously being the emotional reaction of a man hurt by rejection:

> I want to avoid anything that savours of advertisement. I know that my work is odious to most people. So long as I behave perfectly correctly, my opponents are at a loss. If I once start doing the same as they do, they will regain their confidence that my work is no better than theirs. . . . So I think the most advisable course is quietly to accept the *Rundschau's* refusal as an incontrovertible sign of public opinion (10).

As we well know, authors are not always so prideful, and their desire to spread their ideas is not usually held against them. But Freud seemed more concerned with "correct" behavior before his medical colleagues than in convincing a generally educated audience. "Odious" was certainly not to be the response in lay periodicals to psychoanalytic dream theories. And equally certainly, publication in the *Rundschau* was not seeking a mass audience of the commonest denominator.

At any rate, Freud bears a small measure of responsibility for the fact that five years later the *Rundschau* published a laudatory article hailing the significance of Freud's work on dreams, but with nary a mention of his name (11). Without question, the author, Jentsch, was referring to Freud's work. The clearest proofs of this are Jentsch's acknowledgment that dreams are the fulfillment of wishes (p. 882) and his entitling his article *"Traumarbeit"*—Freud's very own phrase for the dream mechanisms he had discovered. Jentsch praised the dream studies and interpretations as being "serious . . . scientific . . . legitimate and rational." The work had been carried out with "virtuosity and acumen." He envisioned that the studies would probably lead to the "important, practical elucidation of both general and specific psychological theories about people."

The kinds and the timing of reviews of Freud's works rarely satisfied Freud. In this he was a victim of his own unrealistic expectations as well as of the novelty of the behavioral sciences at the turn of the century. Freud (and Jones, too), convinced of the greatness of his discoveries, considered as acceptable only those reviews that might best be described as adulatory. The careful, sober, or probing critiques which frequently appeared were designated as "uncomprehending," "base," or "disgraceful." Freud agonized over what seemed lengthy intervals between the publication of a work and its reviews. Just six weeks after the publication of his dream book, Freud began to complain to Fliess about the quality and quantity of his notices. He wrote to Fliess on December 21, January 8, January 26, March 11, March 23, May 7, May 16, June 12, and July 10 to "bewail [the] fate" of the book. The last mention of the subject was confined to a postscript in a letter of October 14 which simply announced that the book had been reviewed in the *Münchner Allgemeine Zeitung*. Freud did not bother to elaborate that the review was enthusiastic and appreciative (12).

I have studied the time that elapsed between publication and review of the works of other authors which were reviewed in the same journals as were Freud's. Freud suffered no discrimination in this regard. Ilse Bry and Alfred Rifkin have also investigated the attention that was paid to Freud's earliest publications. Not only did they find appreciative reviews that Jones' biography never mentioned, but they pointed out that Freud's works faced a unique difficulty in securing reviews in the professional journals. Because of the wide scope of Freud's subject matter, as well as its novel combinations, it properly belonged in very few journals of the day. Though interdisciplinary journals had already ap-

peared at the turn of the century, they were still few in number. Psychoanalysis was a pioneering discipline, and Freud was the founder of one
of the new behavioral sciences. Accordingly, Freud's works received less
publicity than they would have if there had been adequate vehicles for
their review.

Particularly with *The Interpretation of Dreams* Freud

> unwittingly experienced early significant clashes between the evolv-
> ing behavioral sciences and the tradition-bound structure available
> in the organization of science. . . . *The Interpretation of Dreams* was
> reviewed in nonmedical journals because the topic was not suitable
> for the medical review literature. The essay *On Dreams,* however,
> was reviewed in medical and psychiatric journals because it ap-
> peared in a series with the word "nervous" in its title (13).

The reactions of Freud to his reviews were matched by Jones' reactions to medical meetings where psychoanalysis was discussed. Let me
recount one incident which will not only illustrate this point, but will
also tell you something about the problems psychoanalysis encountered
in the German psychiatric community.

On December 14, 1907, the Berlin Psychiatric Society was treated to
its first psychoanalytic paper by Otto Juliusburger, who reported on two
cases he had treated with the psychoanalytic method (14). One case was
that of a twenty-two-year-old girl who was a compulsive jewelry thief.
Juliusburger traced the etiology of her kleptomania to a seduction at
five years of age and to a sensual arousal at six years connected with
gold and precious jewels. Juliusburger pointed out that through the
use of psychoanalysis one could see that the girl was reliving her past
by her stealing.

In the discussion immediately following, Theodor Ziehen (Chief of
Psychiatry at the University of Berlin) and Hugo Liepmann (a well-
known neuropathologist at the Berlin suburban hospital of Dalldorf)
were unimpressed and mildly critical. They both regarded the case as an
example of fetishism, "interesting, but not so rare," as Ziehen said.
Ziehen acknowledged that in such cases both conscious and unconscious
associations apply. Liepmann, however, could not understand why the
Freudian method was at all necessary in this case. The etiological childhood incidents were both conscious. No repressed sexual experience
lying in the unconscious was involved. Liepmann sought to diminish
Freud's contribution by pointing out that the "formative" role of youth-

ful sexual experiences was commonly recognized in certain circumstances. This "formative" role, however, was not the same as Freud's "original, sensational" theory in which these experiences are supposed to be the "cause" of illness. Certainly, Liepmann admitted, sexuality plays just as enormous a role in pathological individuals as in normal persons. But that was known before Freud. On the other hand, "it should be recognized that as a result of his work, in spite of its many exaggerations, insight into the more sensitive and secret connections between the pathologic and the erotic has been sharpened" (15).

Two other physicians were eager to point out the similarity of their experiences and Juliusburger's, even though they said the situations were not identical. A Dr. Schuster reported a case like Juliusburger's but said that it had not even been necessary for him to use the method Juliusburger had described. The patient had spontaneously explained that she believed her symptoms could be traced back to a sexually arousing childhood experience of watching other girls being physically punished at school.

Dr. Paul Bernhardt, who worked under Liepmann at Dalldorf, reported that he tried to get to the unconscious roots of mental illness through the use of Freud's theories. He had not yet succeeded but he still did not think it "wholly improbable" that one could do so. What he wished to make known that night, however, was that "a few years ago" he had observed "proof for one of Freud's basic ideas, i.e., for the conversion of sexual excitation into anxiety." Bernhardt had been unable to discover the unconscious childhood derivatives for his patient's hysterical symptoms (roaring in the ears, weakness, inability to work). But the patient herself had told Bernhardt that she suffered her symptoms when she could not satisfy her sexual feelings which were aroused when she was angry. The patient traced her hysteria back to the time when she had to hold back the anger she wished to express against her relatives when they excluded her on account of her fiancé. "The woman herself told me," concluded Bernhardt, "that since she didn't let out the anger then, it was still stuck in her" (16).

The response of these Berlin psychiatrists to Juliusburger's paper offers some valuable insight into the medical reception of psychoanalytic methods as well as psychoanalysis in general. First, Freud's method was obviously more difficult to accept than his theories. Physicians did recognize the sexual significance of early childhood events. But they questioned whether psychoanalytic techniques were necessary to uncover them.

Second, opposition was rarely total. Liepmann's comments illustrate that he did not understand Freud's theories very well. But though he was critical of what he considered their overly broad application, he still praised Freud for having sharpened the insight of his colleagues into the connection between pathology and sexuality.

Third, physicians were not always afraid to state their agreement with aspects of psychoanalysis, and such agreement did not necessarily result in damage to one's career. Paul Bernhardt was Liepmann's assistant at Dalldorf but publicly disagreed with his superior. Juliusburger, an open Freudian, continued a profitable professional association with the famous Swiss psychiatrist Forel, whose enmity to psychoanalysis is well-known. The year after the Berlin meeting, Juliusburger and Forel collaborated on a paper for the *Zeitschrift für Sexualwissenschraft* on germ cell degeneration. Forel was a leader in the temperance movement, and in 1904 he had written the introduction to a short book on alcoholism by Juliusburger. Perhaps their common great interest in alcoholism overrode their divergent views about psychoanalysis.

Fourth, as is common, the psychoanalytic literature has misleadingly labeled Juliusburger's reception. Obviously Juliusburger's paper did not not encounter the "unanimous opposition" Ernst Jones unaccountably reported (17).

I think that, in many respects, early psychoanalysis shared similar problems of acceptance in both Europe and America, although I do believe there were some important differences, which I shall consider. In both the Old and New Worlds, a medical theory that relied primarily on psycho-etiologic explanations of illness was bound to face resistance. Medicine in the late nineteenth and early twentieth centuries was materialistic and everywhere in the West had a strongly organic basis. "Science" as then defined was enshrined in the dissecting rooms, operating theaters, and laboratories of Western physicians and psychologists. The Cartesian dualism of knowledge, which separated mind from body, was a strong intellectual force, carried forward in the indigenous philosophic concerns of the various Western nations. Indeed, Freud was striking a revolutionary blow in asking scientists, physicians, psychologists, and philosophers to accept a monistic view of mental health and illness. Freud said there was no sharp dichotomy between emotionally healthy and sick individuals. All human beings shared a common psychosexual development. This view was especially distasteful to the European class-conscious, bourgeois physician and scientist who saw the world neatly—and inevitably—divided into "we" and "them": the rich and the poor, the healthy and the sick, the doctor and the patient. The democratic ethos in our country militated against this view somewhat, but in actual practice not very strongly.

I think we can discern cultural differences between Europe and America in three areas:

1. The strictly established channels for the dissemination of scientific information in Europe, especially the importance of high-level academic approval, retarded the spread and acceptance of psychoanalysis.

2. The greater European stress on "nature" in the "nurture-nature" controversy fueled a strong general pessimism about the likelihood of change and the physician's ability to affect the course of illness. There was widespread medical and lay belief that mental disturbance occurred as the result of a tendency towards "degeneracy" or "hereditary taint." The French psychiatrist Morel, although originally interested in the emotional life of his patients, had become convinced that mental illness was the result of hereditary weakness. In 1857 he proposed a precise method for discovering the great variety of physical, intellectual, and moral "stigmata" which indicated "degeneration." Pierre Janet also favored "hereditary neuropathic predisposition" as an etiological explanation of mental illness; so did the German physicians Otto Binswanger, P. J. Möbius, Albert Moll, Emil Kraepelin, and Albert von Schrenck-Notzing. While some American psychiatrists and neurologists also believed in theories of degeneration, this belief was not sustained at the high pitch that it was in Europe, where it was common to feel that European civilization was decadent.

Though the United States boasted a Social Darwinist movement as vigorous as that in Europe, it also had a strong reaction against Social Darwinism, as exemplified in the Harvard Metaphysical Club founded in the early 1870s by Charles Sanders Peirce and attended by William James and Oliver Wendell Holmes. The pragmatist philosophers, social scientists, and reformers were a further outgrowth of a trust in the strength of the environment to temper, if not to conquer, heredity.

The Americans' conviction in their power to change humankind for the better is splendidly exemplified in the opposite reactions of the

Germans and the Americans to Freud's concept of sublimation. The Germans reacted indignantly to Freud's notion that the highest artistic, literary, and religious productions of their civilization could be reduced to something so "base" as sexual or aggressive drives. While the Americans did not enthrone sexuality or aggressivity, the idea that it was possible to convert men's "baser" instincts into "higher" achievements had tremendous appeal, and was one of the chief attractions of psychoanalysis.

3. Marie Jahoda, the social psychologist, has suggested that psychoanalysis had to have a lesser appeal to European societies where acceptance of one's class of origin was still the prevailing ethos. Not that a person could not be ambitious in Europe; but if one tried and failed it was a great deal easier to view one's failure as inevitable and blame it on the faulty social structure. It was not incumbent to look into oneself to discover the causes of failure. There was not as great a demand for the kind of soul-searching upon which psychoanalysis thrives (18). Thus the German physician, psychologist, and later politician, Willy Hellpach, could counter Freud's infantile sexuality theory of the etiology of hysteria with his social theory that a faulty educational system produced "docile" young men who cracked up when faced with the prospect of succeeding in the adult world (19).

I would like to note not only the varying patterns of the reception of psychoanalysis but also its institutionalization based on its European origins. The American manner of training psychoanalysts is modeled very much on the methods developed in Berlin after World War I (20). All training centers today are called "institutes," but the first institute for the teaching of psychoanalysis was founded in conjunction with a low-cost out-patient clinic, and in the early years the stress was on the clinic and public service. Karl Abraham gave the first lecture of a course on the elements of psychoanalysis at the *clinic*, not at an "institute." It was not until February 1922 that the word "institute" was first used at a meeting of the Berlin Psychoanalytic Society, and that was two years after the clinic was officially opened. The word occurred in a discussion of "the instructional activity of the institute of [the] polyclinic." Finally, at the International Psychoanalytic Congress at Salzburg in April 1924, the Berlin analyst Ernst Simmel spoke of the "Berlin Psychoanalytic Institute"—four years after the founding of the out-patient clinic.

In Berlin in the twenties, the lecture courses were open to anyone who wished to attend. All instructors granted admission to anyone who asked permission to attend their classes. Although there were courses meant for physicians and courses for laymen, particularly teachers (21), in practice there was no distinction between professional courses and extension courses; there was no enrollment as a "student" at the institute and no prerequisites were required. The Berlin Society was strongly bent on disseminating information about psychoanalysis to the public and inaugurated a series of radio talks. The Society was partly motivated by the desire to attract patients to the clinic and kept careful count of the number of patients treated annually. Thus, for a number of years, the Berlin group thought of itself basically as a society with an out-patient clinic. This is because teaching had been going on since 1908 in Abraham's apartment and soon afterwards in rented space, so the Society (since 1910) had always offered courses. It was actually the clinic that was new and that served to institutionalize the courses.

This pattern of the founding of an institute in conjunction with a preexisting out-patient clinic was repeated in Vienna, London, Chicago, Frankfurt, and Budapest, and was not broken until 1931 by the New York Psychoanalytic Society. At that time Sandor Rado was specifically brought there to head the new Institute. The "treatment center" of the New York Psychoanalytic Institute was not organized until after World War II. Boston and Baltimore-Washington followed the New York example.

The institute in Berlin also inaugurated all the educational devices now in use in American institutes: the training analysis, supervised or "control" analyses, and case seminars. By 1920, a personal analysis was regular procedure among those who expected to practice psychoanalysis professionally. But it was still up to the individual, and American societies admitted unanalyzed members as late as 1925. The training analysis was originally called by the German title, *Lehranalyse,* and also *didaktische Analyse*. This later became transformed into an English cognate, the "didactic analysis."

Supervised analyses started as common practice in Vienna and Berlin: a younger analyst would ask an older colleague for consultation or advice. At first there were no regulations to cover the number of such analyses, the length of time, or the number of hours now stipulated by the various American institutes. A "control case" or a "control analysis" is another English cognate, deriving from the German word *Kontrolle* which means supervision or inspection and not "control" in the sense of "rule." So a "control analysis" is an analysis done by a candidate supervised by a graduate analyst. Even the word "candidate," used by many institutes to designate students, is an English cognate of the German *Kandidat*. In Germany and Austria, a *Kandidat* is a certain grade of university student, close to receiving the degree.

Case seminars or formal surveys of the psychoanalytic literature were a later addition to the curriculum of the Berlin Institute. Initially students depended mainly on their own reading, which was possible since there was not so much to read.

The era of laissez-faire in psychoanalytic training came to an end by a decree of the Bad Homburg Congress of 1925. This set up the International Training Commission as well as the education committees which eventually would wield great power in the institutes. At Bad Homburg it was decided that "psychoanalytic training could no longer be left to the private initiative of individuals . . . when a candidate presents himself for training . . . the psychoanalytic society of the country in which he lives must collectively make itself responsible for him" (22). Thus, in 1925, the "admission to training" system was started. Each society was asked to appoint its own training or education committee "of not more than seven members." In many places it became the practice that students were admitted to the society upon recommendation by the education committee, there being no formal "graduation."

European psychoanalysis bequeathed much more to the Americans than methods and organizations for training new psychoanalysts. Starting as early as 1909, Freud and his colleagues began to edit their own journals and yearbooks, creating a publishing tradition copied by the Americans. The first university lectureship on psychoanalysis was European, and not American, as is commonly supposed. This was the position held by Sandor Ferenczi in Budapest in 1919. The Americans also seem to have inherited the Europeans' penchant for in-fighting and schisms. One has only to read the Freud-Jung correspondence, published in 1974, to be plunged into a world of Oedipal rivalries truly worthy of the man who so named them. This collection of letters, incidentally, is the first complete and unexpurgated Freud correspondence to be published.

The fights of Freud with Stekel, Adler, Jung, Rank, Ferenczi, and others are well-known. Once Freud decided that a follower had turned into a dissenter, his fundamental tactic was all-out war, and his wrath was ill-concealed. Of Adler, after their break, Freud said to Fritz

Wittels, "I have made a pigmy great." To Abraham, Freud wrote about Adler's "venom and meanness." To Lou Andreas-Salomé he declared that Adler was "a loathsome individual." Hanns Sachs, a devoted disciple to the end, stood in awe of Freud's battle with Adler: "In the execution of this duty he was untiring and unbending, hard and sharp like steel, a 'good hater' close to the limit of vindictiveness" (23).

American psychoanalysts have remained loyal to the litigious inheritance of the founding father. As early as 1933, Ernest Jones wrote to Anna Freud, after a visit to New York, that he thought the New York Psychoanalytic Society was so full of intrigue that psychoanalysis itself was being neglected (24). He was at least right about the personal intrigue. Karen Horney and Sandor Rado were to leave in the early forties, creating two new psychoanalytic havens. The most recent split occurred in Boston as recently as 1974.

Moreover, in the realms of theory and treatment, the Europeans proposed ideas at variance with the Freudian orthodoxy that seemed to appeal to the Americans. Ferenczi was one such European. He held the view that there were no bad children, only bad parents. This was a divergence from Freud's belief that instinctual problems faced by all children led to later neurosis. By 1923 Ferenczi (who analyzed Clara Thompson, who in turn analyzed Harry Stack Sullivan) stressed the importance of current reality in treatment, the interpersonal relations between patient and analyst, and greater activity and involvement on the part of the therapist. The Pandora's box of "classical" versus "nonclassical" analysis was first opened to the Americans by Ferenczi. In 1926 Ferenczi lectured at the New School for Social Research and did a great deal to promote interest in psychoanalysis in America. He also gave classes on treatment techniques for the New York Psychoanalytic Society and conducted some analyses. Back in Europe five years later, Ferenczi was kissing patients and being kissed in return. How far had Ferenczi's influence extended in his New York visit?

Jung also provided enticements for the Americans. American psychiatrists were interested in applying psychoanalytic ideas to the treatment of psychosis as the Swiss were doing. This was a technique about which Freud was quite pessimistic. Jung, like Ferenczi, also wished to pay more attention to the patient's current problems, an approach that continued to appeal to the Americans. And Jung disagreed with Freud's ideas about the value of religion. Very early James Jackson Putnam had expressed the belief of some Americans that religion was a positive and necessary force of men's lives, leading them to be better human beings.

There were European influences and trends the Americans did not have to deal with. Except for brief encounters, they escaped the tarnish of Freud's pessimistic outlook and aloofness. His authoritarian control of the European psychoanalytic movement did not affect them as deeply. Americans did not have the problematic nineteenth century German psychiatric tradition. In the early nineteenth century, German psychiatry had been steeped in mysticism and metaphysics; in the late nineteenth century it was struggling to "modernize" itself. Under such circumstances, psychoanalysis was seen in Germany as a regressive step, pulling psychiatry back into an era of philosophical speculation at best, and prescientific superstition at worst. To the Americans, psychoanalysis may have had its flaws, but there was no doubt that it was "modern." Furthermore, the Americans were never as caught up in the entanglements of the rival European schools. When Harvard wanted to bestow on Freud an honorary doctorate in 1936, Freud was unable to accept for reasons of health. Wasting no time, the commencement committee turned right around and offered the honor to Jung. Freud or Jung, *who* was not crucial. Either way Harvard was assured of having a "psychoanalyst" to display.

To Sigmund Freud there fell the misfortune of disliking the country that was to give psychoanalysis its most widespread acknowledgment. He once joked hollowly: "America is a mistake; a gigantic mistake it is true, but nonetheless a mistake" (25). Freud disliked American food, toilets, manners, sexual mores, lack of culture, alcoholic habits, publishing customs, ideas of sexual equality, women. He wrote that "the contributions to our science from that vast country are exiguous and provide little that is new" (26). Thus, Freud was never able to recognize or take pleasure in his role in a 500-year-old saga: the Europeanization of the world.

The influence of Central European psychoanalysts on psychoanalysis in this country is one of the final chapters of the expansion of Europe that began in the fifteenth century. This influence occurred in two steps. The preliminary one took place in the 1920s when large numbers of American psychiatrists went abroad to study psychoanalysis and to be analyzed at Berlin or Vienna. The major step took place in the 1930s, when large numbers of European psychoanalysts fled the Nazis. In this country they often became leaders in their local societies and institutes and were sought after as training and supervising analysts. Through both routes, American psychoanalysis, American psychiatry, and indeed, all American culture have been deeply affected.

NOTES

1. Sigmund Freud, "On the History of the Psycho-Analytic Movement," *Standard Edition of the Complete Psychological Works of Sigmund Freud* (henceforth *S.E.*) Vol. XIV, p. 32.

2. See Ilse Bry and Alfred Rifkin, "Freud and the History of Ideas: Primary Sources, 1886-1910," *Science and Psychoanalysis*, 1962, Vol. V; Henri Ellenberger, *The Discovery of the Unconscious*, New York: Basic Books, 1970; and my book, *Freud in Germany: Revolution and Reaction in Science*, to be published by International Universities Press. This paper is based on my doctoral dissertation, "The Reception of Psychoanalysis in Germany, 1893-1907," Columbia University, 1971.

3. Felix Gattel, *Ueber die sexuelle Ursachen der Neurasthenie und Angstneurose*, Berlin: Verlag von August Hirschwald, 1898, p. 68.

4. Adolf von Strümpell, Review of Breuer & Freud, *Studien über Hysterie* in *Deutsche Zeitschrift für Nervenheilkunde*, VIII, Dec. 30, 1895, p. 160.

5. Ernest Jones, *The Life and Work of Sigmund Freud*, New York: Basic Books, 1955, Vol. II, p. 114

6. *The Origins of Psychoanalysis. Letters to Wilhelm Fliess, Drafts and Notes: 1887-1902 by Sigmund Freud*, Marie Bonaparte, Anna Freud, Ernst Kris, Eds.; trans. by Eric Mosbacher and James Strachey, New York: Basic Books, 1954, pp. 72, 76, 120.

7. Freud, *The Interpretation of Dreams*, *S.E.*, Vol. IV, pp. 63-64.

8. Freud, *The Origins of Psychoanalysis, op. cit.*, p. 280.

9. Paul Roazen, *Freud and His Followers*, New York: Alfred A. Knopf, 1975, pp. 174-175.

10. Freud, *The Origins of Psychoanalysis, op. cit.*, p. 316.

11. Ernst Jentsch, "Traumarbeit," *Neue Rundschau*, 1905, 16, 875-882.

12. Freud, *The Origins of Psychoanalysis, op. cit.*, pp. 306, 307, 309, 311, 313-314, 323-324, 325.

13. Bry and Rifkin, *op. cit.*, pp. 22-23.

14. Juliusburger, "Zur Lehre von der Psychoanalyse," *Allgemeine Zeitschrift für Psychiatrie*, LXIV, 1907, 1002-8 (discussion, pp. 1008-10) and *Neurologisches Centralblatt*, XXVII, Jan. 16, 1908, 89-90 (summary; discussion, pp. 90-91).

15. *Neurologisches Centralblatt*, 1908, p. 90.

16. *Ibid.*, p. 91.

17. Jones, *op. cit.*, Vol. II, p. 113.

18. Marie Jahoda, "The Migration of Psychoanalysis: Its Impact on American Psychology," *Perspectives in American History*, 1968, Vol. II, pp. 432-33.

19. Willy Hellpach, "Die Hysterie und die moderne Schule," *Internationales Archiv für Schulhygiene*, I, 1905, 222-251.

20. Much of the following is based on Bertram D. Lewin and Helen Ross, *Psychoanalytic Education in the United States*, New York: W. W. Norton, 1960.

21. *A Psycho-Analytic Dialogue. The Letters of Sigmund Freud and Karl Abraham, 1907-1926*, Hilda C. Abraham and Ernst L. Freud, Eds.; transl. by Bernard Marsh and Hilda C. Abraham, New York: Basic Books, 1965, pp. 304, 305, 307, 311, 314, 337, 339, 341.

22. Quoted by Lewin and Ross, *op. cit.*, p. 30.

23. Fritz Wittels, *Sigmund Freud: His Personality, His Teaching, and His School*, trans. by Eden and Cedar Paul, London: George Allen and Unwin Ltd., 1924, p. 225; *A Psycho-Analytic Dialogue, op. cit.*, p. 182; *Sigmund Freud and Lou Andreas-Salomé: Letters*, Ernst Pfeiffer, Ed., trans. by William and Elaine Robson-Scott, London: Hogarth Press, 1972, p. 19; Hanns Sachs, *Freud: Master and Friend*, Cambridge: Harvard University Press, 1945, p. 69.

24. Roazen, *op. cit.*, p. 382.

25. Jones, *op. cit.*, Vol. II, p. 60.

26. Freud, "Introduction to the Special Psychopathology Number of *The Medical Review of Reviews* (1930)," *S.E.*, Vol. XXI, 254.

CHAPTER 2

The New Psychiatry: Medical and Behavioral Science, 1895-1921

Barbara Sicherman, Ph.D.

PSYCHOANALYSIS CAME TO THE UNITED STATES on the crest of a medical psychotherapy movement. In the 1890s, a few neurologists had become interested in the pioneer work on the subconscious by Pierre Janet and Sigmund Freud. James Jackson Putnam, Harvard's first professor of nervous diseases and later Freud's most eminent American convert, endorsed psychic treatment of the psychoneuroses in 1895; he also urged his colleagues to treat the man rather than the disease and to assume responsibility for the patient's moral and social well-being. Yet two decades earlier, Putnam had criticized a fellow neurologist for endorsing "mental therapeutics," a subject he then considered unscientific, ineffective, and deceitful. Putnam's personal odyssey from medical materialism to psychotherapy anticipated the wave of interest in psychic healing that swept the medical profession in the first two decades of the twentieth century (22).

The translation of Paul Dubois' *The Psychic Treatment of Nervous Disorders* in 1905 by William Alanson White and Smith Ely Jelliffe—soon to become Freudians—sparked medical and popular interest in

Presented November 13, 1975. Barbara Sicherman is Editor of *Notable American Women*, Radcliffe College, Cambridge, Massachusetts. Research for this paper was supported in part by a fellowship (MH-18,887) from the National Institute of Mental Health, U.S.P.H.S.

psychoanalysis. The following year, Janet spoke at the opening of Harvard's new medical school, and in 1909 Freud himself made the visit to Clark University that not only launched the psychoanalytic movement in the United States, but also marked his first official recognition. *The Index Medicus* listed "Psychotherapy" as a title in May 1906—its predecessors "Suggestion" and "Hypnosis" had been established in 1903—and in the next fourteen months included 79 articles and 10 books on the topic. Medical societies across the nation debated the various schools of psychotherapy—suggestion, reeducation, persuasion, and of course psychoanalysis. The first psychotherapeutic clinic under the auspices of a medical college was established at Cornell. Morton Prince introduced the first course on psychopathology at Tufts Medical School in 1908, and the same year Putnam delivered public lectures on the psychoneuroses (9, 21, 56).

Psychoanalysis was unquestionably the most radical of the new therapies, and the fact that it received a serious hearing attests to the openness of American medicine and psychiatry. Psychoanalysis did not become a majority movement, but many who were later repelled by its emphasis on sexuality initially viewed it as one of several promising techniques for helping patients with functional nervous complaints. For, as Nathan Hale has demonstrated, the American interpretation of psychoanalysis before 1917 was consistently more optimistic and environmentalist than Freud's. American analysts not only played down the sexual component of psychoanalysis—a popular book on dream interpretation was deemed fit for use "in a young ladies' seminary"—they also considered children more innocent than Freud did and sublimation an elevating, if painful, method of self-improvement (12).

This version of psychoanalysis resonated with prevailing cultural and medical trends in the Progressive era, a period of social and political reform at the beginning of the twentieth century. A new intellectual outlook made physicians and laymen less willing to tolerate disease, poverty, and other evils long considered inevitable. The idea that humans could control their environment, instead of passively submitting to it, was of central importance to men and women of this generation. It provided a rationale for such diverse reforms as the elimination of large trusts, establishment of school hygiene programs, well baby clinics and public playgrounds, and legislated public standards of health and welfare. Physicians supported many of these ventures and cooperated with laymen in the new voluntary health organizations that sprang up after

1904 to eliminate tuberculosis, infant mortality, mental illness, cancer, and venereal diseases (46, 48, 8). Optimism ran so high that some physicians proclaimed disease "largely a removable evil" (67). Americans hoped not just to cure or even to prevent illness, but to enhance the quality of life itself (16).

In this context, psychotherapy and the new developments in psychiatry promised assistance in treating the individual, including the emotional, factors in disease that had acquired greater importance as infectious diseases came under control. The editor of a prominent medical journal declared: "Tuberculosis and cancer may conceivably disappear in the not distant future, but the problems of the individual are just as sure to increase with the development of urban life and the increasing complexities of so-called civilization" (57). The tremendous interest of physicians and even surgeons in psychic healing reflected the changed outlook toward disease and health in psychiatry and medicine. Three developments are of particular importance in understanding the medical setting in which psychoanalysis was introduced:

1. The revolution in psychiatric theory associated with Adolf Meyer, second professor of psychiatry at Cornell University Medical College. More than any other individual, Meyer helped move American psychiatry away from an exclusively neurological to a broadly behavioral model, one that was closely linked to medicine.

2. New therapeutic models that extended the domain of psychiatry. While distinctly medical, they reflected the broad reforming spirit of the Progressive era.

3. New medical interests that gave legitimacy to psychiatry and psychotherapy.

I

American psychiatry as we know it came into being in the first two decades of the twentieth century. New professional structures, theories, and objectives created a specialty beyond the imagination of all but a few visionaries in the nineteenth century. Psychiatry had initially been a medical specialty exclusively concerned with the institutional care of psychotic patients; its practitioners were medical superintendents of asylums and later hospitals. Isolated from the community and the rest of the profession, the superintendents would not even cooperate with specialists in the burgeoning field of neurology who in the 1870s began treating neurotic patients on an out-patient basis and whose research on the brain and nervous system so closely related to their own (14, 52).

Perspectives on mental illness and its treatment were restricted by the somatic orientation of psychiatry and medicine in the late nineteenth century. At a time when a "legitimate" illness needed a certifiably somatic etiology, course, and therapy, those concerned with disorders in which bizarre behavioral symptoms sometimes seemed more fittingly tended by a priest than a physician took no chances. Superintendents in the last third of the century favored rest, drugs, and diet—all designed to minister to the patient's physical condition. John P. Gray, superintendent of the Utica State Lunatic Asylum, expressed relief that such therapies had replaced "moral reasonings and difficult and vexed theological problems" (18). Gray, the first superintendent to appoint a pathologist, further observed that the physician who treated insanity "becomes more and more indifferent to the mental symptoms as expressed in delusions and delusive ideas." Once the physical lesions were removed, he claimed, "we do know that these [mental] states disappear" (19). At a time of overcrowding and small staffs, this approach further encouraged the neglect of hospitalized patients.

By 1921, psychiatry had expanded its subject matter and domain. As defined by E. E. Southard, the influential director of Boston Psychopathic Hospital: "Psychiatry must be conceived to include the minor psychoses, the smallest diseases and the minutest defects of the mind as well as the frank psychoses and the obvious feeble-mindednesses" (53). Psychiatry even had a message for the normal, and some considered the practitioner's chief task "preparation of the individual for successful adaptation for life" (50). Well might psychiatry be considered the "most inclusive of the sciences connected with medicine" (57). A psychiatrist —the term had replaced alienist and medical superintendent—might now work in an outpatient clinic in a general or psychiatric hospital, or in a private office; or in the latter case he would still most likely have been called a neurologist. Some also worked in non-medical settings, including schools, prisons, courts, and industry, where they expected to detect early signs of mental disturbance and—so they hoped—prevent deterioration.

The decision in 1921 to change the name of their professional organization to the American Psychiatric Association—the original title had been in 1844 the Association of Medical Superintendents of American Institutions for the Insane—symbolized the transformation in professional identity. The new name signified that all physicians interested in mental disorders could join. It also reflected the growing interest in the mental or behavioral as distinct from the purely physical aspects of these illnesses. A quarter of a century earlier, the designation "psychiatric association" had seemed "too embarrassing" to employ (3).

The man most responsible for changing the direction of American psychiatry was not even a psychiatrist. Adolf Meyer, who was born in 1866 in Switzerland, arrived in the United States in 1892 with outstanding credentials as a neuropathologist (26). He had studied neurology both in Zurich and with Hughlings Jackson and had completed his thesis on the forebrain in reptiles under the Swiss psychiatrist August Forel.

Perhaps only someone so well schooled in the rigorous laboratory science of neuropathology—and aware of its limitations in solving clinical problems—could have led American psychiatry away from its preoccupation with what Meyer called the "neurologizing fallacy." Temperamentally opposed to dogmatism, Meyer found the American environment personally liberating. His early friendships with humane social reformers, including John Dewey and Julia Lathrop, encouraged his search for new solutions and awareness of the relationship between social environment and mental illness.

Meyer's interest in psychiatry, a profession for which he initially thought himself unsuited, was stimulated by his depressing contacts with the "old psychiatry" in two American institutions for the mentally ill in the 1890s. As pathologist successively at Illinois Eastern Hospital for the Insane at Kankakee and at Worcester State Hospital in Massachusetts, he encountered custodial rather than curative institutions. They were overcrowded, short of medical personnel and, by European standards, too dependent on drugs and mechanical restraint. Meyer at first had little to do with patient care, but he found the scant attention to patients scientifically unsound as well as inhumane. Case records consisted of brief entries in bound books, often separated by hundreds of pages (44, 43). Insisting that staff members take scrupulous care in gathering "all the facts" about each patient, Meyer introduced the "life chart" which he regarded as the central clinical procedure of medicine. Each patient received a thorough interview and physical examination; staff members then discussed the case at several conferences. Meyer insisted that clinical observation take its place with experiment as an instrument of science: "True medical study must begin before the patient

is dead." It was a telling commentary on the failure to correlate pathological research with clinical observation (43). When Meyer moved on
in 1902 to coordinate research for the New York State hospital system,
he transferred the headquarters of the Pathological Institute, which had
been isolated, to the site of Manhattan State Hospital. He also changed
its name to the Psychiatric Institute.

When he turned to clinical problems, Meyer initially found much to
admire in the work of Emil Kraepelin, whose nosology culminated the
descriptive efforts of nineteenth-century psychiatry and brought order to
the vagaries of psychiatric nomenclature. Meyer introduced a modified
version of Kraepelin's system at Worcester in 1897, but later became
convinced that Kraepelin's emphasis on an inevitable cause, course, and
outcome obscured the individual factors in mental illness. Rejecting the
"dogmatism of disease entities," by which patients were "pigeonholed in
one of a limited number of dogmatic classes or 'diseases,'" Meyer believed that Kraepelin's prognosis of almost certain deterioration could
only undermine the search for constructive modes of treatment (41, 36).

Between 1903 and 1910 Meyer published several influential papers on
dementia praecox—his first clinical studies—which led eventually to his
own distinctive theory, "psychobiology." The two essential premises of
this system—"the biological conception of man" and the unity of mind
and body—had informed Meyer's thinking since his student days with
Hughlings Jackson and T. H. Huxley, and were later reinforced by the
work of William James. Evolutionary theory early led him to the conclusion that "all life is reaction, either to stimuli of the outside world or
of the various parts of the organism." From the biological viewpoint,
mind was the supreme instrument for accomplishing man's adaptation to
his environment rather than an automatic function of the brain or a
simple reflex mechanism. Meyer hoped to show that medicine's rejection
of the study of mind was unscientific; he always defined mind as the
"organ of behavior," whose soundness could only be judged by observing
human activity (42).

From this evolutionary perspective, Meyer redefined psychiatry and
mental illness. Adopting the outlook of "natural history," the psychiatrist
became essentially "a user of biography" whose central task was to study
the "whole man interacting with a total environment." In Meyer's view,
the ultimate test of mental well-being was *"adequate or efficient function"*; mental illness was simply the inability of some individuals to perform the activities necessary for a satisfying life in a given environment

(30). The mental—or behavioral—functions of such individuals became more or less severely undermined. "What is vaguely called insanity," Meyer observed, "is really a wide range of greatly differing conditions and diseases all playing havoc with our organ and functions of conduct and behavior" (35).

For the disease concept of Kraepelin, Meyer substituted the view that mental illness was a behavioral disorder. The disease could not be detached from the patient, like so many germs, but was part of his life history. Meyer maintained that individuals who exhibited the same clinical picture had followed similar patterns prior to their illness; certain "reaction types" tended toward the same forms of mental illness (40, 30). Unable to respond directly to their circumstances, such individuals resorted to "substitutive" forms of behavior which became "harmful and uncontrollable" (33).

What caused the deterioration in a given individual? Meyer considered this the central question for psychiatric research. In an effort to answer it, he developed a new approach to "pathology" which differed fundamentally from the pathology of brain lesions. In Meyer's view, pathology was the study of the conditions under which all abnormal changes— mental and physical—occurred, how the changes manifested themselves, and how they might be modified. Constitutional endowment, environment, physical health, and personality traits each contributed to the "causal changes or conditions" that produced a psychiatric disturbance. Although Meyer never regarded psychogenic factors as the only cause of mental illness, he found them often the "controlling" ones (33).

In his insistence that the patient's life history was central to psychiatric study, Meyer's work paralleled Freud's. He incorporated into his own eclectic system those psychoanalytic concepts that he found useful. As early as 1907 he encouraged staff members in New York State hospitals to use psychoanalysis in diagnosing and treating psychotic patients. He also drew on Jung's idea of "complexes" and Freud's theories of "wish fulfillment" and "repression." But he found Freud's emphasis on the unconscious and sexual origins of psychopathological behavior too restrictive. As the popularity of psychoanalysis increased, Meyer feared that its one-sided and premature systematizing would obscure the uniqueness of individuals and subvert the study of other facts of mental life (32).

Where Freud focused mainly on internal psychodynamics, Meyer made much of the patient's social environment. He believed that psychiatrists must try to understand why certain types of mental disturbance appeared more frequently in some communities and among certain ethnic groups. Meyer even proposed that the psychiatric hospital become a center for mental health for "a fairly well circumscribed unit of population," ranging from 200,000 to 500,000 (29). The psychiatrist, working closely with public schools, courts, police, charity and other district agencies, became an agent for public health:

> Just as bacteriology studies the water supply and the air and food of communities, schools and homes, so we psychopathologists have to study more effectively the atmosphere of the community and must devise safeguards in the localities from which the patients come, and to which they are to return (38).

If Meyer provided a rationale for community psychiatry, he never neglected his medical roots. In 1913, at the end of the three-day ceremony that marked the opening of the Phipps Psychiatric Clinic, a model institution linked to the Johns Hopkins Hospital and University in Baltimore, Meyer declared that recent progress in psychiatry came from medicine as well as psychology. Medicine had shed light on the relationship between the internal secretions and the nervous system, the nutritional disease pellagra, and the syphilitic origins of paresis. These important discoveries suggested to Meyer "how unlikely it is that we should ever come to distinguish sharply between a mind and body in our field, because after all, we face one large biological problem." The psychological work simply takes "the general medical foundations for granted, and turns directly to the reactions of the organism as a whole" (31).

II

Meyer's redefinition of the psychiatrist's role as social and preventive was reinforced by the expansive approaches to health care in the Progressive era, a time of flourishing new approaches to the treatment of psychoses and neuroses. In the diverse settings in which psychiatry came to be practiced, two considerations were paramount: early treatment of emotional disturbances, and educational efforts directed to physicians, patients, and the general public. The new institutions—including psychopathic hospitals and outpatient clinics of various sorts—were essentially medical. But, like other medical undertakings of the era, they had a strong social component. Both proponents and opponents of psychoanalysis, with common enthusiasm and an American indifference to theoretical consistency, endorsed virtually identical programs for the care and prevention of mental illness.

Physicians placed enormous faith in the new psychopathic hospitals. Long an established part of German psychiatry, three of these institutions were built between 1907 and 1913—the Psychopathic Hospital of the University of Michigan, Boston Psychopathic Hospital, and the Phipps Psychiatric Clinic. They were designed to do for mental disorders what general hospitals did for other ills: provide diagnostic services and short-term care for patients with any type of disorder, without a declaration of insanity. They also served as de facto community mental health centers and teaching institutions for general practitioners and the public as well as for medical students and specialists.

Boston Psychopathic Hospital exemplified the new trends in psychiatry. It was dominated by the personality of E. E. Southard, as Phipps was by Meyer (17). Like Meyer, Southard was a neuropathologist; unlike Meyer, he always remained one. Indeed, he was considered America's leading organicist, and attempted to correlate brain lesions with specific types of illnesses and even with specific delusions. But between 1910 and his premature death in 1920, Southard became an enthusiastic supporter of the mental hygiene and social service movements, which he considered manifestations of the art rather than the science of psychiatry. Art or science, they were central to the hospital's program. For all their intellectual differences, Meyer and Southard shared the optimistic assumptions of their era and supported the same programs. If Southard was rhapsodic about mental hygiene, he also was cheered by the recent determination that syphilitic infection caused paresis and by the discovery of a partially effective treatment for syphilis. "If we can be optimistic as to paresis," Southard declared, "we can be optimistic about anything" (55).

Boston Psychopathic was required by law to admit all patients in the community with "acute, incipient and curable" mental disorders for diagnosis and possible treatment. Up-to-date laboratory facilities aided the process of diagnosis. There were separate rooms for bacteriology, chemistry, spinal fluid work, and histology, and a special research laboratory for metabolic studies. Wassermann tests were routinely administered and social service workers helped to round up the families of those with positive results. Psychologists administered the Binet-Simon tests to measure intelligence and Jung's "association" test to uncover hidden complexes.

In its first year, Boston Psychopathic admitted 1500 individuals who stayed on an average of three to four weeks. Patients with physical illnesses received appropriate short-term treatment—hydrotherapy for the delirious (including alcoholics), food for the severely undernourished, rest for the exhausted. Those diagnosed as syphilitic would be started on a more arduous course of salvarsan therapy. While convinced that psychological therapies took longer than others, Southard agreed that the psychiatrist must help clarify the "relation of the patient to himself." Despite his opposition to Freud, he employed Lydiard Horton, a psychopathologist interested in psychoanalysis who studied patients' dreams. The least hopeful cases—approximately 40 per cent—were sent on to state hospitals, thereby reinforcing the view that these institutions were for the incurable.

The outpatient clinic at Boston Psychopathic provided comparable services for those who did not need hospitalization. By developing close links with local physicians, community agencies, and patients and their families, the clinic became a "first aid station" and "pivot point" of community mental health. Staff physicians and social workers collaborated in providing after-care for patients discharged from the wards, and helped the troubled individual to "carry on his work, continue to dwell in the family circle, and be rehabilitated in the environment in which he must continue to live in order to play his part in the social scheme of things" (58). Southard and Mary Jarrett provided a collaborative model for psychiatrists and social workers. They also helped to establish the first school of psychiatric social work (25).

Children under fourteen constituted 24 per cent of all patients treated at Boston Psychopathic's outpatient clinic between 1913 and 1918, and adolescents, another 16 per cent. The clinic added new programs as need arose, including a "voice clinic" for the large number of children and adults with speech defects and a social club for formerly hospitalized alcoholics. Still another offshoot was a "habit clinic," established under the auspices of the Baby Hygiene Association in a local settlement house (7). So promising did outpatient work seem that New York in 1913 and Massachusetts in 1914 required each state hospital to establish departments.

General hospitals also began to concern themselves with psychiatric problems, primarily the psychoneuroses. The case of Massachusetts General Hospital is most instructive. Inspired by Richard C. Cabot, who had made a reputation as a master diagnostician, the outpatient department became a center of medical social work. In October 1905, estimating that 40 per cent of the patients suffered from functional complaints, which he defined as those which could be "ameliorated chiefly by a change in the patients' habits and by the correction of hygienic faults," Cabot employed a social service worker at private expense. The idea took hold and volunteers and other paid workers joined the staff. Within seven years, over a hundred hospitals and dispensaries had similar departments (51, 11).

James Jackson Putnam was in charge of the clinic's neuropsychological program. The emphasis on this work in a general hospital reveals how far psychiatry had emerged from its traditional isolation. Most of those attending the clinic were poor and foreign born, among whom disability from nervous complaints often produced severe distress, but little sympathy. Special programs included a clay modeling class, placement of patients with families, and vacations in New Hampshire. But the core of the work was the department's "profound respect for the healing possibilities of good talk," and the close relationship of physician or social worker to the patient. Clinic patients were given blank books in which to write down their thoughts about themselves or others; in some cases a team approach to family problems involved as many as three staff members (28). And in 1911, Putnam found the funds to hire L. Eugene Emerson, a young psychologist interested in psychoanalysis. Patients confided their sexual behavior and dreams to him with surprising frankness. Diagnosis and therapy blended psychoanalysis with common sense. Of one patient Emerson noted: "Obsessions and compelling ideas due to repressed ambitions. Was advised to leave factory and go to school" (15).

Under inspired leadership, even a traditional mental hospital might be transformed. William Alanson White's modernization of the Government Hospital for the Insane in Washington, D. C., renamed Saint Elizabeths, was particularly impressive. Remembered today primarily as a popularizer of psychoanalysis and mental hygiene, as the teacher of Harry Stack Sullivan, and sometimes as an expert in forensic psychiatry, White actually began and ended his career as "a hospital man." The blandness of his published work has obscured the fact that he was an efficient and shrewd administrator and an inspiring therapist and teacher.

White did everything possible to individualize patient care at Saint Elizabeths, an institution that grew from almost 2500 patients when he took charge in 1903 to 5700 patients and 1700 staff members at the time of his death in 1937. He initiated a training school for nurses, encouraged a patient newspaper and orchestra, started a beauty parlor and cafeteria. He also took advantage of the hospital's size to provide specialized services. In 1907 he appointed separate clinical and scientific directors and in 1917 two full-time psychotherapists, the first to be employed in a mental hospital and among the first Americans to try psychotherapy with psychotic patients (60, 65, 47). But White did not neglect new developments in medicine—dietary treatment of pellagra, salvarsan for paresis, even endocrine therapy for dementia praecox—and took special pride in establishing a department of internal medicine in 1919, the first in a psychiatric hospital (61, 64).

Probably nothing better illustrates White's commitment to patients than his response to a questionnaire designed by a former assistant:

> You have . . . on the last page a whole host of character traits set forth, such as hypochondriacal, sympathetic, tender, frank, domineering, sensitive, etc., with just enough space after them to put in a mark indicating whether the patient shows this trait or not. Now my contention has always been that when such a list gets to the doctor, who has not seen the patient, it is pretty thoroughly robbed of all life. What, for example, can you possibly know about a person about whom someone says they are domineering? I don't believe you can know anything (62).

In a similar vein, White urged that a patient's healthy as well as diseased ancestors be included by those compiling pedigree charts to investigate the hereditary basis of mental illness (63).

Proponents of the new psychiatry agreed that the general practitioner was potentially the most important agent of prophylactic work. Psychopathic hospitals, outpatient clinics, and more traditional psychiatric hospitals tried to become educational centers for their communities. Because Phipps was fully integrated into the Johns Hopkins Medical School, Adolf Meyer was able to develop the most comprehensive psychiatric curriculum for medical students as well as specialists, and later established the first psychiatric residency program. But even institutions not attached to medical schools, like Saint Elizabeths, offered local physicians opportunities to learn about new diagnostic tests and to consult with hospital staff members about the mental difficulties of patients under their care. White maintained that this work was vital not only for prophylaxis but for increasing public confidence in the hospital: "I cannot possibly do anything more substantial to establish that confidence than by first securing the cooperation of the medical profession" (66).

III

White was undoubtedly correct in his assessment; he was also an extraordinarily effective envoy to the medical and lay worlds. But he would not have made much headway had not physicians already been interested in expanding their therapeutic horizons. By 1910, smallpox, yellow fever, typhus, and cholera had virtually disappeared from the western world, while deaths from tuberculosis and typhoid had fallen sharply. Most striking was the decline in infant mortality as diphtheria, croup, enteritis, diarrhea, and scarlet fever yielded to medical control. Indeed, life expectancy for males at birth increased by almost thirteen years between 1880 and 1915, that of females by slightly more (24).

Although improvements in living standards and in hygiene probably had more to do with these developments than did science, enthusiasm for laboratory research and scientific medicine ran high; certainly the Flexner report on medical education in 1910 gave great weight to them. But thoughtful physicians recognized that science had as yet contributed little to therapy. What then was the practicing physician to do? For those aware of the harmfulness of many drugs and challenged by the quack dispensers of nostrums, the answer was clear: utilize nature's own resources, with the help of such natural healing agencies as hygienic regimens, hydrotherapy, physiotherapy, and psychotherapy.

Physicians had self-interested motives for endorsing psychotherapy. They were sometimes quite explicit in their efforts to counter the popularity of Christian Science, New Thought, and the other forms of mind cure that flourished in the early years of the century. One prominent neurologist noted that "an enormous number of mentally sick people are running around and get their psychotherapeutics from the wrong well" (2). The popularity of lay healing in the United States goes a long way toward explaining the insistence of American physicians that psychotherapy—and later psychoanalysis—become exclusively medical prerogatives.

New intellectual and scientific developments also made physicians more receptive to the study of emotions and other individual factors in disease. By the turn of the century, physicians were turning away from the extreme somaticism exemplified in the doctrine of cellular pathology and Rudolf Virchow's dictum that "there are no general diseases, there are only diseases of the cell." Walter B. Cannon's laboratory demonstration of the effects of fear and rage on digestion and respiration generated interest in psychosomatic medicine. So did studies on hormones and their relationship to moods. This work seemed to confirm the central hypothesis of psychopathologists—that emotions could induce physical illness—and prompted physicians to turn to psychiatrists and neurologists for assistance in understanding human personality. Lewellys F. Barker, the chief of medicine at Hopkins who introduced psychotherapy on the wards, claimed: "Psychiatry . . . is a large and very important chapter of Inner Medicine. Every internist should have at least some training in psychiatry, and every psychiatrist should be well-versed in the fundamental facts and methods of general medicine" (4).

It would be easy to exaggerate medical endorsement of psychiatry and psychotherapy. In his speech at the opening of Harvard's new medical school in 1906, President Charles W. Eliot ignored potential advances in knowledge about behavior and concentrated entirely on the biological achievements to come. The new Rockefeller Institute had no place for psychiatry. And even the School of Public Hygiene established at Johns Hopkins in 1919 by William H. Welch, Dean of the Medical School and a strong supporter of psychiatry, did not initially include a division of mental hygiene.

Still, psychiatrists and neurologists emerged from World War I confident about the future. Together they had participated in a massive screening and rehabilitative effort to avert and minimize the effects of war-related psychological casualties. The physicians who engaged in this work believed that henceforth psychiatry would occupy an important place in American medicine and society. Thomas Salmon, first medical director of the National Committee for Mental Hygiene and head of neuropsychiatric work with the American Expeditionary Force, later observed that the medical profession welcomed psychiatric views "with a warmth that is sometimes embarrassing" (49).

Salmon was one of those who made expansive promises for the new psychiatry. He apologized that so much of the National Committee's early work had been concerned with hospitals, which he considered a "less important" field of mental hygiene. Salmon believed that in his "dual capacity as psychologist and physician" (50), the psychiatrist could provide solutions to many of the social problems of the day—in education, immigration, and criminology, among others (52). Elaborating on this new role, a prominent neurologist urged the physician who treated the functional neuroses to become an "educator, preacher, sociologist." He must show people "how to live happily and to use with scientific efficiency the forces which nature has given them." He must become a "social and economic neurologist . . . a kind of superman" (13).

With exhortations like these, it was easy to forget that little progress had been made in therapy (although in this psychiatry differed little from general medicine). In fact, the one pessimistic note in an era that otherwise celebrated psychiatric progress was the low recovery rate of psychotic patients. Only about 20 per cent of the patients in state hospitals recovered (59). Small wonder then that a prominent psychiatrist exclaimed: "With all our boasted scientific advancement, our therapeutics is simply a pile of rubbish" (23). This was an extreme position. But discouragement about cures undoubtedly fueled interest in prophylaxis.

Historians have tended to link psychoanalysis with the optimistic and environmentalist approaches to mental illness so evident in the early twentieth century. The reality is more complex. Supporters of what Southard facetiously dubbed the brain spot theory could be just as imprudent in their claims as those who favored the mind twist view (54). None more so than Southard, who maintained that psychiatrists could explain—and perhaps also prevent—strikes, labor turnover, and other social problems (53). Others claimed that through mental hygiene, war might give way to peace, and despair to hope. Southard once acknowledged that "it was difficult to prove that this work actually prevented committable insanity." But, he added, "the work certainly . . . was productive of great social and individual good" (1). Psychiatrists thus found themselves on dangerous grounds. By claiming more than they could deliver, they set the stage for subsequent disenchantment—their own perhaps most of all.

Contemporary disillusionment with psychoanalysis constitutes another stage in the cycle of hope and despair that has plagued American psychiatry since the 1840s. By probing the history of the movement, these seminars provide the occasion for understanding the sources of the current dilemma. They may also point the way to a useful, and less clouded, future.

REFERENCES

1. American Medico-Psychological Association, Proceedings, *Amer. J. Insanity*, 1916, 73, 127.
2. American Neurological Association, *J. Nerv. and Mental Diseases*, 1908, 35, 783.

3. Association of Medical Superintendents of American Institutions for the Insane, Proceedings, *Amer. J. Insanity*, 1891, 48, 105-106.

4. Barker, L. F., The Relations of Internal Medicine to Psychiatry, *Amer. J. Insanity*, 1914, 71, 27.

5. Barrett, A., The State Psychopathic Hospital, *Amer. J. Insanity*, 1921, 77, 309-320.

6. Bond, E. W., *Thomas W. Salmon, Psychiatrist*, New York: W. W. Norton, 1950.

7. Briggs, L. V., *History of the Psychopathic Hospital, Boston, Massachusetts*, Boston: Wright & Potter, 1922.

8. Burnham, J. C., Medical Specialists and Movements Toward Social Control in the Progressive Era: Three Examples. In: Jerry Israel, Ed., *Building the Organizational Society*, New York: The Free Press, 1972, pp. 19-30.

9. Burnham, J. C., *Psychoanalysis and American Medicine 1894-1918: Medicine, Science, and Culture*, New York: International Universities Press, 1967.

10. Cabot, R. C., An Appreciation of Elmer E. Southard, *Bulletin of the Massachusetts Commission on Mental Diseases*, 1920, 4, 14-29.

11. Cannon, I. M., *Social Work in Hospitals: A Contribution to Progressive Medicine*, New York: Russell Sage Foundation, 1917.

12. Coriat, I. H., Papers, Francis A. Countway Library of Medicine, Boston. Review of Isador H. Coriat's *The Meaning of Dreams* in *The Nation*, 1915, "Scrapbook," No. 1, p. 16.

13. Dana, C. L., The Future of Neurology, *J. Nerv. and Mental Diseases*, 1913, 40, 753-757.

14. Deutsch, A., The History of Mental Hygiene. In: *One Hundred Years of American Psychiatry*, New York: Columbia University Press, 1944, pp. 325-365.

15. Emerson, L. E., Papers, Francis A. Countway Library of Medicine, Boston, Case No. 40.

16. Fisher, I., *Report on National Vitality: Its Wastes and Conservation;* Bulletin 30 of the Committee of One Hundred. Washington: Government Printing Office, 1909.

17. Gay, F. P., *The Open Mind: Elmer Ernest Southard, 1876-1920*, N.p.: Normandie House, 1938.

18. Gray, J. P., The Dependence of Insanity on Physical Disease, *Am. J. Insanity*, 1871, 27, 381.

19. Gray, J. P., Insanity, and Its Relations to Medicine, *Am. J. Insanity*, 1868, 25, 162.

20. Grob, G. N., Adolf Meyer on American Psychiatry in 1895, *Am. J. Psychiat.*, 1963, 119, 1135-1142.

21. Hale, N. G., Jr., *Freud and the Americans: The Beginnings of Psychoanalysis in the United States, 1876-1917*, New York: Oxford University Press, 1971.

22. Hale, N. G., Jr. (Ed.), *James Jackson Putnam and Psychoanalysis: Letters between Putnam and Sigmund Freud, Ernest Jones, William James, Sandor Ferenczi, and Morton Prince, 1877-1917*, Cambridge: Harvard University Press, 1971.

23. Hill, C. G., Presidential Address, *Am. J. Insanity*, 1907, 64, 6.

24. Hoffman, F. L., American Mortality Progress during the Last Half Century. In: Mazyck P. Ravenel, Ed., *A Half Century of Public Health*, New York: American Public Health Association, 1921, pp. 94-117.

25. Jarrett, M. C., The Social Service, 1913 to 1918. In: Briggs, *History of the Psychopathic Hospital*, pp. 172-183.

26. Lidz, T., Adolf Meyer and the Development of American Psychiatry, *Am. J. Psychiat.*, 1966, 123, 320-332.

27. Lubove, R., *The Professional Altruist: The Emergence of Social Work as a Career, 1880-1930*, New York: Atheneum, 1969.

28. Massachusetts General Hospital. *Annual Reports*, 1905-1919.

29. Meyer, A., The Aims of a Psychiatric Clinic (1913). In: Eunice E. Winters, Ed., *The Collected Papers of Adolf Meyer*, II. Baltimore: The Johns Hopkins Press, 1951, pp. 192-202. (All citations from Meyer's work are taken from this volume, hereafter cited as *CPM*, II.)

30. Meyer, A., An Attempt at Analysis of the Neurotic Constitution (1903). *CPM*, II, 322.

31. Meyer, A., Closing Remarks (1913). *CPM*, II, 180.

32. Meyer, A., A Discussion of Some Fundamental Issues in Freud's Psychoanalysis (1909-1910). *CPM*, II, 604-617.

33. Meyer, A., The Dynamic Interpretation of Dementia Praecox (1909). *CPM*, II, 443-458.

34. Meyer, A., The Nature and Conception of Dementia Praecox (1910-1911). *CPM*, II, 461.

35. Meyer, A., Opening of the Henry Phipps Psychiatric Clinic (1913). *CPM*, II, 177.

36. Meyer, A., Pathology of Mental Diseases (1916). *CPM*, II, 299.

37. Meyer, A., Plans for Work in the Phipps Psychiatric Clinic (1913). *CPM*, II, 185-192.

38. Meyer, A., The Purpose of the Psychiatric Clinic (1913). *CPM*, II, 178.

39. Meyer, A., The Relationship of Hysteria, Psychasthenia, and Dementia Praecox (1912). *CPM*, II, 441.

40. Meyer, A., Remarks on Habit Disorganizations in the Essential Deteriorations, and the Relation of Deterioration to the Psychasthenic, Neurasthenic, Hysterical and other Constitutions (1905). *CPM*, II, 421-431.

41. Meyer, A., A Review of Recent Problems of Psychiatry (1904). *CPM*, II, 355.

42. Meyer, A., A Short Sketch of the Problems of Psychiatry (1897). *CPM*, II, 274-275.

43. Meyer, A., Special Reports of the Medical Department, Worcester Lunatic Hospital (1898). *CPM*, II, 63.

44. Meyer, A., The Treatment of the Insane, (1894). *CPM*, II, 37-49.

45. Meyer, A., Twenty-Fourth Anniversary of the Henry Phipps Psychiatric Clinic (1937). *CPM*, II, 210-233.

46. Mowry, G. E., *The Era of Theodore Roosevelt and the Birth of Modern America, 1900-1912*, New York: Harper & Row, 1962.

47. Overholser, W., An Historical Sketch of Saint Elizabeths Hospital. In: *Centennial Papers, Saint Elizabeths Hospital, 1855-1955*. Washington, D.C.: Centennial Commission, Saint Elizabeths Hospital, 1956, pp. 1-18.

48. Rosen, G., *A History of Public Health*, New York: MD Publications, 1958.

49. Salmon, T. W., Presidential Address, *Am. J. Psychiat.*, 1924, 4, 5.

50. Salmon, T. W., Some New Fields in Neurology and Psychiatry, *J. Nerv. and Mental Diseases*, 1917, 46, 90-99.

51. Sicherman, B., The New Mission of the Doctor: Redefining Health and Health Care in the Progressive Era, 1900-1917, *Papers and Proceedings of the Dialogue Group on Humanistic Social Science and Medical Education of the Institute for Human Values in Medicine* (in press).

52. Sicherman, B., The Quest for Mental Health in America, 1880-1917, Ph.D. dissertation, Columbia University, 1967.

53. Southard, E. E., Cross-Sections of Mental Hygiene, 1844, 1869, 1894, *Am. J. Insanity*, 1919, 76, 109.

54. Southard, E. E., The Mind Twist and Brain Spot Hypotheses in Psychopathology and Neuropathology, *Psychological Bull.*, 1914, 11, 117-130.

55. Southard, E. E., The Outlook for Work at the Psychopathic Hospital, Boston, 1913, *Bost. Med. and Surg. J.*, 1913, 169, 427-428.

56. Taylor, E. W., The Attitude of the Medical Profession Toward the Psychotherapeutic Movement, *Bost. Med. and Surg. J.*, 1907, 157, 843-850.

57. Taylor, E. W., The Widening Sphere of Medicine, *Bost. Med. and Surg. J.*, 1909, 161, 40.

58. Thom, D. A., The Out-Patient Department. In: Briggs, *History of the Psychopathic Hospital*, 168-169.

59. Tourney, G., A History of Therapeutic Fashions in Psychiatry, 1800-1966, *Am. J. Psychiat.*, 1967, 124, 787.

60. White, W. A., *The Autobiography of a Purpose.* Garden City: Doubleday, Doran, 1938.

61. White, W. A., Letter to L. F. Barker, October 28th, 1919. Personal Correspondence of William Alanson White, 1906-1937, Record Group 418, Records of Saint Elizabeths Hospital.

62. White, W. A., Letter to B. Glueck, October 14, 1916, *ibid.*

63. White, W. A., Letter to S. E. Jelliffe, June 4, 1910, *ibid.*

64 White, W. A., Letter to T. W. Salmon, May 9, 1919, *ibid.*

65. White, W. A., The New Government Hospital for the Insane, *Am. J. Insanity*, 1910, 66, 523-528.

66. White, W. A., The Relation of the Hospital for the Insane to the Medical Profession and to the Community, *Government Hospital for the Insane, Bulletin No. 1*, 1909, 10.

67. Winslow, C.-E. A., *The Life of Hermann M. Biggs: Physician and Statesman of the Public Health.* Philadelphia: Lea and Febiger, 1929.

68. Winters, E. E., Adolf Meyer's Two and a Half Years at Kankakee, May 1, 1893-November 1, 1895. *Bull. Hist. Med.*, 1966, 40, 441-458.

I wish to thank Saint Elizabeths Hospital for permission to quote from the Personal Correspondence of William Alanson White, 1906-1937, Record Group 418, Records of Saint Elizabeths Hospital, National Archives.

CHAPTER 3

American Psychology and Psychoanalysis: William James and G. Stanley Hall

Dorothy Ross, Ph.D.

HANNAH DECKER, who opened this lecture series with a discussion of the response to psychoanalysis in Europe, noted Freud's rather stubborn and ungrateful disparagement of the American "professors and superintendents of mental hospitals" who showed an early interest in psychoanalysis. Last month Barbara Sicherman talked here about those "superintendents of mental hospitals" whose eclectic and hopeful use of psychoanalysis ran against the grain of Freud's powerful and stoical mind. Today, I would like to talk about the American professors, chiefly, Freud must have meant, the professors of psychology, some of whom he met when G. Stanley Hall brought him to lecture and receive an honorary degree at Clark University in Worcester in 1909. I am afraid we will find that the psychology professors, too, did not meet Freud's fastidious standards.

Like the psychiatric profession, psychology in America was undergoing a major transformation during the period from about 1880 to 1910 (1). Prior to that time, psychology had developed in the religious atmosphere of the American colleges as part of an edifying amalgam of mental

Presented December 11, 1975. Dorothy Ross is Assistant Professor of History, Princeton University, Princeton, New Jersey.

and moral philosophy. Beginning in the 1870s, as the religious domination of the colleges began to collapse, psychology as well as the new social disciplines began to forge independent identities. Such pioneers as William James at Harvard and George Trumbull Ladd at Yale introduced courses in scientific psychology and, after 1880, they were joined by even more scientifically oriented students and younger colleagues, often with German university training.

Fortunately, the colleges were ready to receive them. Under pressure from alumni and trustees for more secular and "relevant" education, and supported by the largesse of the new class of industrial rich, the colleges began to expand and modernize. In the decentralized American educational system, the growth and prestige of each new university set off competitive shock waves which stimulated all the others to match the leader. Under this spur of competition, all the new social and behavioral sciences made rapid headway, but psychology grew even more rapidly than the others. Within the first decade of growth, almost two dozen psychology laboratories were established in the new universities, and by 1897 there were more doctorates in psychology being awarded in the United States than in any other science except chemistry. Perhaps psychology inherited the respect accorded the older mental philosophy and the new authority of science. For men themselves enacting the transition from one to the other, the new psychology offered scientific strategies for coming to terms with earlier religious and philosophical allegiances.

Academic psychology during the period 1880 to 1910 was quite distinct from the philosophical psychology which prevailed before 1880, and also quite distinct from the kind of behavioristic academic psychology which developed after 1910 under the impress of a still younger generation. The positive reception which Freud's work received in some quarters of American academic psychology was a product of the unique set of conditions which prevailed in American psychology during this period.

For one thing, the new psychology was decidedly Europhile, and even more particularly, Germanophile, in orientation. In revolt against the provincial culture which had prevailed in American colleges during the nineteenth century, the new psychologists were eager to assimilate the latest European developments. Attracted by the German universities, then the most advanced in science in the world, they remained, even after they returned home, attuned to a broader range of European work than probably was the case within any of the European countries themselves. This internationalism in outlook suffered a severe blow from the First World War, and American psychology, even granting the later input from European emigrés in the 1930s, was probably never again as cosmopolitan.

Secondly, the new psychology looked to natural science, but in this interim period before behaviorism set in, the conception of science was still fairly loose. The psychologists revolted against the older philosophical psychology in the name of a more thorough commitment to empiricism and laboratory experimentation. But their conception of empirical observation was still rooted in broader "naturalistic" conceptions of science, and their laboratory orientation had not yet hardened into a primary focus on methodological rigor. This was particularly true of the functionalists among the new psychologists, like William James and G. Stanley Hall, who turned the Wundtian study of consciousness toward the study of mental process, in a biological, evolutionary framework.

Third, the new psychology—again particularly its functionalist wing—was eclectic in a way that only a new and newly institutionalizing subject could be. It was forging an identity from many strands of converging interest not only from the older mental and moral philosophy, but also from the new evolutionary biology, from medicine, physiology, anthropology, and even psychical research. The new psychologists could move relatively easily into problems in mental illness and associations with psychiatry. After about 1920, when firmer patterns of professionalization and specialization had been established, the natural eclecticism of the pioneer generation was not possible.

Finally, the rebellious stance of the new psychologists against their own provincial roots, their openness to novelty, made them sympathetic to the kind of heretical doctrines Freud was propounding. The intellectually adventurous figures who played the pioneer role in American psychology would be peculiarly open to Freud's "anti-establishment science" (2). If we look more closely at the work of William James and Stanley Hall that prepared the ground for Freud's reception in America, will see these factors at work.

Of the two, James was certainly the more important figure for the development of American psychology, though his influence in the direction of psychoanalysis was more indirect than that of Hall (3). James came by his vivacious idiosyncrasy quite naturally. His father, a Swedenborgian, and amateur philosopher on the fringes of the Transcendental movement, had been crippled in his youth. Living off an inheritance, he devoted his mature life to the unconventional rearing of his five children. I do not mean to be unkind when I note that the result of his intense efforts was the creation of two neurotic geniuses—William and his younger brother Henry—and perhaps three, if we count their sister Alice, a talented woman early confined to the life of an hysterical invalid.

James' schooling was wide-ranging and shaped by the intellectual atmosphere of his home, but it was also haphazard, compiled under a succession of tutors and schools as his father moved the family bewteen New York City, Europe, and finally Cambridge. The elder James' avocation was that of religious philosopher, but he wanted his son to become a scientist. In America in the 1860s and 1870s, when the rising authority of science appeared to threaten not only religious truths but the natural foundations of morality as well, the younger James felt the need to reconcile the claims of both science and religion. He studied physiology on a tour of the German universities in the 1860s, where he encountered Wundt's new psychology; got a medical degree at Harvard's Lawrence Scientific School, intending to use the degree as a credential in basic science rather than medical practice; and began teaching at Harvard as an instructor in physiology. But he was already personally involved in working through philosophical problems, deeply read in the British associationists and engaged in working out the implications of the latest physiological and biological knowledge for psychology.

As James' interest moved first to physiological psychology, then psychology, and finally to philosophy again, he always subordinated the claims of science to his own rich sense of the variety and richness of experience. He argued that religious intuitions had, under certain circumstances, a claim to our belief. And within the realm of psychology, he always limted the scope of the new German laboratory psychology. He drew more on the older British philosophical psychology, on French and English medical traditions, as well as on his own rich perceptions of the inner world.

James' catholic and cosmopolitan background opened him to an interest in psychopathology as a crucial area of psychological observation. But he was drawn to this area by personal problems as well. During his own prolonged adolescence, James suffered long bouts of depression and psychosomatic illness, and was finally plunged into a terrifying fear of being rendered wholly impotent. James worked his way out of the abyss by a philosophical determination to believe in the possibility of free will, but he remained forever after closely attuned to the ebb and flow of inner terrors and to the close and subtle connections between normality and abnormality.

James was an important participant in the growing interest in psychotherapy which was developing in Boston after 1890. As Nathan Hale has shown in his fine study of *Freud and the Americans,* the Boston movement was led equally by such physicians as Morton Prince and James Jackson Putnam, and by the Harvard psychologists like James. They took up chiefly the ideas of Pierre Janet, who explained psychopathological behavior as the product of the dissociation of consciousness, but they were also aware of Freud's work. James reviewed the Breuer and Freud study on hysteria as early as 1896 and he, like his Boston colleagues, cited Freud among the contributors to the growing interest in subliminal consciousness opened up by Charcot and Janet (4).

To carry the story of Freud's reception in America further, we need now to turn to James' student, G. Stanley Hall (5). In the case of Hall, we can see the same kind of cosmopolitan, eclectic and anti-establishment science at work, as well as distinct personality factors. Hall's prickly personality and his appetite for heretical ideas worked not only against the older provincial psychology but also against his teacher and colleague, William James.

Hall was born in a small village in northwestern Massachusetts in 1844 of nine generations of modest Congregational ancestors. His father was a farmer, and he was almost twenty when he enrolled in nearby Williams College. Though he went on to Union Theological Seminary in New York, and then a year in Germany, he still felt somewhat the provincial when he arrived in Boston in 1876 to study psychology with William James and encountered the intellectual milieu in Cambridge, a group closely knit by ties of family and acquaintance. Hall was already the kind of personality who felt himself constantly threatened, martyred, and abused. Most of the young Cambridge men, in their turn, never got closer than to consider him, as Henry P. Bowditch remarked, a kind of "queer genius."

His relations with James, the teacher to whom he owed so much, grew particularly torturous as their careers developed. After taking a Ph.D. degree with James in the subject of psychology in 1878, the first such degree awarded in this country, Hall returned to Berlin and Leipzig for two more years of study. Here he continued to explore both the experimental work and the interest in psychopathology he had learned under James. He made himself one of the most widely, if not deeply, schooled Americans in the new field of physiological psychology. But when he came back again to America, he could barely support himself with academic odds and ends. In just a few more years the reform of American colleges and universities would create a burgeoning market for new Ph.D.'s with some scientific expertise, but he was still some years ahead of his time.

Finally, in 1884, at the age of forty, Hall was appointed professor of psychology and pedagogy at Johns Hopkins University, then the apex of America's educational system. Here he outlined a wide-ranging view of psychology, with emphasis on the "physiological and psychiatrical." Hall's psychiatric work included lectures on abnormal psychology and clinics at the Bay View Asylum, Baltimore's institution for the pauper insane, which he helped to reform. Later, at Clark, he would continue such ties by sending his students to Adolf Meyer, then at the nearby Worcester State Hospital.

But Hall's new eminence did not quiet his anxieties. He began to champion what he called a "strictly scientific" psychology, as opposed to the kind of "arm-chair" psychology practiced by James and the older philosophically oriented theorists. Although he himself had sever doubts about an empirical psychology limited only to the narrow range of laboratory experimentation that was then available—indeed precisely because he did doubt that narrow framework—he attacked James and the philosophical psychologists cleverly and mercilessly. He was determined to make psychology a rigorous science and to capture the leadership of the new profession from that height.

When, in 1887, Hall left Hopkins to become the founding president of Clark University in Worcester, Massachusetts, he had still another and nearer base from which to challenge James. Hall hoped to make Clark University into a solely graduate university, dedicated to advanced scientific research. From 1889 to 1892, Hall came very close to fulfilling his ideal with an exceptionally talented group of young scientists, including Albert A. Michelson in physics, H. H. Donaldson in physiology, Franklin P. Mall in neuroanatomy, and Franz Boas in anthropology. Hall was unable to keep this band together, however, and as seemed often to be the case with Hall, the circumstances under which he lost his brilliant faculty led to personal recriminations and quarrels which seriously damaged his reputation in the academic world.

Before and after this turning point at Clark in 1892, Hall continued to quarrel publicly with James, and now Harvard too, about issues of rivalry between their institutions. Hall let it be known that he considered Clark far more "advanced" an institution than Harvard, a contention James was hardly ready to admit. Things came to such an impasse that Robert M. Yerkes, the animal psychologist, recalled that when he had been at Harvard around the turn of the century, he was "given to understand that it was either indiscreet or bad form for a Harvard psychologist to try to cultivate friendly professional relations with G. Stanley Hall and his Clark associates."

During the late 1890s and the first two decades of the twentieth century, Hall largely withdrew from psychological combat into the tiny institution at Clark he had managed to salvage. Hall ran the institution during all those years on an annual budget of $28,000 (except for separate library funds). Beleaguered, victim of the hostilities from his colleagues he himself had set off, Hall also, and this is most important, gave up the attempt to form a strictly scientific psychology. He turned his interest to subjects which his psychological colleagues considered marginal and heretical, and which could not be studied with the exactitude his laboratory colleagues increasingly required. But they were subjects which he felt to be of genuine moment in the lives of people— sexuality, psychopathology, the study of child development, and adolescence. The man who brought Freud to America in 1909, therefore, was decidedly a maverick whose actions were always suspect by his professional peers and whose institution clung precariously to existence.

Yet Hall also managed to preserve in himself and Clark University genuine intellectual values, and the high quality of some of the work done there was appreciated elsewhere. The combination of wide-ranging psychological interest, cosmopolitan outlook and intellectual daring which characterized Hall's work at Clark was typified by the conference he arranged in 1899 to celebrate the tenth anniversary of the founding of the university. Hall brought five distinguished foreign scientists to Clark at that time, among them Santiago Ramon y Cajal, of the University of Madrid, whose work in histology was one of the principal sources of the neurone theory; Antonio Mosso, of the University of Milan, pioneer student of psychiatry and development; and August Forel, professor of psychiatry at Basel and director of the Burghölzli Asylum. When the twentieth anniversary of Clark drew near, in 1909, Hall wanted to arrange a conference of equal intellectual distinction.

At the same time, Hall recognized the rising interest in the subject of psychotherapy in Boston and Cambridge. He was still largely cut off from Boston psychological and medical circles, but he followed the new literature of psychotherapy with interest. Since he read widely in German, he was aware of Freud's work with Breuer on hysteria by 1899 and there are references to Freud's work in his books and lectures in the years following. With typical aplomb, Hall apparently sensed that this was the right moment to upstage Boston and to make a major intellectual coup, both for himself and Freud. This is undoubtedly what Freud sensed when he remarked later that "there was a touch of the 'King-maker' about [Hall]." Hall brought to Clark for the 1909 conference other distinguished European and American scholars, and spoke of Freud as representing "the psychology of the future." James attended for a day, had a long talk with Freud, and according to Ernest Jones' memory, told Jones that the future of psychiatry belonged to psychoanalysis. The conference proved to be a turning point not only in Freud's life but in the whole American reception of psychoanalysis.

The particularly catholic and unorthodox character of the pioneer generation of scientific psychologists in America can go a considerable way toward explaining the positive early reception Freud received in America. But these factors operated in the context of the new psychology of the period, and of American culture. In an account of psychoanalysis in America, we must consider two other factors, the influence of Darwinian ideas and the changing sexual morality among the American middle class.

David Shakow and David Rapaport have argued persuasively, in their superb study of the influence of Freud on American psychology, that what influence psychoanalysis has been able to exert on American psychology came into the discipline through the channel of the functional psychology of this first generation, and through the lingering effects of functionalism on the margins of the behaviorism which followed (6). The functional psychologists were influenced by Darwin in their revolt against the structuralist analysis of consciousness into its elements. The functionalists emphasized instead the study of mental processes—the dynamic purposes which directed human behavior, and the character of mind as an organ useful in the adaptation of the organism. Functionalism was a loose orientation rather than a developed theory; almost everyone to whom the label can be applied developed a rather individual theoretical framework.

When, in the middle 1890s, Hall gave up the attempt to follow a rigorously scientific psychology, he began to work out his own genetic version of functional psychology. His devotion to genetic psychology was probably the single most important factor in his sympathetic recognition of psychoanalysis. Hall had always been attracted to evolutionary ideas, and had become impressed with the developmental approach through his studies of historical religious criticism, and of Hegel, Comte, and Herbert Spencer—that is, through the many sources of historical and evolutionary consciousness in the nineteenth century prior to Darwin. He had also been early schooled in romantic literature and such dynamic philosophies as those of Schopenhauer and Von Hartmann. When he studied Darwinian biology seriously, it confirmed inclinations of long standing.

Hall formulated a psychology based on the central role of what he called "feeling-instincts." These feeling-instincts, he believed, were native to the individual, but acquired through experience in the long history of the race. As each individual developed, these instincts appeared in sequence. Ontogeny recapitulates phylogeny. But Hall studied this process in the context of individual development and thus came to concepts *somewhat* similar to Freud's; he talked, for example, about repression, reversion, and sublimation, which he called irradiation. The result of these processes, he believed, was a psyche which "seems built layer upon layer of partly isolated yet strangely interacting strata," a psyche in which much of the dynamic structure is unconscious and ill-coordinated, yet acts powerfully on behavior.

These unconscious layers, Hall said, revealed themselves in "the many-voiced comments, the sense of assent and dissent, pleasure and pain, the elation of strength or the esthetic responses, the play of intuitions, the impulses to do or not to do, automatic tensions or contractions" which run along beneath the conscious stream of images; and, he added, the "mild or incipient insanities [which anyone] that is honest and has true self-knowledge will . . . confess to recognizing in his own soul . . ." Hall obviously was sensitive to the troubled workings of his own mind. Evolutionary and biological conceptions allowed him to see these many strangely-interacting layers as deposits of past developmental stages. Unlike Freud, however, Hall traced these stages to the distant racial past and not to the dynamics of the living individual. Hall concluded that what was needed to understand the psyche was, quite literally, an "archeology of mind" (7).

Hall was thus in a position to recognize the power of Freud's genetic theory and to appreciate the clarity it brought to processes he had only vaguely sensed. He was also, of course, in a position to distort Freud's theory by melting it into his own phylogenetically oriented geneticism. After 1909 Hall wavered back and forth a good deal in his estimate of Freud's theories. At first declaring to Freud that he would "ring the bell" for him, he then balked at what he regarded as Freud's pervasive overemphasis on sexuality. Eventually he returned to a very positive view of the importance of psychoanalysis, but he continued to regard it as one facet, if the central one, of his own larger genetic psychology (8).

James' psychology was not built on a genetic theory, nor did Freud's psychoanalysis have such central importance to his overall functional framework. Many of the positive insights in James' work, which historians have pointed to as showing his sympathy to Freudian ideas, reflect however the same kind of genetic and romantic influences which we have already seen at work in Hall. James, too, postulated an instinct psychology and he was also aware of multiple layers of the mind and the way in which these stray forms of consciousness could be linked to earlier developmental stages. James had, however, one further source of interest in the unconscious—indeed it may have been his chief one— and that was his religious interest. James always regarded the subconscious states which appeared in psychopathology as peculiarly close to religious revelation. The most substantial psychological use to which he put the concept of the unconscious—or as he called it, the subliminal consciousness—was in his study of *The Varieties of Religious Experience.* James' biological, Darwinian interest served as a bridge linking his religious roots and his openness to Freudian psychopathology (9).

James himself never served directly as an advocate of Freud's views. Now wholly taken up with philosophy, he did not live long after the Clark conference. Just what he thought of psychoanalysis has been disputed, for the positive words he reportedly left with Ernest Jones were not echoed in letters he wrote after the conference. In these letters he said that Freud personally impressed him as a "man obsessed with fixed ideas" and "I strongly suspect Freud, with his dream-theory of being a regular hallucine." "Dream symbolism," he said, "was a most dangerous method." Still, James hoped that "Freud and his pupils will push their ideas to their utmost limits, so that we may learn what they are." Undoubtedly they "cover some facts, and will add to our understanding of 'functional' psychology, which is the real psychology" (10). James' response to Freud was in fact very similar to Hall's—both showed a distaste for the pervasive sexual symbolism which Freud proposed in his dream theory; both registered enthusiasm over the other directions of Freud's insights; and both accepted psychoanalysis only within the larger framework of their own, functional psychology.

Probably the most important aspect of Jamesian psychology to influence the American reception of psychoanalysis was one which had little direct connection with the springs of James' interest in Freud: the concept of habit. Indeed, the great influence of James' chapter on habit in his *Principles of Psychology* is a revealing curiosity. James himself, when he published the chapter as a separate article three years before the *Principles,* described it to a correspondent as "a mere potboiler, which I had long had, written, in my drawer. No new thing in it, so I hardly advise you to read it" (11). James is quite right, if we judge the chapter by itself. Yet James must have sensed three years later, when he made the essay on habit the fourth chapter in the *Principles,* just after his basic opening chapters on the psychology of the brain, that the concept of habit was essential to his whole conception of psychology.

For James, habit was the basic behavioral unit of learning. It could easily be conceived as rooted in the stimulus-response mechanisms he described at the base of nervous function on the one hand, and on the other, it transformed the elemental associationism of the older British atomists and the newer structuralists into a functional category of mental process. Habit was not only the basic unit of psychological functioning, but it moved easily toward behaviorism. It is no accident that James began his chapter on habit with the observation, "When we look at living creatures from an outward point of view, one of the first things that strike us is that they are bundles of habits" (12). However much or little James recognized the significance of his treatment of habit at the time, his functionally oriented colleagues and behaviorist successors recognized it at once. The concept of habit became perhaps the central concept of the new psychology for decades thereafter.

The changing use of the concept of habit from James to behaviorism is an area which historians need to explore in greater depth. By means of the concept of habit American psychologists could rework some of Freud's basic ideas within the context of a behavioristic learning theory, but they could also eschew or obscure thereby a great deal of Freud's dynamic intentions. The concept of habit is one key to the slow and partial acceptance of psychoanalysis which ultimately occurred in American psychology—what Shakow and Rapaport describe as the heavy influence of Freud's "conceptions" but the lack of influence of his specific "concepts."

Finally, I would like to consider the transformation in sexual morality which was beginning to occur in America during the first two decades of the century. Nathan Hale has argued that by the end of the nineteenth century the American business and professional classes were under the grip of a peculiarly virulent form of "civilized morality," a rigid code which prescribed sex for procreation only, so as to shore up the late marriages, smaller families, and work-orientation required by a mature industrial society still ignorant of scientific birth control (13).

As Hale has shown, many of those who early appreciated the power of Freud's ideas were sensitive to the way this civilized morality had inhibited sexually and crippled personality. Both James and Hall were victims of this Victorian code and both of them, particularly Hall, participated in the effort to treat the subject of sexuality with greater candor, to break down public reticence on the subject and thus to secure a more healthful sexual development. James expressed this attitude occasionally in comments and in his general demeanor; Hall worked actively in the public purity movement which attacked prostitution and venereal disease; he lectured and wrote on the importance of sexuality in development, particularly in adolescence; and for a while, he urged sex education in the schools.

Although psychologists of the generation of Hall and James did not realize it at the time, their modest efforts at enlightenment inadvertently contributed to a more profound change in sexual behavior than they bargained for. This change in sexual behavior, documented by Kinsey, and related to the more hedonistic values of the new consumption economy, broke into public view during the 1920s. During the progressive period, before this change in sexual behavior had gone very far, Hall and James could be optimistic about the ability of more enlightened attitudes to guide the sexual instinct into respectable channels. Historians have noted the importance of this progressive optimism in the positive reception of Freud in this period (14). Psychologists like Hall echoed the new psychiatrists and analysts in their faith in sublimation and the usefulness of psychoanalysis in facilitating the healthful sublimation of sexuality into monogamous marriage and the higher civilized pursuits of art, religion, and so on.

Progressive optimism was not the only response to Freud's theories, however. After 1912 and particularly during the 1920s, as the sexual revolution gained momentum, anxiety about the new code of sexual behavior was rising among the American middle class, and the anxiety generated, I believe, a resurgence of puritanical attitudes toward sex. John B. Watson's behaviorism was in part a source and reflection of this "new Puritanism." Watson had been initially attracted to Freudian theory and he developed behaviorism not only in dialogue with the older functional and structural psychology, but in dialogue with psychoanalysis. His accounts of behaviorism in the twenties, and particularly his behavioristic prescriptions for child-rearing, which were very widely distributed, betray a distinct fear of the sexuality which Freud had disclosed at the dynamic core of human nature (15).

So great was his anxiety that he prescribed a rigid, ascetic regimen for infants and children. Watson urged, and most of the child-rearing manuals of the twenties agreed, that parents must not fondle, kiss, or stimulate their infants in any way, lest their sexuality be overly aroused. Pacifiers were out, but so was almost any kind of physical contact, except the unavoidable functional handling, which must be done in a matter-of-fact way, and outgrown as soon as possible. The increasing anxiety in the 1920s over sexuality is one subject which needs further investigation by historians. I believe it contributed to Watson's turning away from psychoanalysis and his development of behaviorism. It may have affected the quick acceptance of behaviorism by other American psychologists as well and hence the less congenial attitude towards psychoanalysis which came to prevail in American psychology.

By 1920 academic psychology had lost the eclectic and heretical caste, the loose functional outlook, and the scientific flexibility which had opened it to Freudian influence for a few brief decades. The outcome was unfortunate both for academic psychology and for the increasingly sectarian development of psychoanalysis.

NOTES

1. A standard source on the history of American psychology during this period is Edwin G. Boring, *A History of Experimental Psychology*, New York: Appleton-Century-Crofts, 1957. See also Dorothy Ross, *G. Stanley Hall: The Psychologist as Prophet*, Chicago: University of Chicago Press, 1972, Chaps. 9 and 10.

2. Ernest Jones, *The Life and Work of Sigmund Freud*, New York: Basic Books, 1955, Vol. II, pp. 214-15.

3. On William James and his psychological career, the standard source is Ralph Barton Perry, *The Thought and Character of William James*, Boston: Little, Brown, 1935, 2 vols.

4. Nathan G. Hale, Jr., *Freud and the Americans: The Beginnings of Psychoanalysis in the United States, 1876-1917*, London: Oxford University Press, 1971.

5. On Stanley Hall, see his revealing, but often inaccurate, autobiography, *Life and Confessions of a Psychologist*, New York: D. Appleton, 1923, and Ross, *op cit.*

6. David Shakow and David Rapaport, *The Influence of Freud on American Psychology, Psychological Issues*, Vol. IV, no. 1, 1964.

7. Ross, *op. cit.*, pp. 370-74.

8. *Ibid.*, p. 395ff.

9. William James, *The Varieties of Religious Experience*, New York: Longmans, Green, 1902.

10. Perry, *op. cit.*, Vol. II, pp. 122-23.

11. *Ibid.*, p. 90.

12. William James, *The Principles of Psychology*, New York: Henry Holt, 1890, Vol. I, p. 104.

13. Hale, *op. cit.*, ch. 2.

14. *Ibid.*, ch. 13.

15. On Watson, see David Bakan, "Behaviorism and American Urbanization," *Journal of the History of the Behavioral Sciences*, II, 1966, pp. 5-28.

CHAPTER 4

The Influence of Psychoanalysis
Upon American Culture

John C. Burnham, Ph.D.

LATE IN THE 1960s an era ended when, in both medicine and American culture in general, psychoanalysis increasingly came under attack. Competent eyewitnesses were agreeing that, as California psychiatrist Judd Marmor put it, "the prestige of psychoanalysis in this country appears to have dropped significantly in academic and scientific circles." Substantial numbers of psychiatrists hastened to dissociate themselves from a strictly analytic stance, and the analyst was no longer so often the ideal of youngsters in the profession. Other intellectuals felt free to portray Freud's work as an undesirable holdover from the past. The shifting opinions of medical and cultural leaders may well have reflected merely the total victory of psychoanalytic thinking, a point in time beyond which attack was not a real threat to those in and near psychoanalysis. Or a real change, to something new, may have occurred. Not enough time has passed yet to reveal which. But in either case, the historical turning point affords some perspective on the impact of psychoanalysis upon American culture (1).

Freud's work came upon Americans in two different waves. The first

Presented January 22, 1976. John C. Burnham is Professor of History and Lecturer in Psychiatry, Ohio State University, Columbus, Ohio. Preparation of this paper has been supported in part by NIH Grant LM02539 from the National Library of Medicine.

wave coincided with Progressive reform, psychotherapy, and new ideas about the place of children and sexuality in American society. The second wave came with the bureaucratic society that developed in the 1930s and after, especially following World War II, when the numbers of people increased so as to move American society to a new scale and when new groups with new values became dominant.

In both periods, the primary carriers and disseminators of Freud's teachings were the physicians; increasingly, as the years went on, those who practiced psychoanalysis. The various patterns are documented by other contributors to this volume.

Well before World War I the followers of Freud clustered together in a few cities, reinforcing each other and attempting to convert others to the psychoanalytic viewpoint. Fifty years later the conversion experience and ways of holding beliefs among Freudians still suggested religious institutionalization and commitment. Members of analytic groups, usually later formalized into psychoanalytic societies and institutes, performed two important functions. First, they acted as apostles who could persuade others to join the ranks, for, as in all other major innovations in science, true belief and conversion almost invariably required personal explication before a potential believer made a commitment to new views. Second, they presented relatively undistorted versions of what Freud taught (2).

The influence of psychoanalysis was of course not limited to propagation of orthodox Freudianism by the best qualified analysts and their immediate lay adherents. Far more often Freud's influence was partial and piecemeal, carried by cultural agents who had little or no comprehension of the total work of Freud, its internal consistency, or its significance. Nevertheless the analytic groups represent initial influence and provide indications of the general direction of the flow of events. And it would be as much a mistake to underestimate the analysts' influence as to overestimate it.

The two phases of psychoanalysis in America are in fact most easily delineated by internal changes in both content and personnel in the analytic movement. During the 1920s the initial propagators of psychoanalysis lost much of their effectiveness. The most prestigious Freudian, J. J. Putnam of Boston, died in 1918. The most loyal and vigorous disciple, A. A. Brill of New York, went through a period of bad personal relations with Freud. Illness incapacitated Horace W. Frink, the most promising of the Yankees. Trigant Burrow developed his own ideas.

Many others tended to retreat into more general psychiatry, particularly in the guise of mental hygiene.

By the end of the 1920s, the analytically sophisticated understood that Freud had turned aside from his earlier emphasis on instinctual drive and repression as such. Within a decade or two, most of Freud's close adherents were building on his new structural scheme of id, ego, and superego to work within what was called ego psychology, in practice emphasizing the strengths and competences of the psychical apparatus. These new ideas were often carried by distinguished refugees who came to dominate American psychoanalysis, ably seconded by a new group of Americans who had studied directly with Freud or some other European in the twenties and early thirties. The combination of new versions of analysis and new personnel represented essentially a fresh departure and furnished a burst of energy that pushed the second wave so fast and so far as to overshadow completely the substantial continuity from the initial group of Americans who took up Freud's ideas (3).

By 1940, in fact, as people at that time recognized, the center of world psychoanalysis had shifted to the United States. The refugee analysts were self-confident and extraordinarily able. The ease with which they moved into the analytic community, moreover, reflected the substantial success of the psychoanalytic movement in maintaining an international character. This transit of endeavor, ideas, and personnel was facilitated markedly by a new and particular receptivity of American culture to international viewpoints (4).

Since the discontinuity within organized psychoanalysis coincided with major shifts in American culture, the impact of the analysts has to be viewed in terms of rapid changes in social groups. The formerly dominant cultural groups, both Progressive and conservative, consisted mostly of persons narrowly American, often dominated by New England consciences. By 1940, however, the nation's cultural life was dominated by a new elite, a Jewish and WASP group in revolt against ethnic provincialism—the WASPs against "100 per cent Americanism" and all that it stood for, the Jews against the village culture of the ghetto. The new ideal was a cosmopolitan culture, and the rise of Hitlerism made this American aggregation feel like the inheritors of Western civilization and humaneness, a feeling intensified as European emigrants joined the group (5).

The new liberal intelligentsia played the essential role in popularizing psychoanalysis and broadening the influence of Freud's teachings. Relatively direct evidence exists in the form of known personal contacts and, perhaps even more important, personal analyses. A similar, and in part identical, group dominated the mass media, especially those originating in New York and Los Angeles, and these leaders exerted a similar influence on a lower level of American culture. Many major figures in the entertainment world were in fact psychoanalyzed. Brill held back from writing an autobiography for fear that it might turn out to be something of an exposé involving many well-known members of the art and literary world (6). So close were the contacts between the analysts and the new arbiters of culture that it was more than coincidence that the end of dominance of the liberal intelligentsia in the 1960s came at the same time as troubled questioning among the analysts.

Within this very concrete and specific social context of direct influence, it is possible to suggest how powerful the impact of psychoanalysis was and to go on and suggest that, in fact, changes that occurred could represent actual influence. In the context of the intelligentsia as the embodiment of Western civilization, for example, the importance of the analyst's image as cultured cosmopolitan emerges. Many intellectuals saw discussions of literary interpretation in analytic scientific literature as lamentable demonstrations of analysts' softheadedness, or at least tender-mindedness (read: "unscientific"). But to the liberal intelligentsia, the analysts represented scientists who were sensitive to the values of other intellectuals who shared the intellectuals' concern with preserving Western civilization and at the same time with denying those traditional standards that were merely ethnocentric and self-serving. Franz Alexander sensed the core belief when he wrote in 1956, "Psychoanalysis is a true product of that phase of Western civilization which had deep respect for individual differences that people actually have in our complex free societies" (7).

Examination of the second phase of the penetration of Freud's influence into the United States is particularly important because there already exist competent historical accounts of much of the first phase (8). In that first phase, psychoanalysis was carried primarily within two successive, more general movements, psychotherapy and mental hygiene, and popularization was confounded with both general intellectual rebellion and a myriad of books and articles for "the nervous." The second phase of psychoanalysis is complicated by the fact that intellectual avant gardism, books for the nervous, and mental hygiene persisted for many decades even though no longer as significant, or at least only percolating down to those Americans subject to cultural lag. Despite such obcurity and uncertainty, contributed by the continual alterations of the social matrix, it still appears that first phase knowledge did not necessarily contribute to or even facilitate second phase psychoanalysis. Rather, persistence and lag merely added another, contemporaneous version of influence—and distortion.

The core group from whom influence in American culture emanated, the analysts, never numbered more than several hundred. In the heyday of analysis, the 1950s, the various institutes were turning out fewer than a hundred new analysts a year (and the institutes were turning down, and often embittering against psychoanalysis, many times that number of psychiatrists who sought admission) (9). The pressures on the lives of those few hundred were very great. Many agreed with Karl Menninger of Topeka, who asserted in 1944 that there was need in the world for "psychiatric counseling" and that psychoanalysts had important insights they "can and should give to the world." Yet most analysts in fact resisted pressures to involve themselves in various outside causes and reforms. An analyst mostly, as Lawrence S. Kubie lamented in 1950, "practices analysis all day and teaches analysis all night." Such an analyst also worked to maintain skepticism and detachment rather than dedication and belief—except, of course, belief in psychoanalysis (10). The number of the core group, even very late, then, who were active in influencing American life was very small indeed. The more is the wonder that their impact was so great. Magnification occurred not only because of their effects upon elites, especially the WASP-Jewish cultural leaders, but because of two further factors: the institutional setting and the general cultural readiness for Freud's teachings.

The analysts were first of all psychiatrists. Earlier in the twentieth century they had also been neurologists or, more generally, nervous and mental disease specialists. After World War I, the profession of "neuro-psychiatry"—soon generally shortened to the conventional "psychiatry"—developed, with half of the psychiatrists no longer in hospital practice by 1930 and the specialty of psychiatry no longer necessarily identified with psychotic patients. Although still under the domination of hospital psychiatrists until World War II, increasingly the profession took on a public aspect of possessing both wisdom and omnipotence, particularly as preventive mental hygiene moved into many public arenas, including business and education, in the 1920s. The image of the psychiatrist in the 1930s was augmented by widespread publicity given to physiological determinants of behavior, such as endocrine activity, and to new medical procedures, such as electroencephalography and shock therapies (11).

Despite the physical orientation of most psychiatrists, it was the psychotherapy and psychological manipulation advocated by conspicuous specialists, including the analysts, that caught the imagination of the public and, eventually, of the specialty itself. The critical event was World War II. By the late 1940s, the by then familiar figure of the psychiatrist was very frequently identified as an analyst, complete with couch and, to the distress of the analysts, a note pad. This was the cartoon stereotype, and despite the ambivalence he represented, he embodied an astonishing popular belief in his knowledge and power (12).

It is only fair to observe that this idealization of the psychiatrist as analyst was in part based upon the attitudes of the psychiatrists themselves. The bulk of American psychiatrists in the post World War II years often utilized approaches based upon psychoanalytic formulations, the strategy generally referred to as dynamic psychiatry. The extreme in this direction was the analyst, and he increasingly was functioning as an ideal as well as, to a diminishing minority, a devil. And while the ranks of analysts were limited to a few hundred, psychiatrists increased in number to tens of thousands by the 1960s. For years, many of the best students in medical school were becoming interested in psychiatry, and in turn the best residents in psychiatry tended to go on into analytic training (13).

What happened in World War II therefore had two aspects. First, psychiatry gained immense importance in the eyes of both physicians and the general public. Second, everyone, both within and without psychoanalysis, traced to psychoanalysis the content that made such an impression. While a good deal can be shown of the way in which the war experience left a popular impact, exactly what happened to open the door to dynamic, or psychoanalytic, interpretations in medicine and popular thinking remains obscure. One basic fact, with innumerable instances applicable to both medical practice and public awareness, was the personal contact of physicians and service personnel with psychiatric disabilities and psychiatric treatment. While similar experience with so-called shell shock in World War I had led to substantial popularizing of mental hygiene and neuropsychiatry, the scale and conspicuousness of psychiatry in the World War II experience had much more far-reaching effects. Conventional wisdom of the day, both lay and medical, remarked about the large number of cases of "battle fatigue" and the excessive proportion of exclusions and discharges for psychiatric reasons. The great influx of psychoanalytic thinking came, presumably, in explaining to officers, physicians, public, and patients *why* the mental disability occurred and was to be taken seriously (14).

It was in this situation that the analysts, despite their small numbers, clearly gave the most satisfying answers. And they had the chance. At the beginning of the war, the screening instructions for recruits had their origins with Harry Stack Sullivan, who had his own version of dynamic psychiatry. By the end of the war, the man in charge of Army psychiatry and most effective in selling it was William C. Menninger, a member of the Topeka Psychoanalytic Society. John M. Murray, of the Boston Psychoanalytic Society, headed up the Army Air Force psychiatric service. Many a physician or layman who saw the results of psychotherapy or group psychotherapy or especially narcoanalysis, in which the abreaction effects were strikingly like those reported by Freud in his earliest period, decided that there was validity in dynamic explanations of inexplicable behavior and even of some physical problems. The demand for psychiatric treatment and consultation far outran supply, and the hard core of hospital psychiatrists was swamped and passed by (15).

While institutional factors in the 1930s and after account for the propagation of dynamic ideas that were fundamentally Freudian in origin, the readiness of Americans to take up those dynamic explanations is not so easy to explain. Menninger himself noted that the time was ripe for what he was fostering. In May 1945 he reported that "psychiatry, for better or for worse, is receiving a tremendously increased interest. This is manifest on all sides by articles in magazines, in the newspapers, frequent references to psychiatry and psychiatric problems on the radio and in the movies. It is reliably reported that at least six pictures currently being made in Hollywood have a psychiatric tone or overtone. This interest is widely manifest in government agencies, and . . . we have had inquiries and requests for help from a wide variety of such agencies and also from civilian groups" (16).

Despite persistent publicity in the 1930s, pre-war America offered no adequate foundation for a mass movement in favor of psychoanalysis or even psychiatry such as Menninger reported in 1945. The dominant hospital physicians of the late thirties were conservative and tended to view even mental hygiene suspiciously (17). Indeed, in 1945 a number of progressive specialists felt constrained to form the Group for the Advancement of Psychiatry in order to get around the still powerful conservatives in the profession. During the 1930s, psychoanalysis itself was not conspicuous in the mass media, however sophisticated the liberal intelligentsia was in the use of analytic terms, and in the early war years popularization ebbed further, if the *Reader's Guide* is an accurate index. Yet by 1948 psychoanalytic and other varieties of popularization of psychological dynamics caused Frederic Wertham to write in *The New Republic* that "the tremendous amount of popular reading in psychopathology is an important social phenomenon." He himself thought that it distracted people from pressing world problems to what he termed a "cult of personal contentment" (18). By 1950 the frequent appearance of couch situation jokes not just in *The New Yorker* but even in cheap cartoon magazines was the best indicator that the man in the street, even he who was not quite up to illustrated magazines, was expected to know the psychiatrist/psychoanalyst.

For those who not only looked at the pictures in *Life Magazine* but read the articles, there was an official—and well informed—article in 1947 in that weekly:

> A boom has overtaken the once obscure and much maligned profession of psychoanalysis. It is part of the larger boom which simultaneously has engulfed the whole science of psychiatry, in which psychoanalysis is a special therapeutic technique, and which has made the 4,011 accredited psychiatrists about the most sought-after members of the entire medical profession. From the horde of outright psychotics who now occupy more than half of all the hospital beds in the country to the simple-minded folk who seek guidance and solace from the phony tea-leaf "psychiatrists" in Los Angeles and elsewhere, the story is the same—a mass demand for psychiatric help which has swamped facilities and practitioners alike. And of all psychiatrists, the comparative handful of analysts—there are only about 300—seem to be the most heavily besieged.
>
> In part this reflects the alarming prevalence of mental and emotional disorders in the population today; in part, it merely reflects the increase in popular knowledge and acceptance of psychiatry, and especially psychoanalysis, as a cure. During the war millions of service personnel had direct contact with psychiatry for the first time and large numbers of them received more or less elaborate psychiatric treatment. Meantime, a whole new literary genre became popular, with the learned Freudian and the analytic couch as its symbols. Novels about mental illness (*Private Worlds, The Crack-Up, Brainstorm, Snake Pit*, etc.) were frequent. Hollywood quickly followed suit, and numbers of "big" pictures of late have had psychiatric overtones. Indeed it is rare to find a Hollywood musical

these days without some sort of pseudo-Freudian "dream sequence," a convention dating from the huge success of Moss Hart's *Lady in the Dark,* which concerned the efforts of a mixed-up editor of a fashion magazine to solve her difficulties through psychoanalysis.

All this has happened quite suddenly. Several decades ago, to be sure, a few psychoanalytical terms—notably *ego* and *libido*—were part of the vocabulary of the country-club set, and moralists were complaining that the loose conduct of the times was due to Sigmund Freud's engaging theory that sex makes the world go 'round and that it might be dangerous to harbor repressions in this sphere. As far as the average man was concerned, however, psychoanalysis remained dark science, with no apparent usefulness except to the neurotic idle rich . . . (19).

Similar evidence of the widespread popularization of psychoanalysis continued in the following decades. By the 1960s, there were at least three *children's* books alone devoted entirely to Freud. In the 1940s, mental hospital reform flourished in many states and the federal government began heavy subsidies of mental health research and personnel training. By 1963, before a whole new federal program was undertaken, the budget of the National Institute for Mental Health was almost seventy million dollars. Part of the public support for these massive efforts grew out of sympathy for the mentally ill; but a more significant segment involved American hopes for the overall benefits psychiatry might bring (20).

To explain this acceptance, conventional wisdom of that day and since suggested that the psychiatrist had become the priest or authority figure in American culture within a new secularism. But the development of a new authority figure did not take place in a vacuum, nor did World War II destroy religion. A better explanation is that the enthusiasts of dynamic psychiatry and psychoanalysis, like the Menninger brothers, were asserting that they and their colleagues could contribute to a better world because they knew the causes of human unhappiness. Later a conservative cult of contentment—as Wertham suggested—may have been important, but for the decades coinciding with the high tide of psychoanalytic influence in America, the analysts, the deviant analysts, and many of their psychiatric and lay followers persisted in describing the benefits of psychoanalytic treatment and applied psychoanalytic psychology in terms of glowing promises. The public acceptance of psychoanalysis/psychiatry mushroomed in that brief moment of expansive optimism of the 1940s when many Americans really did believe that they could make the postwar social environment a significantly better place in which to live. In 1947 members of the New York Psychoanalytic Institute predicted that 20,000 psychiatrists would be needed for preventive work alone (21). The members of a number of analytic splinter groups were particularly devoted to social reform and wrote eloquently on the subject, drawing substantial public attention. But more than just psychiatry was involved.

Beyond psychiatry, the analysts were involved in medicine and science, and in the image of each one. The rise of psychoanalysis coincided almost exactly with the spectacular transformation of medicine, and the care that Americans took to keep formal psychoanalysis within medicine helped shape the direct influence. Increasingly, descriptions of the functions of medicine in society included not only curing the ill but bringing happiness by means of both physical and mental manipulation. "It is increasingly evident," reported the Rockefeller Foundation as early as 1934, "that physicians generally are being looked to for knowledge that will help in interpreting as well as in guiding the behavior of man . . ." (22). The idea that physicians could work miracles with surgery and pharmacology carried over to the psychiatric realm, and once again the analyst was portrayed as the ultimate wise man and manipulator. One sign of medical acceptance was the number of physicians and members of their families who were analyzed; in the 1950s over half the analytic patients in Los Angeles, for example, fell into this category (23).

But in fact the increasing prestige of science, especially after the advent of atomic energy, endowed anyone who wore a white lab coat with a special kind of authority. And within medicine and science, the second wave of psychoanalysis had a particular claim to prestige: Freud's work, and psychoanalytic literature in general, emphasized the theoretical—far more than comparable medical, scientific, or psychological publications. In another day the theoretical content of Freudian literature had alienated many Americans who preferred that their science be highly empirical. The most damaging criticism of psychoanalysis had always been that it was unscientific. Analysts were deeply offended, for example, when the 1925 president of the American Association for the Advancement of Science, psychologist J. McKeen Cattell, asserted: "Psychoanalysis is not so much a question of science as a matter of taste, Dr. Freud being an artist who lives in the fairyland of dreams among the ogres of perverted sex" (24). To combat the unscientific image, American proponents of Freud in fact showed an extreme readiness to work with psychological testing, with psychosomatic medicine, and with neurology to try to connect Freudian theory with the concrete, the material, the statistical, and the replicable. But as theoretical science became more and more prestigious in the United States, the situation reversed, and the analysts shared in that prestige and were called upon to join, and offer insights and theory to aid the work of, organismic holists and other very "respectable" scientists.

Despite the analysts' attempts to keep their subspecialty within medicine, another discipline, psychology, became almost as important in disseminating knowledge about the work of Freud and his successors. The profession had two rather separate aspects, both of which involved members in spreading the influence of psychoanalysis. The first was as teachers of, ultimately, hundreds of thousands of college students who took elementary courses in the subject each year. As early as 1916 a general textbook had mentioned Freud's ideas, and various teachers, most importantly Edwin B. Holt at Harvard, had even earlier discussed psychoanalytic ideas in lectures. Yet by and large most psychology teachers remained hostile, in general emphasizing their methodological objections and agreeing with Madison Bentley, an experimentalist, who in 1921 commented on the Freudian unconscious that "this confusion of hypothesis with observed and verifiable fact is extremely common within psychology today . . . an illegitimate substitution of forces and faculties for the empirical existence of mind" (25). But the relentless urge of the academic psychologists to gain students and influence led to a steadily increasing inclusion of psychoanalytic ideas in even elementary instruction. Once again, World War II seemed to bring a critical transformation. Textbooks changed to meet what one set of authors described frankly as an alteration in point of view, associated with the war, so as to require material on "problems of personal adjustment." The only obvious event that might have been a cause for any of these new attitudes, beyond the psychological testing of all service personnel, was the production of an extremely widely distributed popular paperback book, *Psychology for the Fighting Man* (1943)—"What you should know about yourself and others." As that book engendered new images and expectations, so increasingly in elementary expositions postwar psychologists concerned themselves with motivation, emotion, abnormality, and personal problem solving with increasingly frequent discussions of psychological therapy and allusions to psychoanalysis. Over the years, as psychology classes proliferated, a substantial fragment of the population had

had at least some exposure to material and vocabulary that had its origin with the Freudians (26).

Even more spectacular in growth was the second aspect of psychology, clinical psychology. After World War II, for every new psychiatrist added to the ranks, two clinical psychologists sprang up, with about the same effectiveness in spreading some knowledge of psychoanalysis. Although many clinical psychologists were attached to school programs, many more were undertaking psychotherapy and sometimes psychoanalysis, in spite of the analysts' attempts to restrict their own numbers to M.D.'s only. Even many relatively well educated people did not discern much difference between a psychiatrist, a psychologist, and a psychoanalyst—and very often there wasn't much, in terms of actual functioning (27). In fact popular interest—again as reflected in the *Reader's Guide*—increased in the postwar decades in the psychology headings far more than in those for psychoanalysis. Such psychologist psychotherapists as Carl Rogers were portrayed in texts and popularizations as equal and competitive with Freud. And unhappy as the Freudians were about it, all psychotherapy brought knowledge of Freud's work, however partial and distorted, from 1905 to the 1970s (28).

The expanding role of psychologists in using and spreading Freud's ideas came to be based increasingly on the changing content and theory of psychology itself. The influence of behaviorism had been to inhibit attention to intrapsychic events but to encourage both adaptive and genetic viewpoints. Because Freud's psychology helped so much in conceptualizing emotion and motivation, however, psychoanalysis was not far from the interests of many psychologists. By the forties and fifties, the learning theorists, who represented the most prestigious element in the discipline, were finding that their concerns, problems, and formulations were startlingly like those of the ego psychologists within psychoanalysis who had inherited the mantle of theoretical orthodoxy among the Freudians—each emphasizing the way a person adjusted to both internal and external reality, and developed competence (29). Much of this change represented Freud's influence on the psychologists. By persistently standing for an ideal or extreme position—as with the psychiatrists—the Freudians helped to give courage to hardheaded experimentalists in dealing with difficult problems such as contexts of perceptions, or motivation and drive. Curiously, the influence in psychology grew on itself: the selfsame group of psychologists who joined Clark Hull's seminars on psychoanalysis and learning at Yale in the 1930s (initiated by

Neal Miller, an analysand) were the leaders in the movement to establish and expand clinical psychology after World War II—using government money and existing, usually experimental, departments of psychology for training the new personnel (30).

All of this specific activity by the analysts, the psychiatrists, and the psychologists provides a set of social structures through which Freud's influence can be traced in definite ways as it came into the United States. The reaction of the dominant WASP-Jewish intelligentsia further shows how receptive were cultural institutions, formal and informal, especially just before, during, and after World War II. Indeed, the confluence of signs of influence in the early 1940s raises the question of what psychoanalysis had to offer Americans at that time, for the phenomena were too striking to represent merely general cultural compatibility.

The obvious need that was met was described by psychiatrist Henri Ellenberger after a visit to the United States in 1952: "In Europe," he observed, "people go to the psychiatrist because of a *symptom*, in America because of a *problem*." The European patient wishes to be restored, Ellenberger continued, while the American wants to have a problem solved, and the psychiatrist therefore becomes a person "who solves problems." And in the United States, Ellenberger observed, the ideal treatment for such patients was psychoanalysis, "acknowledged in America as the therapeutic method par excellence." For whatever reasons, social or personal, post World War II Americans were willing to spend large amounts of money themselves and through their government in the pursuit of a happiness that consisted of solved problems (31).

The cartoonists' ambivalent portrait of the omnipotent analyst, the enthusiasm for social control, first noted in the Progressive era and then surfacing again in the 1940s, and the anti-mental health campaign of the McCarthy period and after—all suggested the power of psychiatry, and especially psychoanalysis, to give people hope that problems could be solved, indeed that people should be happier (32). Advocates—and opponents—of psychoanalysis were all well aware of the possibilities in Freud's teachings. He had himself explored some of them as they affected social processes as well as individual concerns. Freudians were among the leaders in questioning pressures to conform, in suggesting that nonconformists could be happy and well adjusted (although, of course, within analysis there was a vigorous debate on this and kindred issues). The promise of happiness and normality, as philosopher

Walter Kaufmann of Princeton pointed out in 1960, was based on the leveling tradition inherited from Freud: "Like no man before him, he lent substance to the notion that all men are brothers. Criminals and madmen are not devils in disguise, but men and women who have problems [the common heritage] similar to our own; and there, but for one experience or another, go you and I" (33).

Focusing on personal problems and solving them, as a number of observers pointed out, was a particularly effective tactic employed by managers of the increasingly bureaucratic American society, a tactic to head off, indeed, deny, the existence of social discontent (34). The most brilliant of the post-Freudian theorists, Erik Erikson, showed that every culture developed more or less adequate social institutions to accommodate every developmental stage and drive in the life cycle of human beings—all of whom, in every culture, shared life cycles that embodied the universal human so vital in the assumptions of the liberal intelligentsia. Erikson's teachings were easily corrupted into the conservative assumption that any changes that needed to be made were on a one-by-one, individual basis—as in psychoanalytic psychotherapy—and in that individual, not in the culture (35). Similarly, the stress of the ego psychologists on competent, non-disruptive functioning fit precisely into the needs of the bureaucratic society for citizens who were function-oriented and played their assigned social roles in the complex machinery of production, distribution, and gratification. Indeed, the idea that Freud's teachings were merely the agencies of social forces raises directly the possibility that psychoanalysis was a symptom of historical change rather than a cause of it. Surely the distortions of Freud's ideas in the United States, in the direction of making them both more medical and more social than in Europe, suggests the powerlessness of ideas to mold rather than to be used by presumably deeper historical currents.

One sensible way of testing the impact of psychoanalysis on American culture is to examine very specific areas where the influence can be demonstrated, most notably the learned disciplines. In psychiatry the impact was fundamental, and in psychology also. In anthropology and sociology, from William I. Thomas's four wishes to recent social psychological theory, again competent studies suggest basic influence (36). Other students have demonstrated impressive use of the ideas of Freud and his followers in literature and art and religion (37). In short, such evidence covers all of what is conventionally known as culture, both high and, as noted earlier, popular culture. The positive evidence that psychoanalytic ideas affected those who embodied both cultures is profound and impressive (38).

But in order to assess possible negative evidence—the changes attributed to psychoanalytic thinking that can be accounted for as well or better by other historical forces—a different approach is appropriate. A brief test of two alleged influences, which can be called, respectively, hidden motives and sex, suggests much use of the name and vocabulary of psychoanalysis to cover the effects of other forces—and at the same time much real influence (39).

Americans learned about the hidden motives of men from many sources in Western culture besides Freud. The most concrete and contemporary was Marxism. Bohemians and intellectuals who began uncovering hidden motives, presumably in the Freudian mode (in fact usually crudely sexual in the early days), had before that learned the technique of analyzing economic motives hidden behind common, socially accepted rationalizations. Yet the mechanisms of motive conversion that Americans did learn from Freud made analysis of hidden motives more systematic and more convincing (40).

The discussion and to a lesser extent the acceptance of sexual feelings and behavior presumably so characteristic of twentieth century America have often been attributed, for good or ill, to Freud. In this case the social hygiene movement was clearly antecedent in time and was in part —because Freud was one of the few authors available in English who had touched on the subject—the agency through which Freud's ideas were popularized. Certainly during the first wave of psychoanalysis Freud was the rationale, not the cause of events. As Waldo Frank recalled, girls who came to Greenwich Village wanting to be seduced would have given in just as easily to persuasion couched in terms of social liberation as they did to warnings about the dangers of being inhibited. Like those young ladies, writers favoring or opposing what they imagined to be changes in American sexual attitudes and actions blamed and praised Freud. In later years it was common to overlook the analysts' emphasis on the intrapsychic functioning of sexuality and rather—and inaccurately—to connect the analysts with perceived behavior and with the stress on undifferentiated "outlets" found in the works of Alfred Kinsey and his successors (41).

If, then, these examples are expanded to a systematic evaluation of the influences of psychoanalysis on the United States, account must be taken not only of multifarious levels and types of influences but of possible concurrent cultural changes in which Freud's work was merely incidental. What can be made, for instance, of the fact that Freud was stressing intrapsychic conflict just when the writers of novels were shifting their focus from external actions and social relationships to inner feelings and psychological development? Or, again, if Freud's ideas of the unconscious and instinctual drives were utilized to verbalize a new theory of evil in the world, that is, to provide a way of articulating an awareness of irrationality in human affairs, how much influence does that mere use of a psychoanalytic vocabulary signify? Contrary instances, in which concepts are used without vocabulary, are equally complicating. The most important is the evidence of A. Michael Sulman that the influence of psychoanalysis was profound indeed in the work of Benjamin Spock and other child rearing advisers who utilized many psychoanalytic ideas without the terminology, including concepts previously absent from child rearing literature, such as penis envy and sibling rivalry (42).

When all of the filtering of the complications is completed, the evidence reveals a number of modes in which psychoanalysis affected American culture—even discounting the ability of Americans to read Freud as they read the Bible, namely, picking out parts and interpreting the text so as to be able to cite passages in defense of almost any position at all (43).

In many areas, such as changes in sexual attitudes or the need to have problems solved, larger forces than psychoanalysis *were* determining the general direction of change. What psychoanalytic ideas contributed was some of the form that the changes took. The causes of apparently inexplicable behavior, for example, were often found in instinctual drives and defense mechanisms rather than the devil or economic man. On quite a different level, the patient-analyst relationship became an important model for social interaction and for suggesting human relationships in the process of overcoming difficulties (most conspicuously and formally in the pastoral counseling movement). While Freud's work was not the cause of much social change as such in many areas, he and his followers did influence the ways in which historical forces worked themselves out in American society (44).

As in both psychiatry and psychology, one fundamentally important function of psychoanalysis in American life was that of representing an extreme position. Political historians have long since pointed out the role of extremists in social processes in the United States. An extremist to either left or right makes a substantial shift in position toward the extreme appear to be "moderate," and moderate, middle-of-the-road positions are those which command the consensus necessary for Americans to take action. So psychoanalysis, a well thought out, generally consistent position, enabled basically conservative people in many fields to move at least some distance toward Freud's position—and to take it seriously. Such partial acceptance may represent distortion—but it does also represent influence (45).

This role of psychoanalysis as extreme or ideal was particularly important in helping the dominant cultural group maintain important values—those encapsulated in the Western civilization conception. The perceptive Chicago analyst, Maxwell Gitelson, who chose to speak for the most orthodox Freudians in 1955, believed with considerable justification that in practice his work and that of his colleagues created "a bastion of creative individualism" (46).

Freud was influential in the culture because he made sense within that Western tradition. People have been puzzled to understand the force that caused many important and central literary people and scientists alike to repeat in print elementary formulations of psychoanalysis as if trying to convey some of Freud's basic ideas to the reader. So often the id, ego, and superego, or the list of so-called mental mechanisms, were entirely alien to previous—and successive—work of such thinkers. Some of the interest of course can be written off in ad hominem terms as merely the attempt of a person to solve his own personal problems, or perhaps an aberration, like a temporary interest in Marilyn Monroe or genealogy. But the list of such cultural leaders, including those who were not analyzed, was over the years far too long to be dealt with on an individual level. In the mass, interest in even the detailed structure of the Freudian schema was a cultural phenomenon, symptomatic not necessarily of cultural attraction so much as of the awesome power of the intellect of Sigmund Freud. Good minds recognized that power, and in that recognition they translated it into an historical force. Such a major thinker who was widely read could influence any civilization in which surpassing intellectual achievement commanded respect.

NOTES

1. Marmor, J., "The Current Status of Psychoanalysis in American Psychiatry," *Amer. J. Psychiat.*, 1968, 125, 679. Other examples include Frankel, F. H., "Psychiatry Beleaguered: Or the Psychiatric Identity Crisis," *Psychiat. Quar.*, 1969, 43, 410-413; Vispo, R. H., "Psychiatry: Paradigm of Our Times," *Psychiat. Quar.*, 1972, 46, 208-219.

A particularly well balanced assessment is Mora, G., "Recent Psychiatric Developments (Since 1939)," in Arieti, S., Ed., *American Handbook of Psychiatry*, 2nd ed., New York: Basic Books, 1974, Vol. I, pp. 43-58. One of the most significant attacks was Millett, K., *Sexual Politics*, Garden City, New York: Doubleday, 1970, *passim*.

2. Discussion of the sociology of psychoanalytic groups is in Burnham, J. C., *Psychoanalysis and American Medicine, 1894-1918: Medicine, Science, and Culture*, New York: International Universities Press, 1967. See also Knight, R. P., "The Present Status of Organized Psychoanalysis in the United States," *J. Amer. Psychoanal. Assoc.*, 1953, 1, 197-221.

3. The history can be traced in Oberndorf, C. P., *A History of Psychoanalysis in America*, New York: Grune & Stratton, 1953, supplemented by Burnham, *Psychoanalysis and American Medicine, op. cit.*, and by Millet, J. A. P., "Psychoanalysis in the United States," in Alexander, F., Eisenstein, S., and Grotjahn, M., Eds., *Psychoanalytic Pioneers*, New York: Basic Books, 1966, pp. 547-596. Contemporary observations are in Zilboorg, G., et al., "Present Trends in Psychoanalytic Theory and Practice," *Bull. Menninger Clinic*, 1944, 8, 3-17.

4. See, for example, Alexander, F., "Psychoanalysis Comes of Age," *Psychoan. Quar.*, 1939, 8, 299-306; Fermi, L., *Illustrious Immigrants, The Intellectual Migration from Europe, 1930-41*, Chicago: University of Chicago Press, 1968, especially chap. VI.

5. Hollinger, D. A., "Ethnic Diversity, Cosmopolitanism and the Emergence of the American Liberal Intelligentsia," *Amer. Quar.*, 1975, 25, 133-151. *Perspectives in American History*, 1968, 2.

6. Burnham, J. C., "Psychoanalysis in American Civilization Before 1918," unpublished doctoral dissertation, Stanford University, 1958, chap. IX. It would be easy but to some extent in bad taste to assemble the remarkable roster of the analyzed.

7. Alexander, F., "Psychoanalysis in Western Culture," *Amer. J. Psychiat.*, 1956, 112, 694.

8. In addition to works already cited, see Matthews, F. H., "The Americanization of Sigmund Freud: Adaptations of Psychoanalysis Before 1917," *J. Amer. Stud.*, 1967, 1, 39-62; Hale, N. G., Jr., *Freud and the Americans, the Beginnings of Psychoanalysis in the United States, 1876-1917*, New York: Oxford University Press, 1971; Burnham, J. C., "The New Psychology: From Narcissism to Social Control," in Braeman, J., Bremner, R. H., and Brody, D., Eds., *Change and Continuity in Twentieth-Century America: The 1920's*, Columbus: Ohio State University Press, 1968, pp. 351-398; and Covert, C. L., "Freud on the Front Page: Transmission of Freudian Ideas in the American Newspapers of the 1920's," unpublished Ph.D. dissertation, Syracuse University, 1975.

9. See *Bull. Amer. Psychoan. Assoc.* and Lewin, B. D., and Ross, H., *Psychoanalytic Education in the United States*, New York: Norton, 1960.

10. Menninger, K., "Present Trends in Psychoanalytic Theory and Practice," *Bull. Menninger Clinic*, 1944, 8, 14-17; Kubie, L. S., "The Dilemma of the Analyst in a Troubled World," *Bull. Amer. Psychoan. Assoc.*, 1950, 6, 1-4.

11. Burnham, J. C., "The New Psychology," *op. cit.;* Burnham, J. C., "The Struggle Between Physicians and Paramedical Personnel in American Psychiatry, 1917-41," *J. Hist. Med. Allied Sci.*, 1974, 29, 93-106. An important example of popularization is Ray, M. B., *Doctors of the Mind, The Story of Psychiatry*, Boston: Little, Brown, 1942.

12. Redlich, F. C., "The Psychiatrist in Caricature: An Analysis of Unconscious Attitudes Toward Psychiatry," *Amer. J. Orthopsychiat.*, 1950, 20, 560-571; Plank, R., "Portraits of Fictitious Psychiatrists," *Amer. Imago*, 1956, 13, 259-268; Winick, C., "The Psychiatrist in Fiction," *Journ. Nerv. Ment. Dis.*, 1963, 136, 43-57.

13. Gitelson, M., "Psychoanalyst, U.S.A., 1955," *Amer. J. Psychiat.*, 1956, 112, 700-701,

was one among many who commented on this phenomenon. See, too, such discussions as Benjamin, J. D., "Psychoanalysis and Psychoanalytic Psychotherapy," *Psychoan. Quar.*, 1947, 16, 169-176.

14. Anderson, R. S., et al., Eds., *Neuropsychiatry in World War II*, 2 vols., Washington: Office of the Surgeon General, Department of the Army, 1966-1973. Important examples were Stern, E. M., "Don't Let the Big Word Scare You," *Reader's Digest*, May, 1944, 104-106; Cooke, E. D., *All But Me and Thee, Psychiatry at the Foxhole Level*, Washington: Infantry Journal Press, 1946; Rennie, T. A. C., and Woodward, L. E., *Mental Health in Modern Society*, New York: The Commonwealth Fund, 1948.

15. Menninger, W. C., "Psychiatry and the Army," *Psychiatry*, 1944, 7, 175-181; Menninger, W. C., "Psychiatric Objectives in the Army," *Amer. J. Psychiat.*, 1945, 102, 102-107; Grinker, R. R., and Spiegel, J. P., *Men Under Stress*, Philadelphia: Blakiston, 1945; Anderson, *Neuropsychiatry in World War II, op. cit.*

16. Menninger, "Psychiatric Objectives in the Army," *op. cit.*, 102. See, similarly, *Psychoan. Quar.*, 1947, 16, 294.

17. E.g., see Myerson, A., "The Attitude of Neurologists, Psychiatrists and Psychologists Toward Psychoanalysis," *Amer. J. Psychiat.*, 1939, 96, 623-641. One of the important events of the 1930s was the campaign of the Rockefeller Foundation to build up the specialty of psychiatry and fund research in that specialty and cognate disciplines. Although Rockefeller money was extremely important to psychoanalysts in particular cases (especially the Chicago group), most of the funds went to biologically oriented studies and to the older psychiatric establishment.

18. Wertham, F., "The Cult of Contentment," *The New Republic*, 1948, 118, 22-25.

19. Wickware, F. S., "Psychoanalysis," *Life*, Feb. 3, 1947, 98; Haveman, E., *The Age of Psychology*, New York: Simon & Schuster, 1957.

20. See such works as Redlich, F. C., "What the Citizen Knows About Psychiatry," *Ment. Hygiene*, 1950, 34, 64-79, and the important document, Joint Commission on Mental Illness and Health, *Action for Mental Health*, New York: Basic Books, 1961; Brand, J. L., "The National Mental Health Act of 1946: A Retrospect," *Bull. Hist. Med.*, 1965, 39, 231-245.

21. *Psychoan. Quar.*, 1947, 16, 597. The best known document is Menninger, W. C., *Psychiatry in a Troubled World, Yesterday's War and Today's Challenge*, New York: Macmillan, 1948.

22. *The Rockefeller Foundation Annual Report*, 1934, 78.

23. Medical acceptance, at least in part, of psychoanalysis was of great importance. Gregg, A., "The Place of Psychoanalysis in Medicine," in Alexander, F., and Ross H., Eds., *20 Years of Psychoanalysis*, New York: Norton, 1953, p. 47, made the point this way: "To begin with, medical men have for years regarded psychiatry as an island lying off the coast of the mainland of medicine, doubtless connected geologically with the mainland but not very accessible to less than adventurous spirits. For the past ten years psychiatry has been a sort of St. Michel, an island only when the tides of feeling are at flood. You need no reminder of the somewhat similar status accorded by psychiatrists to psychoanalysts."

24. Cattell, J. M., "Some Psychological Experiments," *Science*, 1926, 63, 5.

25. Bentley, M., et al., "Dynamical Principles in Recent Psychology," *Psychol. Monographs*, 1921, 30, 16.

26. For complete examination see Shakow, D., and Rapaport, D., *The Influence of Freud on American Psychology*, New York: International Universities Press, 1964; Boring, E. G., Langfeld, H. S., and Weld, H. P., *Foundations of Psychology*, New York: Wiley, 1948, pp. vii-viii; Burnham, "Psychoanalysis in American Civilization," *op. cit.* 1971, 233.

27. Kubie, L. S., "The Pros and Cons of a New Profession: A Doctorate in Medical Psychology," *Texas Rep. Biol. Med.*, 1954, 12, 692-737.

28. See Reisman, J. M., *The Development of Clinical Psychology*, New York: Appleton-Century-Crofts, 1966; Garber, R. S., "The Relationship of Psychiatry to Medicine," *Psychiat. Digest*, 1969, 30, 11-15. And on Rogers, see Harris, H. I., review of White, *The Abnormal Personality*, in *Psychoan. Quar.*, 1948, 19, 259.

29. The central document is White, R. W., "Motivation Reconsidered: The Concept of Competence," *Psychol. Rev.*, 1959, 66, 297-333. Earlier examples are represented by Levy, D. M., "Animal Psychology in Its Relation to Psychiatry," in Alexander, F., and Ross, H., Eds., *Dynamic Psychiatry*, Chicago: University of Chicago Press, 1952, pp. 483-507.

30. Boring, E. G., et al., *Psychoanalysis as Seen by Analyzed Psychologists*, Washington: American Psychological Association, 1953; Shakow and Rapoport, *The Influence of Freud*, op. cit., Reisman, *Development of Clinical Psychology*, op. cit., 296-303.

31. Ellenberger, H., "A Comparison of European and American Psychiatry," *Bull. Menninger Clinic*, 1955, 19, 43-44, 51. One well-known illustrative document was Rolo, C., Ed., *Psychiatry in American Life*, New York: Dell, 1966 [1963].

32. E.g., Auerback, A., "The Anti-Mental Health Movement," *Amer. J. Psychiat.*, 1963, 120, 105-111.

33. One collection of typical statements is Nelson, B., et al., *Psychoanalysis and the Future. A Centenary Commemoration of the Birth of Sigmund Freud*, New York: National Psychological Association for Psychoanalysis, 1957; Kaufmann, W., "Freud and the Tragic Virtues," *Amer. Scholar*, 1960, 29, 469.

34. Burnham, "The New Psychology," op. cit.; Lasch, C., *The New Radicalism in American (1889-1963): The Intellectual as a Social Type*, New York: Knopf, 1965, p. 146.

35. The basic document is Erikson, E., *Childhood and Society*, New York: Norton, 1950. Erikson himself of course harbored no such conservative ideas.

36. E.g., Hinkle, G. J., "The Role of Freudianism in American Sociology," unpublished doctoral dissertation, University of Wisconsin, 1951; Jones, R. A., "Freud and American Sociology," *J. Hist. Behav. Sci.*, 1974, 10, 21-39.

37. Examples are: Muller, H. J., "The New Psychology in the Old Fiction," *Sat. Rev. Lit.*, Aug. 21, 1937, 3-4; DeVoto, B., "Freud's Influence on Literature," *Sat. Rev. Lit.*, Oct. 7, 1939, 10-11; Hoffman, F. J., *Freudianism and the Literary Mind. 1909-1949*, 2nd ed., New York: Grove Press, 1959 [1957]; Sievers, W. D., *Freud on Broadway, A History of Psychoanalysis and the American Drama*, New York: Hermitage House, 1955; Fraiberg, L., *Psychoanalysis and American Literary Criticism*, Detroit: Wayne State University Press, 1960.

38. See, for example, Brosin, H. W., "A Review of the Influence of Psychoanalysis on Current Thought," in Alexander and Ross, *Dynamic Psychiatry*, op. cit., pp. 508-553, and the evidence offered in such works as Kubie, L. S., "Psychiatry and the Films," *Hollywood Quar.*, 1947, 2, 113-117, and Fearing, F., "Psychology and the Films," *Hollywood Quar.*, 1947, 2, 118-121.

39. Instinctual drive has been discussed in Burnham, J. C., "The Medical Origins and Cultural Use of Freud's Instinctual Drive Theory," *Psychoan. Quar.*, 1974, 43, 193-217.

40. Burnham, "Psychoanalysis in American Civilization," op. cit., 368-371.

41. Burnham, J. C., "The Progressive Era Revolution in American Attitudes Toward Sex," *J. Amer. Hist.*, 1973, 59, 885-908; Burnham, "The New Psychology," op. cit. See, for example, Benedek, T., review of Kinsey, et al., *Sexual Behavior in the Human Female*, in *Psychoan. Quar.*, 1954, 23, 272-279.

42. E.g., Taylor, G. O., *The Passages of Thought, Psychological Representation in the American Novel, 1870-1900,* New York: Oxford University Press, 1969; Sulman, A. M., "The Freudianization of the American Child: The Impact of Psychoanalysis in Popular Periodical Literature in the United States, 1919-1939," unpublished doctoral dissertation, University of Pittsburgh, 1972.

43. Many good examples are discussed in King, R., *The Party of Eros, Radical Social Thought and the Realm of Freedom,* Chapel Hill: University of North Carolina Press, 1972.

44. For example, Tyler, P., "An American Theater Motif: The Psychodrama," *Amer. Quar.,* 1963, 15, 140-151.

45. This problem is discussed in some relevant detail in Burnham, *Psychoanalysis and American Medicine, op. cit.* See Havens, L. L., *Approaches to the Mind: Movement of the Psychiatric Schools from Sects Toward Science,* Boston: Little, Brown, 1973.

46. Gitelson, "Psychoanalyst, U.S.A., 1955," *op. cit.,* 705. One of the most widely quoted documents was Trilling, L., *Freud and the Crisis of Our Culture,* Boston: Beacon Press, 1955. Norman Mailer in 1968 traced the beginnings of disenchantment with psychoanalysis back to a time when "people in analysis began to be subjected to men who were no longer cultivated, poetic, deep and engaged in intellectual activity. . . ." Quoted in Leo, J., "Psychoanalysis Reaches a Crossroad," *The New York Times,* Aug. 4, 1968.

CHAPTER 5

The New York Psychoanalytic Society and Institute: Its Founding and Development

Samuel Atkin, M.D.

IT IS FITTING—and a pleasant coincidence—that this paper is being presented on the 65th anniversary of the New York Psychoanalytic Society. On February 11, 1911, to be precise, Abraham Arden Brill, together with a handful of doctors interested in the revolutionary ideas of Freud, met in Brill's home to found the New York Psychoanalytic Society (1). Its purpose was to be "the study and advancement of the Psychoanalytic Science, and its application to the study and treatment of nervous and mental diseases, as well as to pure psychology." Any physician in good standing and actively engaged in the work of psychoanalysis was eligible for active membership, which was limited to fifty. No limit, however, was set on the number eligible for associate membership, conferred "only on those individuals who take an active interest in psychoanalysis." Honorary membership, limited to 25, "may be conferred upon those persons who have furthered the cause of Psychoanalysis. They may be either residents of the United States or of foreign countries" (2).

Presented March 11, 1976. Samuel Atkin is on the faculty, and formerly president, of the New York Psychoanalytic Institute and formerly president of the New York Psychoanalytic Society.

73

A. A. Brill

Before proceeding further I would like to pay tribute to that remarkable human being, A. A. Brill, to whom the establishment of psychoanalysis in America is forever indebted. Born in 1874, in Galicia (then part of Austria-Hungary), Brill came to the United States at the age of thirteen, alone, penniless, knowing no English. On arrival he found work doing odd jobs in a saloon, in return for which he was allowed free lunch and the privilege of sleeping on the floor. He worked his way through grammar school, the Eron Preparatory School on 2nd Avenue (which I myself later attended), and college, eventually earning a medical degree at the age of twenty-nine from the College of Physicians and Surgeons in 1903. He spent the next four years at Central Islip State Hospital. Brill's eagerness to learn more about mental illness led him in 1907 to Bleuler's clinic in Burghölzli, Switzerland, where psychoanalysis was making a strong impact. Here he worked with Jung, Abraham, and Jones and through them met Freud. (Years later, in his reminiscences, he described how the residents would gather at the breakfast table and tell their dreams and interpret them according to Freud's theories.)

Freud made a profound impression on Brill. When he returned to the United States, Brill dedicated himself not only to the practice and teaching of psychoanalysis but to proselytizing for this new science whenever and wherever he could. For the next forty years—until his death in 1948—he did just that. He expounded Freud's theories primarily at psychiatric and neurological meetings; but he never passed up an opportunity to speak before lay audiences as well.

Picture, if you will, this stocky little bearded fellow passionately propounding, in a thick accent, Freud's ideas to anyone who would listen. What impressed me was his direct, forthright, I would say even blunt, approach bespeaking great moral and intellectual honesty and personal independence. Here was a man of great pride and self-esteem who bowed his head to no man. Brill was my idea of a "normal" man. At the drop of a hat he would vigorously debate the skeptics and scoffers over these new, and indeed in those days unsettling, scientific revelations. One can appreciate the resistances that, say, Freud's theories of infantile sexuality would have aroused in that post-Victorian era.

Lest I give the impression of Brill as a combative zealot, let me quickly disabuse you. He was a man of great warmth and personal charm, a leader who attracted many colleagues to the study of psycho-analysis and who did much to create an atmosphere of benevolence toward this new science in the intellectual community.

Perhaps Brill's greatest contribution to psychoanalysis was his auda-cious undertaking, despite a language limitation of which he was aware (he did not know German well), of translating Freud's writings into English, opening Freud's discoveries to all who would read him. When Jones demurred to Freud about Brill as an English translator, Freud is reputed to have replied, "I'd rather have a good friend than a good translator."

The New York Psychoanalytic Society and the American
Psychoanalytic Association (3)

At this juncture I would like to mention something about the rela-tionship of the New York Psychoanalytic Society and the American in this early period. It will be recalled that Freud visited the United States in 1909 to give a series of lectures at Clark University in Worcester, Mass., to which, incidentally, Ernest Jones and Brill accompanied him. In March 1910 the International Psychoanalytic Association was founded at the Nuremberg Congress. Upon Freud's recommendation Jung was elected as president. Freud, who was active in encouraging the forma-tion of branch societies, was eager to have an American Psychoanalytic Association established and, backed by Jones, proposed to the eminent and elegant James Jackson Putnam of Boston that he be its head. Brill, who had ushered in psychoanalysis to this country through New York, its great cultural and ethnic gateway, felt strongly that New York rather than Boston should be the center, and when, on May 9, 1911, the Amer-ican Psychoanalytic Association was established (three months after the New York Psychoanalytic Society) Brill refused to subordinate his or-ganization to the American, despite Freud's urging that he do so. It should be noted that in those days the American was not a federation of societies but a small collection of scattered members who lived outside New York. At the Weimar International Congress held in September 1911 both groups were accepted as equal branches. They remained so until 1932 when the New York Psychoanalytic Society, together with the Boston, Chicago, Washington, and Baltimore groups, became a part of the American Psychoanalytic Association.

Beginnings

In those early days membership in the society consisted more of friendly well-wishers of psychoanalysis than of confirmed practitioners. Members were encouraged to read psychoanalytic papers before various psychiatric and medical groups.

An early enthusiast was Brill's close friend, Clarence P. Oberndorf, then a psychiatrist at Bellevue. "Oby," as he was affectionately called, found Freud's discoveries a useful tool in comprehending his psychotic patients and he became an eloquent advocate of this new science. Even before Brill's return to America in 1908 there was a lively interest in psychoanalysis at Bellevue and other psychiatric centers, including some state hospitals where there were advocates of dynamic psychiatry like John MacCurdy and George Kirby. Adolf Meyer, head of the New York State Psychiatric Institute, became a member of this early band of advanced thinkers and disseminators of psychoanalysis (4).

Members of the Society met in one another's homes or in the private dining rooms of such venerable gastronomic institutions as the Brevoort or Luchow's. One of Brill's favorite meeting places was Rudolf's Beer Saloon, of sainted memory. To give you the flavor of those early days I can do no better than quote from Bertram Lewin's paper, "Reminiscence and Retrospect," which he read in 1961 at the 50th anniversary celebration of the New York Society (5).

> The intimate meetings were not unlike those at Berggasse 19, with perhaps twenty as a maximal attendance—roughly the size of a present-day well attended committee meeting. . . . When there was some special occasion, perhaps a distinguished out-of-town speaker, the meetings were held in the old Academy of Medicine on West 44th St., where I heard Rank, and it was only around 1926 that they began to be held regularly in the new Academy building at 3 East 103rd St. . . . Everybody knew everybody, often very well, and there was much community interest.
>
> Despite the growing popular interest in psychoanalysis, the analytic society grew only slowly. Until 1925 the business sessions were perfunctory. Dues were expended to defray the expenses of the annual dinner. Until I became Secretary of the Institute in 1939, the programs were not printed and notices to members were typed. The dinners were informal affairs, with menu selected by Mr. Beraud, steward of the Brevoort, who was a friend and a civilized man. As a busboy he had taken Mark Twain's meals to him in the house on the corner of 9th St. and Fifth Avenue (since razed).

The Society meetings were very much of the type Freud had in mind in 1918, places to study and learn more about psychoanalysis.

In those days if one wished to learn more about psychoanalysis and become a more thorough practitioner, it was customary to go to Vienna for analysis, usually with Freud. (An analysis in those days took from several months to at most a year or two.) Adolph Stern was the first New Yorker to make this pilgrimage shortly after World War I. He was soon followed by, among others, Oberndorf, H. W. Frink, Leonard Blumgart, Philip Lehrman, Abram Kardiner, and Ruth Mack Brunswick. On their return to New York they formed a nucleus of dedicated teachers of psychoanalysis, laying the groundwork for a training program. In the twenties this nucleus was reinforced by other American returnees —Lawrence Kubie, Bert Lewin, William Silverberg, Clara Thompson, and Gregory Zilboorg—who had received analytic training in the institutes of Berlin and Budapest as well as Vienna. (My own first analyst was Kardiner, who was analyzed by Freud; my first supervisor, Lewin, who was analyzed by Karl Abraham.)

This group was joined by the "early" (i.e., pre-Hitler) arrivals from Europe—Sandor Lorand, Paul Schilder, Fritz Wittels, and Dorian Feigenbaum. From time to time notable European analysts would come for long or short visits to teach, lecture, and do analysis, adding ferment and excitement to the analytic scene. Otto Rank appeared in 1924 and remained for several years, giving some members of the Society an opportunity to be analyzed by him. Ferenczi came in 1926, but in truth he analyzed few physicians. He lectured at the New School for Social Research. (I heard my first words about psychoanalysis from Ferenczi, not at the Institute but at the New School.) Alfred Adler also spent a number of years here and made a great impact on psychiatry at the time.

Growth and Development

By 1930 the New York Society had made great strides in the teaching and dissemination of psychoanalysis through the writings of its members (6). Bertram Lewin, William Silverberg, Thomas French, Sandor Lorand, and Dorian Feigenbaum had already contributed significant papers to the *Internationale Zeitschrift für Psychoanalyse*. In 1931 the New York Psychoanalytic Institute was established, with Sandor Rado, "imported" from Berlin, as Educational Director.

In 1932 the *Psychoanalytic Quarterly* was founded, with Feigenbaum, Lewin, Frankwood Williams and Gregory Zilboorg, all members of the New York Society, as its editors. Williams was a pioneer in applying psychoanalytic concepts to mental hygiene and, with Marion Kenworthy and Bernard Glueck, brought psychoanalysis to the social sciences and social work.

Zilboorg's prolific clinical and theoretical papers ranged over a wide variety of subjects from "unconscious anxiety" to religion. His *A History of Medical Psychology* remains a monument to his fame. Lewin's papers on "The Body as Phallus," on claustrophobia, hypomania, the dream screen, are classics in psychoanalytic literature. His seminal book *The Psychoanalysis of Elation* is a basic text in psychiatry. Rado's papers on pharmacothymia and traumatophobia as well as his classic paper on depression appeared in the *Psychoanalytic Quarterly*.

The great neuropsychiatrist Paul Schilder stirred considerable interest in psychoanalysis among his students at Bellevue, many of whom eventually became psychoanalysts. Among his writings on neurology, psychiatry, and philosophy, those on body image, hysterical conversion factors in somatic disease, and identity remain important contributions to the present day. Indeed, some are masterpieces, especially those on conversion.

From 1933 on, when Hitler and his anti-Jewish laws drove many European colleagues from their homes, members of the New York Psychoanalytic Society worked hard to rescue large numbers of them from Nazi annihilation. Although they were offered opportunities to work in many places throughout America, most of the newcomers settled in New York. Almost from the beginning they began to contribute to psychoanalytic teaching and writing. They did much to make our Society and Institute the outstanding institutions they are today.

To mention a few that come to mind: Robert Bak, Edmund Bergler, Berta Bornstein, Gustav Bychowski, Ludwig Eidelberg, Elizabeth Geleerd, Ruth and Kurt Eissler, Dora and Heinz Hartmann, Salomea and Otto Isakower, Edith Jacobson, Ernst and Marianne Kris, Rudolph Loewenstein, Bela Mittelman, Margaret Mahler, Geza Roheim, Otto and Melitta Sperling, Isidor Silbermann, René Spitz—the list is a long and distinguished one of the refugee analysts who found a haven in New York and who more than amply repaid our country with their invaluable enrichment of psychiatry and psychoanalysis.

The Forties and After

If the thirties witnessed the flowering of psychoanalysis in New York, the forties and fifties ushered in a broadening of the scope of psychoanalytic theory well beyond Freud's discoveries, as well as their modification, restructuring, and refinement.

Separately and together Hartmann, Kris, and Loewenstein clarified and defined psychoanalytic metapsychology and advanced modern ego psychology. Hartmann's work on the conflict-free ego and primary and secondary autonomy profoundly influenced the thinking and practice of psychoanalysis throughout the world. Loewenstein, a great clinician and teacher, wrote extensively on the theory and practice of psychoanalytic technique. His interest in aggression, guilt, and masochism led him to a study of the historical roots of anti-Semitism, brilliantly expounded in his book *Christians and Jews: A Psychoanalytic Study*.

Ernst Kris, originally an art historian, applied psychoanalysis to the study of aesthetics and artistic creation. His interest in the genetic sources of man's psyche led him to the study of infants by direct observation at Yale, a project which his wife Marianne Kris, together with Samuel Ritvo, Albert Solnit, and others, continued after his death to the present day.

Phyllis Greenacre, an early pupil of Adolf Meyer and for many years an attending physician in the psychiatry department at Cornell (7), was —and still is—one of the outstanding contributors to psychoanalytic literature and thought. Her papers on body image and on the dynamisms of the developmental cycles of life, as well as her recent two-volume collection of essays, *Emotional Growth,* are essential reading for every student of psychoanalysis. Greenacre's abiding literary interests found expression in recent years in her enchanting and enlightening psychoanalytic biographies of Lewis Carroll, Jonathan Swift, and Charles Darwin.

Lawrence Kubie was another prolific writer whose papers ranged over a wide territory of psychoanalytic, pedagogic, literary, and scientific subjects. He concerned himself not only with basic issues of psychoanalytic theory and practice but with the relationship of psychoanalysis to medical education. His gracious manner, his elegance, his wide connections, and his felicity of thought and expression made him an ideal spokesman for psychoanalysis to the general public as well as to the medical profession.

During the forties and fifties many members, notably Bak, Bychowski, Eissler, Eidelberg, and Bergler, made psychoanalytic explorations into the psychoses, expanding our insights into schizophrenia and other psychotic processes. Psychosomatic medicine also attracted the scientific interest of many members, the pioneer work of Flanders Dunbar being one of the first in the field.

In 1943 the first of Edith Jacobson's theoretical and clinical papers on affectivity appeared in English, culminating (in 1971) in her magnificent volume of essays, *Depression: Comparative Studies of Normal, Neurotic and Psychotic Conditions*. Her books *The Self and the Object World* and *Psychotic Conflict and Reality* have added much to our clinical understanding and technical management of narcissistic and borderline patients. (Now in her late 70s, Edith Jacobsen is as active and creative as ever.)

During this productive period the field of child analysis took on new significance. In 1945 the *Psychoanalytic Study of the Child* was established. Almost from its first issue it became one of the most important journals of psychoanalysis. Margaret Mahler's papers on autistic and symbiotic children began to appear during this period, as did René Spitz' films on the first year of life.

Mention should be made of two other psychoanalytic publications born during this creative period and edited by members of the New York Society: *The Journal of the American Psychoanalytic Association* (1953) and the *Annual Survey of Psychoanalysis*.

Recent Developments

In the last two decades two outstanding research projects by members of the New York Society have helped to clarify murky areas of psychological phenomena and advanced our psychoanalytic knowledge. I refer to Margaret Mahler's seminal findings on the separation-individuation process, a stupendous ten-year research study based on direct observation of the early mother-child interaction, and to Charles Fisher's laboratory studies on sleep and dream phenomena.

Victor Rosen's work on style, creativity, and the analytic process has had a great influence on analytic thought. His Language Study Group, of which I am proud to have been a member, has contributed much to a psychoanalytic understanding of language and thought processes (8).

In this dry recital of writings I have committed an injustice not only to the many members whose contributions time does not permit me to record but even to those mentioned, of whose works I have scarcely skimmed the surface. The foregoing has been offered merely as evidence of the impact the New York Psychoanalytic Society has had on the intellectual life and practice of psychiatrists and psychologists in this era.

Impact on Adjacent Psychiatric Institutions

Through the years members of the Society have given their services as therapists, teachers, and supervisors at many important psychiatric facilities in the community, among them Mt. Sinai Hospital, Albert Einstein College of Medicine, Hillside Hospital, Bellevue Hospital, Kings County Hospital, St. Lukes, and Roosevelt Hospitals. Many residents from these institutions have come to the New York Psychoanalytic Institute for their psychoanalytic training. Both the Institute and the psychiatric institutions have profited from this cross-fertilization.

The New York Psychoanalytic Institute

The history of the NYPI is inextricably bound to the history of the Society. To try to separate the two is an arbitrary and difficult task, sharing as they do a common membership and overlapping functions. The Society is responsible for the training of students. The Educational Committee, however, derives its authority from both Society and Institute. (It will be recalled that the Educational Committee was established in 1925, before there was an Institute.) The Library and the physical plant at 247 East 82nd Street belong to both. Dues, paid to the Society, confer membership to both organizations. The annual Brill lecture is a function of the Society, the annual Freud lecture of the Institute. Both lectures are given at the New York Academy of Medicine and before essentially the same audience.

The year 1925 was a crucial date in psychoanalytic education. At the Bad Hamburg Congress an International Training Commission was established to bring standards and uniformity to psychoanalytic training, which was to become the function of societies and institutes rather than of the individual analyst.

On October 25, 1925, the New York Psychoanalytic Society formed its first Educational Committee on the authority of the International Training Commission. It was to assume responsibility for training not only for New York but for sanctioning the training of all Americans being trained abroad who, upon their return to America, would become members of the New York Psychoanalytic Society. This arrangement prevailed for five years. During this time the Educational Committee organized the teaching in a relatively loose curriculum. It arranged didactic analysis, supervision of cases, lectures, and courses. (I attended lectures in Brill's home and at the Oliver Cromwell Hotel in 1928 and 1929.) The teaching was all very friendly and informal. Students were invited to membership in the Society without fixed requirements, as to a learned society.

On September 24, 1931, the New York Psychoanalytic Institute was established. It was patterned after the Berlin Psychoanalytic Institute, from whose ranks Sandor Rado came to be the first Educational Director. (I patterned my own clinical conferences after his.) A curriculum took shape under the tutelage of Rado, Feigenbaum, Kardiner, Kubie, Lehrman, Lewin, Lorand, Meyer, Oberndorf, and Zilboorg. It seems to me only yesterday that I saw the introduction of the first dream seminar by Lillian Powers, the first seminar on technique by Albert Slutsky, the first reading seminar of psychoanalytic writers other than Freud by Bert Lewin, and the first continuous case seminar by Edith Jacobson.

The administration of the school, hardly its most glamorous aspect, is an integral part of it and should be mentioned. Monroe Meyer was the first Executive Director from 1931 to 1939. I was the second, from 1939 to 1946. In the early forties, I set up the first records, wrote the first syllabus, established admissions procedures, and organized procedures for progression and graduation.

An event of overwhelming significance escapes containment in an historical sequence. This was the revitalizing of our academic and professional life by the arrival during the Hitler era of our European colleagues. The choice of New York as their home by so many did much toward giving the Institute its eminence.

With the arrival of the child analyst Berta Bornstein and later Marianne Kris, Margaret Mahler, and Mary O'Neill Hawkins (an American child analyst studying in Vienna during that period), the teaching of analytical child psychiatry then being done by David Levy and Edward Liss was reorganized into a faculty in child analysis that prevails to this day.

In 1946 the Society and Institute reached out into the intellectual community by offering interdisciplinary colloquia and seminars through an Extension School of Applied Psychoanalysis. Long before this formal establishment of a school, however, indeed as far back as the early thirties, the Society gathered into its classrooms groups of teachers, social workers, internists, policemen, lawyers, and judges for instruction in applied psychoanalysis. Geza Roheim and Abram Kardiner introduced seminars with anthropologists, among them Alfred Linton, Margaret Mead, Gregory Bateson, and Ruth Benedict. Seminars on scientific methodology were held with philosophers. In the early forties I invited some of the leading biologists, among them Beach and Richter, to a two-day symposium on Instinct Theory. (I had the pleasure of entertaining Adolf Meyer on that occasion.)

It was a time of ferment, of fashioning new tools in the allied sciences and professions. We instructed members of our disciplines and they instructed us. It was all a part of the new intellectual enlightenment inspired by Freud.

As the universities and professional schools in the metropolitan area have more and more assumed the teaching of applied psychoanalysis, the activities of the Institute in this field have diminished.

Specially qualified post-doctoral students in the social or biological sciences are accepted for psychoanalytic training. While most of those who have received training have been psychologists, there have also been sociologists, historians, and political scientists. It is expected that an intimate knowledge of psychoanalysis will enhance the students' research capacity in their own fields.

There has been a considerable growth of post-graduate studies for psychoanalysts. While small private study groups of members have always existed (one of the better known was led for many years by Herman Nunberg), the first official post-graduate study group, led by Hartmann, Kris, and Loewenstein, was set up to study "Psychoanalytic Theory in Relation to Clinical Problems." After Kris's death, a number of seminars, known as the Kris Study Groups, were arranged and continue to this day. Many significant monographs have come out of their deliberations, including ones on "Regressive Ego Phenomena in Psychoanalysis," "Beating Fantasies," "Indications for Psychoanalysis," "Place of the Dream in Clinical Psychoanalysis," "Reconstruction in Psychoanalysis," and "Mechanisms of Denial."

The Library of the New York Psychoanalytic Society and Institute is perhaps the largest psychoanalytic library in the world. It contains more than 10,000 books, periodicals, and reprints dealing with psychoanalysis and related subjects. Among these are rare volumes, including original Freud letters.

No report is complete without a few statistics. Currently the Institute and Society have 327 members. Over the years the Institute has graduated about 500 psychoanalysts. It trains between 80 and 100 students a year.

The Treatment Center

The Treatment Center of the New York Psychoanalytic Institute was established in 1946. (In 1927 Brill had tried to set up a low-cost outpatient clinic patterned after the one run by the Berlin Institute, but he failed to obtain a license.)

From 1946 to 1948 the Treatment Center functioned as a mental hygiene service for veterans. Since 1948 it has operated as a low-cost community psychoanalytic treatment center. It serves primarily as an adjunct to the educational program of the Institute. Patients are selected for treatment who are considered suitable for psychoanalysis by students during their clinical training. Every student psychoanalyzes at least two cases under the supervision of a training analyst. In this past year 51 students psychoanalyzed 60 patients under the supervision of 40 training analysts. Approximately 12,000 analytic sessions were held. Patients pay an average fee of $4.50 per session.

Patients considered unsuitable for analysis but who are in need of psychotherapy are sent to members of the Affiliated Staff—graduate analysts who participate in the Treatment Center program. Affiliated Staff members also take on for treatment patients whose analytic treatment by a student was unsuccessful. Last year Affiliated Staff members held 1,354 psychotherapy sessions and 3,300 psychoanalytic sessions.

The Affiliated Staff takes responsibility with the Director of the Treatment Center for intake, consultation, and referral. There is also a child analysis program with its own staff of examining psychoanalysts and instructors.

A large portion of the membership is actively involved in the program of the Treatment Center as teachers, supervisors of students, intake advisors, participants in conferences, and clinical research projects. Many of the Treatment Center cases are presented in continuous case seminars and clinical conferences as part of the teaching program.

Through the years Society members have utilized the clinical case material for special study. Leo Stone's "The Widening Scope of Psychoanalysis"; Arnold Pfeffer's evaluation of the results of psychoanalysis;

Stephen Firestein's report on "Termination in Psychoanalysis"; Herbert Waldhorn's "Assessment on Analyzability"—these are a few of the studies that have emanated from the Treatment Center.

One of the most outstanding research projects under the direct auspices of the Treatment Center is the *Gifted Adolescent Project,* from which publications by Phyllis Greenacre, Victor Rosen and others on such subjects as creativity, style, and language have been derived.

Two research projects going on currently deserve mention: a recorded analysis and an investigation into the nature of clinical evidence for psychoanalytic interpretation.

Offspring

A paper on the New York Psychoanalytic Society and Institute would not be complete without a report of the branches that have sprung from it. The first was a group that defected—perhaps a gentler word would be "departed"—from its ranks to form a society of its own. In 1940 Karen Horney, who had made outstanding contributions to psychoanalysis, particularly on female sexuality and on the influence of the culture on the development of neurosis, left the Society, along with Clara Thompson, William ("Billy") Silverberg, and several others to form an institute of her own. (Later Thompson and Silverberg split from the Horney group; but that is another story.) Five years later (1945) Rado, Kardiner, Levy, and Daniels left to form a training center at Columbia University, known as the Association for Psychoanalytic Medicine.

In a happier vein, the New York Psychoanalytic Society and Institute have served as a source from which, as membership increased, new societies and institutes grew. In the early days of the Society analysts who lived in Boston, among them M. Ralph Kaufman, Ives Hendricks, and Isidor Coriat, would come to New York to attend meetings. In 1930 they formed the Boston Psychoanalytic Society and subsequently an institute of their own. The New York Institute trained and graduated students from Philadelphia and Western New England, who eventually formed societies and institutes in their own communities. In 1955, Brooklyn members organized their own society and institute, known as the Psychoanalytic Association of New York, under the auspices of the State University of New York, Downstate Division. In recent years members from New Jersey, Westchester, and Long Island have started societies and are planning training programs. Many maintain membership in the New York Society as well as their own.

The birth and growth of the New York Psychoanalytic Society and Institute epitomize the progress of psychoanalysis in America. In 1961, on the 50th anniversary of the Society, Leo Rangell, then President of the American Psychoanalytic Association, said, "The New York Psychoanalytic Society is in many ways a symbol, a model, and an ego ideal. Its strength . . . its standards, its progressive directions toward the future, serve as examples to younger and less well-established groups." I would like to think that this can still be said on its 65th anniversary.

Conclusion

Freud's humanistic psychology has won a secure place in the psychological sciences. At the 50th anniversary of the New York Psychoanalytic Society I could say with conviction that psychoanalysis had replaced the crudely mechanistic and dehumanized psychiatry that had prevailed in Freud's day. Today, fifteen years later, I am not so sure. The reactionary return in many quarters to a mechanistic, soulless psychiatry dismays me. This regressive trend makes it all the more imperative that psychoanalysis maintain its vitality and strengthen its potential for future gains in human welfare.

NOTES

1. Charter members of the New York Psychoanalytic Society were: Doctors L. E. Bish, A. A. Brill, F. J. Farnell, H. W. Frink, C. Garvin, A. Hoch, M. J. Karpas, G. H. Kirby, C. P. Oberndorf, B. Onuf, E. M. Poate, C. Ricksher, J. Rosenbloom, E. W. Scripture, and S. A. Tanenbaum.

2. From the Constitution of the New York Psychoanalytic Society, adopted at its third meeting on March 28, 1911.

3. I am indebted to Dr. Herbert M. Wyman for a review of this early history in a personal communication and bibliography. See also his article, "The 65tn Birthday of the New York Psychoanalytic Society" in *The Newsletter of the NY Psychoanalytic Society and Institute,* Jan. 1976, Vol. 13, No. 1.

4. Dr. Meyer recalled to me how he, together with Bernard Sachs, the eminent Mt. Sinai neurologist who remained a fierce antagonist of psychoanalysis to his death, sat on the same workbench with Freud in Brücke's neurohistological laboratory in Vienna.

5. In: Martin Wangh, et al., Eds., *Fruition of an Idea,* New York: International Universities Press, 1962.

6. For the historical survey of psychoanalytic writings by members of the New York Psychoanalytic Society, I am indebted to the Foreword by Martin Wangh in *The Fruition of an Idea,* New York: International Universities Press, 1962.

7. Other psychiatrists in those days who were active both at Cornell and in the New York Society and Institute were the late Jack Dunn, James Wall, who was director at Bloomingdale, and George Amsden.

8. Rosen's book, *Style, Character and Language,* edited by S. Atkin and M. Jucovy, has just been issued by Jason Aronson.

CHAPTER 6

Orthodoxy and Eclecticism in Psychoanalysis: The Washington-Baltimore Experience

Donald L. Burnham, M.D.

IT IS WELL KNOWN that Freud had serious conflict and more than a few misgivings about how his brain-child, psychoanalysis, might develop in the intellectual and cultural climate of America. On the one hand, he welcomed and encouraged its transplantation to America, and gave considerable impetus to this move with his lectures at Clark University in 1909 and his personal contacts with G. Stanley Hall, William James, Adolf Meyer, and others. On the other hand, he feared that in America psychoanalysis might suffer a variety of weakening, possibly corrupting, influences, among them a too easy acceptance of watered-down, more palatable, less explicitly sexual versions of psychoanalysis. In his *History of the Psychoanalytic Movement* Freud said: "It was characteristic of that country [America] that from the beginning professors and super-intendents of mental hospitals showed as much interest in analysis as independent practitioners. But it is clear that precisely for this reason the ancient centres of culture, where the greatest resistance has been

---

* Presented April 15, 1976. Donald L. Burnham is Research Psychiatrist, Intramural Research Program, National Institutes of Health, Bethesda, Maryland. Portions of this paper are derived from "History of the Washington Psychoanalytic Society and the Washington Psychoanalytic Institute" (Noble and Burnham, 1969).

displayed, must be the scene of the decisive struggle over psycho-analysis" (13).

Psychoanalysis in the Baltimore-Washington region, as it has developed over the past sixty-five-plus years, exemplifies, and possibly even epito-mizes, some of Freud's predictions about psychoanalysis in America. Certainly it would be difficult to find two more apt and outstanding examples of "professors and superintendents of mental hospitals" than Adolf Meyer and William Alanson White. Their combined influence was incalculable in shaping the emergence of psychiatry as a distinct profession in this country. Meyer contributed much to promoting the use of the very term "psychiatrist" as a replacement for the earlier grim term "alienist." An entire generation of psychiatrists looked to Meyer and White for leadership.

One can readily imagine that Freud would have welcomed support for psychoanalysis from these two immensely respected and influential men, just as earlier he had welcomed Bleuler's interest and support in ex-tending psychoanalysis beyond the original Vienna circle. However, he must also have sensed that, like Bleuler, neither Meyer nor White was of a mold to fit easily into the role of disciple for another man's system. Each was too strong and ambitious in his own right. Meyer created his own system and named it "psychobiology." White was eclectic to the point of once being accused of having a case of "phaga-cytosis or overingestion of theories" (19, p. 381). Nonetheless, both Meyer and White contributed tremendously to psychoanalysis' taking hold and flourishing in America, as well as to some of the specific features which have distinguished psychoanalysis in America from psychoanalysis in Europe.

Meyer and White constituted something of a paradox. They were major forces in creating a climate receptive to psychoanalysis, yet neither of them ever became an orthodox Freudian loyalist. The tension be-tween eclecticism and orthodoxy seen in the relationship of Meyer and White to psychoanalysis finds certain parallels in a dilemma which has tended to divide psychoanalysts everywhere, including the Baltimore-Washington breed of analysts. The dilemma hinges on the question of whether psychoanalysis should be a separate and distinct profession, or a sub-specialty of psychiatry or of psychology. Should psychoanalytic knowl-edge and skills be entrusted only to a chosen, select few who constitute a loyal group devoted to preserving the purity of the Freudian heritage, while perhaps limiting the range of their influence? Or should psychoanalysis seek broader membership and applications, but thereby perhaps risk dilution, adulteration, and loss of uniqueness?

This dilemma in all of its complex ramifications certainly has played a significant role in the development of psychoanalysis in Baltimore and Washington. From the beginning, diversity of membership and of approaches was a feature of the psychoanalytic groups which formed in this region. This may have been partly because of their "home-grown" quality. There was less leadership and dominance from analysts who had come originally from Vienna or Berlin. The early Baltimore-Washington analysts came form a variety of backgrounds. Several, including Ernest Hadley and Edward Kempf were from the midwest. A number had been raised as Roman Catholics. Among these were Kempf, Trigant Burrow, Leo Bartemeier, and Harry Stack Sullivan. Even more remarkable was Thomas Verner Moore, trained as both a psychologist and a psychiatrist, but also a Catholic monk who founded the Benedictine Priory in Washington. Moore's textbook, *Dynamic Psychology*, published in 1924 (33), was the first American psychology text to contain extensive discussion of Freud.

Kempf was another outstanding example of diversity. Kempf first came into contact with psychology and psychoanalytic ideas as an undergraduate at Indiana University where his professor was E. H. Lindley, a Clark University Ph.D. and a personal friend of G. Stanley Hall and Adolf Meyer. After medical school and as early as 1910, Kempf applied Freudian principles to the psychological treatment of dementia praecox patients. In 1913 his unorthodox methods prompted his being fired from the Indianapolis State Hospital, and he moved to Meyer's department at Johns Hopkins (26, p. 6). This was the same year as the opening of the Phipps Clinic.

Then from 1914 to 1920 he was a full-time psychotherapist at St. Elizabeths Hospital under White's direction. During that time he served as the second president of the Washington Psychoanalytic Society, which had been founded in 1914 with White as its first president. Kempf also attempted to integrate the psychoanalytic approach with Bechterev's theories of conditioning and with observations made in Shepherd Franz's laboratory of primate psychology at St. Elizabeths. Kempf's book *Psychopathology*, 1920 (28), described in detail his analysis of schizophrenic patients and was for a time enormously influential among young psychiatrists.

Despite his manifest eclecticism, Kempf was assigned important responsibilities in the American Psychoanalytic Association. For example, when in 1926 the time came for a shift from self-selection and self-training of analysts to more official forms of training, Kempf joined Jelliffe and Oberndorf on the committee which drew up the first set of training standards to be promulgated by the American Psychoanalytic Association.

Kempf's interest in the treatment of psychoses by psychoanalytic methods was shared by many of the early Baltimore-Washington analysts. It is an endeavor which continues among the present generation of analysts, many of whom have been on the staffs of Chestnut Lodge, Sheppard-Pratt Hospital and St. Elizabeths Hospital. This interest has, in turn, contributed to fueling the orthodoxy-eclecticism tension. The question of the suitability of psychoanalysis as a means of explaining or of treating schizophrenia is, I believe, an important chapter in the history of psychoanalysis. It played a part in the early splits between Jung and Freud and between Jung and Abraham. Years later it was part of the response accorded the work of such investigators as Sullivan, Frieda Fromm-Reichmann, Dexter Bullard, Ives Hendrick, Lewis Hill, and more recently, Harold Searles and Clarence Schulz.

Meyer's interest in Freud's ideas was sparked to a considerable degree by his seeing in them a basis for the psychogenesis and psychotherapy of psychoses. It is something of an irony that Meyer was more optimistic about the cure of mental illness by psychological means than was Freud. Meyer's convictions took much of their strength from his mother's recovery from a depressive-paranoid illness which had been at least in part precipitated by his leaving his native Switzerland for the United States. His mother's recovery was all the more striking to him because his former teacher at the Burghölzli, August Forel, had pronounced her incurable. Forel, incidentally, was among the numerous European professors of psychiatry who rejected psychoanalysis.

Meyer's paper at the 1909 Clark University conference was entitled "The Dynamic Interpretation of Dementia Praecox" (31); at about the same time he published another paper "A Discussion of Some Fundamental Issues in Freud's Psychoanalysis" (32).

Several of Meyer's students and colleagues also showed early interest in the applicability of Freud's ideas to psychosis. C. Macfie Campbell published in 1910 an article titled, "The Form and Content of the Psychoses: The Role of Psychoanalysis in Psychiatry" (7), and in 1912 another, "The Application of Psychoanalysis to Insanity" (8). Later Campbell became Professor of Psychiatry at Harvard and the Director of the Boston Psychopathic Hospital. He was instrumental in obtaining Commonwealth Fund Fellowships for several young psychiatrists who were thereby enabled to travel to Europe for psychoanalytic training and later to become leaders of the development of psychoanalysis in Boston, among them M. Ralph Kaufman and John Murray.

Another early Boston analyst was Ives Hendrick, who received part of his psychiatric training at Sheppard-Pratt Hospital on the outskirts of Baltimore. Hendrick, author of an important book, *Facts and Theories of Psychoanalysis*, retained throughout his distinguished career an active interest in the psychological treatment of psychoses. On several occasions he lamented the loss in this endeavor among more orthodox analysts as psychoanalysis in America became more formally organized (22, p. 234).

John MacCurdy, one of the eight persons who joined in founding the American Psychoanalytic Association in Baltimore in 1911, and for several years lecturer in psychopathology at Cornell, also was interested in the psychoanalytic study of the psychoses, witness his 1914 paper, "The Productions in a Manic-Like State Illustrating Freudian Mechanisms" (30).

Jung's monograph, *The Psychology of Dementia Praecox*, was first published in 1907, and the translation by F. W. Peterson and A. A. Brill appeared in 1909 as Number 3 in the *Nervous and Mental Disease Monograph Series* (24), which had been inaugurated by Jelliffe and White in 1907. This series was an important vehicle for the dissemination of psychoanalysis in America, as was the *Psychoanalytic Review*, founded by Jelliffe and White in 1913. The latter was the first English-language journal of psychoanalysis. Jung contributed a note to the first issue, after Freud declined in a manner judged by Jelliffe to be "not very cordial." For many years the *Psychoanalytic Review* published official reports of the meetings of the American Psychoanalytic Association.

Jung's 1912 lectures at Fordham University at Jelliffe's invitation were another significant event. Earlier Ernest Jones had declined a similar invitation on the grounds that he did not believe that a Jesuit university would provide a suitable platform for lectures on psychoanalysis (19, p. 358). Jung's acceptance was surprising from another standpoint, namely, Switzerland's official anti-Jesuit position. Jung's lectures revealed substantial deviations from Freud's ideas, particularly concerning childhood sexuality and libido theory (25).

Jung's studies of dementia praecox also played a part in the split which developed between him and Freud. At first enthusiastic, Jung subsequently came to doubt that Freud's libido theory could provide a full and sufficient explanation of dementia praecox, and hence to doubt the general validity of the libido theory. It was partly as a response to Jung that Freud wrote his paper, "On Narcissism. . . ." Also important in the divisions of opinion as to how dementia praecox, or schizophrenia, or paraphrenia, was to be understood and treated was Freud's distinction between "transference neuroses" and "narcissistic neuroses." He was convinced that patients suffering from "narcissistic neuroses" were incapable of forming libidinal transferences to their therapists and hence were unsuitable for psychoanalytic treatment. This conviction, which became a dictum, contributed heavily to many future disputes among analysts, not just as to whether schizophrenia could be investigated and treated by psychoanalytic techniques, but even as to whether those who essayed to do this could properly be called psychoanalysts.

I don't mean to oversimplify the lines of these disputes, for they were extraordinarily complex. Certainly they extended far beyond the Freud-Jung and Abraham-Jung splits. One can quickly cite Federn, Ferenczi, and Groddeck, who, from early on, by example and by teaching, promoted a broad view of the applicability of psychoanalytic treatment to what came to be known as severe character disorders, borderline illnesses, and many types of psychoses. Later Sullivan, Zilboorg, Silberberg, Fromm-Reichmann, Lewis Hill, Bychowski, and Bak, among others, promoted similar views, which, not incidentally, sometimes had divisive effects upon psychoanalytic organizations.

Bernard Glueck was another outstanding example of the eclectic aspect of early psychoanalysis in Washington-Baltimore. His staff service at St. Elizabeths spanned the years 1909-1912 and 1913-1916. At St. Elizabeths he was in charge of Howard Hall, housing the wards for the criminally insane, and in 1916 published an important work, *Studies in Forensic Psychiatry* (15). Then in 1918 he became head of a pioneer psychiatric clinic at Sing Sing prison. A younger brother, Sheldon, went on to a distinguished career as a criminologist at Harvard. In 1924 Bernard was an expert witness in the notorious Loeb-Leopold trial, as was William A. White. Glueck also played a major role in creating the profession of psychiatric social work.

For a time Glueck was enthusiastic about Adler, and while at St. Elizabeths translated Adler's *The Neurotic Constitution* into English (1).

One basis for Glueck's temporary enthusiasm for Adler was his preference for a view of man as goal-seeking, with free will and self-direction, in contrast to Freud's strict determinism. Perhaps American emphasis on optimism and meliorism contributed to this preference, though Glueck himself subsequently became convinced of the superiority of Freud's theories (16, p. 76).

Sparked by White, St. Elizabeths was a beehive of translation activity. Each issue of the *Psychoanalytic Review* contained abstracts in translation of European psychoanalytic articles. The previously mentioned *Nervous and Mental Disease Monograph Series* included translations of major psychoanalytic works by such luminaries as Freud, Abraham, Jung, Rank, Hitschmann, and Von Hug-Hellmuth. The indefatigable passion for translation on the part of White and his close friend Jelliffe also had its eclectic side. As early as 1905 they had translated the Swiss Paul Dubois' *Psychic Treatment of Nervous Disorders* (12). In 1913 Jelliffe translated a book on *Psychotherapy* by Dejerine and Gauckler (10), and in 1917 Silberer's *Problems of Mysticism and Its Symbolism* (37).

White's own books, *Outlines of Psychiatry* (40, 41) and *Mental Mechanisms* (42), provided important early educational vehicles through which American medical students were introduced to psychoanalytic ideas (3, p. 153).

St. Elizabeths Hospital provided the setting for the organization of the first Washington Psychoanalytic Society. This was in 1914, and most of the members of the Society were on the staff of St. Elizabeths, where the meetings were held monthly. The papers presented spanned a wide range of topics and evidently generated great interest. During the first years of the Society White gave papers on "The Unconscious," "Dreams," and "Symbolism." Glueck spoke on "The God-Man or Jehovah Complex." Kempf gave no less than four papers in a span of two years. One was "The Psychoanalytic Study of Regression with a Dual Personality," another "The Social and Sexual Behavior of Some Infrahuman Primates." James Hassall spoke on "The Role of the Sexual Complex in Dementia Praecox."

Several of the speakers came from Baltimore. Trigant Burrow addressed the topic "Repression and Its Influence on Education." Burrow, a charter member of the American Psychoanalytic Association, was one of the first Americans to journey to Europe for psychoanalytic training. This was in Zurich with Jung. Burrow later developed his own theories and forms of treatment, which he called "phyloanalysis." This involved forms of group analysis, which probably constituted at least one branch of the ancestral tree which has proliferated into the multitude of groups—encounter, sensitivity, or whatever—which litter our landscape today.

Another Baltimorian of the time, C. Macfie Campbell, presented to the Society his paper, "Some Familiar Symptoms in Childhood: Their Interpretation and Formulation," a choice subject which reflected Campbell's interest in mental hygiene. Both he and Meyer were very active in the work of the National Committee for Mental Hygiene (9).

Another noteworthy member of the Washington Psychoanalytic Society during this formative period was Ross Chapman, who later, as Medical Superintendent of the Sheppard and Enoch Pratt Hospital and Professor of Psychiatry at the University of Maryland Medical School, contributed greatly to the development of dynamic psychiatry and psychoanalysis in the Baltimore-Washington region. Perhaps Chapman could be counted as another example of the "professors and medical superintendents" whose interest in psychoanalysis was less than completely welcome to Freud.

Still another early member of the Washington Psychoanalytic Society was one whom it is difficult today to imagine as ever having been interested in analysis. This was Walter Freeman, later to achieve notoriety for his allegedly reckless performance of frontal lobotomies.

With the advent of World War I and the departure of many members for military service, the Society lapsed into dormancy and was not reconvened until 1925. Among the papers presented to the Society during that first year of revival were Sullivan's "Erogenous Maturation," Nolan D. C. Lewis' "A Psychoanalytic Approach to Children Under Twelve," and Burrow's "The Group Method of Psychoanalysis."

In 1926 the name of the Washington Psychoanalytic Society was changed to the Washington Psychopathological Society. It is uncertain precisely what considerations prompted the proposal and adoption of the change of name. One reason offered was that the new name would encourage a broader range of scientific pursuits and would better serve the needs of the numerous psychiatric and non-medical members whose primary interests were not in psychoanalysis. Another was that the change would avoid the Society's being confused with the Washington Psychoanalytic Association, which had been organized in 1924 with Ben Karpman as one of its leaders.

Still another explanation advanced was that the change of the Society's name had been instigated by members of the Association so that the Association could become the sole psychoanalytic organization in the region. This allegation was denied by Lucile Dooley, who was highly respected generally and a member of both organizations.

I shall return to discussion of this struggle between the Society and the Association shortly, but for the moment would like to digress to speculate about another possible source of the impetus for the change of the Society's name. My speculation concerns the rivalry between the American Psychopathological Association and the American Psychoanalytic Association and W. A. White's position in this rivalry. The American Psychopathological Association arose in an atmosphere of growing interest in psychotherapy of various types and was founded in Washington, D. C., in 1910. Its membership embraced both physicians and psychologists, and its first president and dominant force was Morton Prince. Prince had founded the *Journal of Abnormal Psychology* in 1906, with Meyer as one of its associate editors.

The American Psychoanalytic Association was founded in 1911, a year later than the Psychopathological Association. Prince sensed a strong rival in Freud; moreover Prince and Ernest Jones clashed more than once during Jones' early efforts to establish psychoanalysis in America, despite James J. Putnam's efforts to mediate between them (20, p. 35).

White, despite his abiding interest in, and many contributions to, psychoanalysis, including his serving four terms as President of the American Psychoanalytic Association (1915, 1916, 1927, 1928), was so eclectic at heart that probably the broader scope of the American Psychopathological Association appealed to him. According to Oberndorf, at the 1919 meeting of the American Psychoanalytic Association White co-sponsored a resolution that the Association be dissolved as a separate entity and incorporated into the American Psychopathological Association. He is quoted as saying, ". . . the time has come to free American psychiatry from the domination of the Pope at Vienna" (35, pp. 135-136). Oberndorf's account must be questioned, however, in light of evidence that White was not at the 1919 meeting; he was elected Secretary-Treasurer in absentia. Oberndorf goes on to credit Meyer, his revered teacher, with a stout and successful defense of the proposition that psychoanalysis had an important contribution to make to American psychiatry and that this contribution could best be assured by the continuance of the American Psychoanalytic Association. Meyer's firmness on this point is an illustration of Phyllis Greenacre's cogent characterization of her early mentor: "Meyer stood for certain things, and he stood for them very firmly" (personal communication, 1976).

This event did not, however, bring a rupture of White's relationship with organized psychoanalysis, for he again served as President of the American Psychoanalytic Association in 1927-1928, and in 1931 was the principal speaker at a banquet in New York honoring Freud's 75th birthday (46). Nonetheless, we can surmise that White's leaning toward the American Psychopathological Association was perhaps a factor in the change of name of the Washington Society. A possible addendum to this surmise is White's subsequent request that the name of the William Alanson White Psychoanalytic Foundation, established in 1933 under the leadership of Hadley and Sullivan, be changed to the William Alanson White Psychiatric Foundation. This was done shortly after White's death in 1937. Brill reacted to the change of name by resigning from the Board of Trustees of the Foundation.

After this digression on "what's in a change of name," I return to the rivalry between the Washington Psychopathological Society and the Washington Psychoanalytic Association as to which would emerge as the official representative of psychoanalysis in the region. This entailed the question of which, if either of them, could obtain formal affiliations with the American Psychoanalytic Association and the International Psychoanalytic Association. This question was further complicated by the intense divergence between the American and the International Associations on the issue of lay analysis. For example, Ferenczi's visit to the U.S. in 1927, during which he lectured at the New School for Social Research in New York and St. Elizabeths Hospital in Washington, added fuel to the lay analysis controversy, since he was well known to favor the training of lay analysts.

All of this came at a time when psychoanalysis was moving away from the informal period in which analysts had largely been self-selected and self-trained into a period of more formal institutionalization of psychoanalytic training. This meant the promulgation of formal standards for training and the establishment of psychoanalytic institutes. A key event in this shift occurred in 1925 at the Bad Hamburg Congress when the first International Training Commission was established for the purpose of formulating standards for psychoanalytic training. In America Brill played a vital part in this shift; it is significant that after succeeding White as President of the American Psychoanalytic Association in 1929, Brill served continuously for the next seven years.

Hence the rival organizations in Washington looked to Brill for official sanction and status within organized psychoanalysis. As it turned out, his blessing was eventually bestowed on those who had been leaders in the Washington Psychopathological Society. Among them were Ernest Hadley, Harry Stack Sullivan, Clara Thompson, and William Silverberg. Hadley was in close communication with Brill, partly by dint of his serving as Secretary of the American Psychoanalytic Association for seven years, six of which coincided with Brill's terms as President. After preliminary negotiations during 1928 and 1929, Hadley sent Brill on May 16, 1930, a confidential report on the potential members for a new psychoanalytic society which might receive official sanction. The report detailed the known qualifications of the prospective members. Concurrently Clara Thompson was asked to send a similar report about prospective members from the Baltimore area. Brill replied favorably by return mail, which suggests that his mind may have already been made up.

Thereupon invitations to an organizing meeting were sent out, and the meeting was held on Saturday evening, May 31, 1930, at Hadley's downtown Washington office. Present were Anna C. Dannemann Colomb, Lucile Dooley, Hadley, Nolan D. C. Lewis, Edward Hiram Reede, Silverberg, Sullivan, and Clara Thompson. Later additions to the roster of charter members were Ross Chapman, Philip Graven, Loren Johnson, Adolf Meyer, G. Lane Taneyhill, and W. A. White. Clara Thompson was elected the first president of the new Society.

Conspicuously absent was Ben Karpman, the leader of the Washington Psychoanalytic Association. Precisely how and why Karpman was omitted or excluded remains something of a mystery. Many years later Silverberg recalled that Sullivan had asked him to serve as secretary pro tem and had given him a list of names and addresses of persons to be invited to the organizing meeting. Karpman's name was on this list, but some months later Silverberg learned that Karpman's invitation had been sent to an outdated address. Another version of the Karpman story has been attributed to Lucile Dooley—that Brill had sent informal advance word the group would receive his approval only if Karpman were excluded.

Karpman was both a colorful and controversial figure. He wrote voluminously and rather luridly about criminal and perverse sexual behavior. He had had some association with Stekel; whether and how much personal analysis by Stekel this entailed is not known. One certainty is that Karpman maintained an abiding hatred for Sullivan for the remainder of his life. An oft-repeated scene at psychiatric meetings in Washington was Karpman's rising from the floor to comment upon the paper of the evening and somehow managing to interpolate the gratuitous remark that Sullivan had never been a true analyst.

After the founding of the Washington-Baltimore Psychoanalytic Society, the activities of the Washington Psychoanalytic Association greatly diminished, though a few of their members continued to meet with Karpman with some regularity for almost thirty years longer.

Not long after the founding of the new Society it began to sponsor a formal training program; in 1932 to be exact, one year after the opening of the New York Psychoanalytic Institute and the same year as the establishment of the Boston and the Chicago Institutes. Hadley, Hill, and Silverberg took the lead in promoting formal training. It is perhaps of note that their origins were not Vienna, Berlin, or Budapest but rather Kansas, Virginia, and New York City, although Silverberg had received personal analysis in Berlin, and Hill had traveled to Budapest for supervision by Ferenczi.

Early in 1933 Silverberg conducted the first formal course, consisting of fifteen seminars on Freud's five published case histories. The next scholastic year, 1933-34, a considerably expanded course list was offered, and the faculty included Dooley, Hadley, Hill, and Nolan D. C. Lewis. Silverberg and Thompson, though they moved from Baltimore to New York in 1933, continued to conduct seminars and supervision in Washington for several more years.

It should be recorded that much earlier courses and lectures had been given by Taneyhill to medical students at Johns Hopkins from 1917 to 1925 and by Dooley to women psychiatric residents at St. Elizabeths Hospital during World War I (11).

Another forerunner of formal courses had been the "Miracle Club." This was an informal case seminar which met Sundays in Baltimore. Reports differ as to whether the club met at Sheppard-Pratt Hospital (18) or at Clara Thompson's apartment (17, p. 355). The members included Thompson, Silverberg, Sullivan, Hill, and Marjorie Jarvis. The club's name derived from the "miraculous" beneficial effects on the patients discussed by the club members.

A similar "Miracle Club" was formed in Washington in 1932 and included Silverberg, Dooley, Graven, Hadley, and Reede (18).

Lewis Hill directed the society's Training Program from 1934 to 1940; in the latter year the Washington-Baltimore Psychoanalytic Institute was founded, with Hill as its first Director. In 1949 he was succeeded by Hadley, who served in that capacity until his death in 1954.

Another important chapter in the history of psychoanalysis in Washington-Baltimore concerns the rather complicated relationship of the Society and the Institute with the William Alanson White Psychiatric Foundation on the one hand and the Washington School of Psychiatry on the other. From the mid-thirties until 1949 the workings of these organizations were intertwined, with much overlap of faculty and administration. The Foundation was established in 1933. The change in its name from Psychoanalytic to Psychiatric at White's request which led to Brill's resignation as a trustee has already been mentioned, and was an omen of future organizational changes, conflicts of purpose, and fallings-out among friends.

Several key persons, including Dooley, Fromm-Reichmann, Hadley, Hill, and Sullivan, shared in the formation of the Foundation and of the school, and subsequently in 1938 of the journal *Psychiatry,* after failure of negotiations to take over the *Psychoanalytic Review* from Jelliffe.

It seems clear that even from the outset they did not all share the same goals for the Foundation. Hadley and Dooley were most interested in establishing an institute for psychoanalytic training within the orthodox Freudian tradition. Sullivan's interests were broader and more varied (2). Ultimately these organizations took on much of the shape he envisioned and provided him with an organizational base. Their aims and purposes were broad and eclectic, and courses in psychoanalysis were to be but one section of the curriculum. For this section an arrangement was made between the Washington-Baltimore Psychoanalytic Society for students enrolled in the Society's training program to take didactic courses provided by the Washington School of Psychiatry. It was envisioned that other students would come to the school via other routes and from other institutions, including St. Elizabeths Hospital, the Veterans Administration, and the military medical facilities in the Washington area. In some of their courses in the school the psychoanalytic candidates would be joined by other students.

It is not difficult to discern that this arrangement created a situation ripe for conflict, especially when one considers how sensitive the issue of purity of discipline vs. eclecticism has been in organized psychoanalysis. The same issue arises around the question of whether training in psychoanalysis should be conducted by a section within a university department of psychiatry.

White's death in 1937, even though his participation had been in considerable part honorary and symbolic, probably left the situation more open to the serious disagreements that developed among Sullivan and various others who had joined him in establishing the Foundation and the School. Sullivan asked Adolf Meyer to succeed White as President of the Foundation, but Meyer politely and firmly declined. Dooley, who had been designated Professor and Head of the Department of Psychoanalysis in the school, resigned in 1941. Hill followed her in 1944. Hadley, who had been a mainstay and co-editor of the journal *Psychiatry*, resigned in 1945, and in 1946 Sullivan became the sole editor.

Meanwhile the activities of Sullivan, the Washington School of Psychiatry, and the Washington-Baltimore Psychoanalytic Society and Institute became entangled in a series of psychoanalytic schisms in New York, in which Karen Horney, Erich Fromm, Silverberg, and even more specially, Clara Thompson, played leading roles.

As background for this piece of history it is important to know of the personal bond of friendship that existed for a time among these powerful personalities and Sullivan. During 1934 they were all located in New York, and met every Monday evening for dinner. After a whim of Sullivan's they dubbed themselves the "Zodiac," and each assumed the name of an animal. Thompson was "Puma," Sullivan "Horse," Horney "Water Buffalo," and Silverberg "Gazelle" (39). Subsequently, Erich Fromm joined the group.

This bond of friendship and shared ideas evidently played a part in Horney's, Thompson's, and Silverberg's resigning from the New York Psychoanalytic Society in 1941 and forming the Association for the Advancement of Psychoanalysis. Sullivan and several other Washingtonians also joined this Association, but resigned after the American Psychoanalytic Association adopted a resolution in December 1941 to the effect that membership in these two rival associations would be considered incompatible with the spirit of the constitution of the American Psychoanalytic Association.

Then in 1943 Clara Thompson split off from the Horney group, and with the collaboration of Sullivan, Fromm, Fromm-Reichmann, and Janet and David Rioch, formed the New York Division of the Washington School of Psychiatry. Later this was to become the William Alanson

White Institute, entirely separate from any organizations in Washington.

However, for several years the Thompson group was closely, even integrally, affiliated with the Washington-Baltimore Psychoanalytic Institute. Thompson, Janet Rioch, and Ralph Crowley were appointed Training Analysts in the Washington-Baltimore Institute, and their students were enrolled as candidates in the Institute. In addition, Sullivan and Fromm-Reichmann traveled regularly to New York to conduct seminars and supervision, while some of the Thompson group's candidates journeyed to Washington for supervision.

A variety of factors caused this liaison between the Thompson group in New York and the Washington-Baltimore Institute to fray and finally to break. One practical problem was that of coordinating the records kept in the two cities, especially as the American Psychoanalytic Association began to require more detailed reports.

The Thompson group had a growing wish for autonomy, yet at the same time needed the sponsorship of the Washington-Baltimore Institute. A step toward independence was taken in 1946 when the Thompson group obtained a provisional charter from the New York State Board of Regents in the name of the William Alanson White Institute of Psychiatry.

However, it proved much more difficult to obtain recognition as an approved institute from the American Psychoanalytic Association and its newly-formed (1946), and increasingly active, Board on Professional Standards. Application for this recognition was made by the White Institute several times between 1948 and 1952. After prolonged efforts by Thompson and her colleagues to rally support from other Institutes and to persuade and negotiate for approval, the application was finally withdrawn in November 1952, and never resubmitted.

Meanwhile the Washington-Baltimore Institute removed the White Institute candidates from its rolls in 1949, and the next year Thompson, Janet Rioch and Crowley were dropped as Training Analysts of the Washington-Baltimore Institute.

This episode produced much frustration and bitterness; it not only created a deep rift between the Thompson group and many former friends in Washington-Baltimore but also contributed to divisions within the Washington-Baltimore group itself. Sullivan's death in 1949 undoubtedly weakened the liaison, since he had been one of the strongest links between the White Institute and the Washington-Baltimore Institute.

Neither Hadley nor Hill was as keenly motivated as Sullivan to maintain this affiliation. In addition, both Hadley and Hill were strong supporters of the American Psychoanalytic Association. Hill had been its President in 1940 and, as previously mentioned, Hadley had served as secretary for seven consecutive terms. Perhaps even more important, Hadley had chaired the committees on a new constitution and on professional standards. Thus he had been instrumental in changing the organization from one comprising individual numbers to one which was a federation of societies. What this meant was less autonomy for the societies and institutes and more central control and regulation by the control body, the American Psychoanalytic Association. This was especially true in the sphere of psychoanalytic training.

During this same period lines of cleavage for future splits were forming within the Washington-Baltimore Society. Numerous factors contributed to this process. For one thing, as numbers of analysts and students increased, it became more feasible for each city to have its own society and institute. World War II and gasoline rationing had made students and faculty more mindful of the inconveniences and difficulties of traveling between the two cities for training. However, there were other, probably more cogent, factors at work, including ideological as well as personality divergencies.

Division into two separate societies occurred in 1946. For another five years training was conducted by a joint institute, with a separate Education Subcommittee in each city. Application for division of the Institute was made to the American Psychoanalytic Association in 1950; action on the application was deferred in 1951, and approval granted in 1952.

One of the sharpest foci of conflict was between Sullivan and Jenny Waelder-Hall, who had arrived in Washington in the mid-1940s from Vienna, with a brief interim stay in Boston punctuated by her divorce from Robert Waelder. Some observers have commented that Sullivan was almost a bête noire for her. However, her disapproval of many features of the Washington component of the Institute extended beyond the person of Sullivan to such issues as whether the centrality of libido in personality development could be questioned and whether three sessions a week might accomplish as good results as four or five a week.

Nevertheless, it is tempting to view Waelder-Hall and Sullivan not only as eloquent spokesmen but as literal personifications of Viennese orthodoxy and American eclecticism and of the difficulty, if not impossibility, of reconciling the two.

For his part, Sullivan certainly was not an orthodox Freudian. In fact, in formulating the concepts and theories of his "interpersonal psychiatry" he was at pains to coin terms which would distinguish his ideas from those of Freud. For example, any student who made so bold as to ask wherein Sullivan's "parataxic distortion" differed from Freud's "transference" was likely to be met by a withering blast of sarcasm, or at best told to figure it out for himself. This had not always been the case, for Sullivan's early papers in the 1920s, when he directed a schizophrenia ward at Sheppard-Pratt Hospital, were distinctly Freudian in their concepts and language. He had also been an active psychoanalytic organization worker; in 1930, when the Washington-Baltimore Psychoanalytic Society was founded, he had been Vice President of the American Psychoanalytic Association. Only later did both he and his critics set him apart from Freudian psychoanalysis.

Nevertheless, even from early in his career many aspects of his professional interests and endeavors were unorthodox. To begin with, he was greatly absorbed in the study and treatment of schizophrenia in a hospital setting, rather than in office treatment of neurotic patients. Certainly he did not subscribe to the dictum that "narcissistic neuroses" were untreatable by psychoanalytic methods. Doubtless he was influenced by Kempf, who was doing his pioneer work at St. Elizabeths when Sullivan came there as liaison officer for the Veterans Bureau. Sullivan's ideas were also influenced by the "Chicago school" of sociology, particularly as exemplified by Charles Horton Cooley and by George H. Mead. Later influences came from Harold Lasswell and Edward Sapir.

Still another strand of unorthodox influence can be discerned in the ideas of Boris Sidis, probably as transmitted to Sullivan by White. Sidis, a student of William James, an associate editor of Morton Prince's *Journal of Abnormal Psychology*, and a prominent member of the American Psychopathological Association, was an early exponent of dynamic medical psychology, of the power of unconscious mental processes, and of psychotherapy. Though Sidis was one of the first in America to refer to Freud's studies when he published a review of Freud's *Psychopathology of Everyday Life* in the first volume of the *Journal of Abnormal Psychology* (1906), later in his career he conspicuously avoided mention of Freud and was concerned to promote his own ideas (36, p. 106). Sidis placed great significance on fear as a central motivating force and as the key to the formation and treatment of neuroses. When Sullivan maintained that quest for security and the deployment of "security operations" were as important as instinctual drives for sexual gratification and defense mechanisms, he was remarkably close to Sidis' ideas about fear, as well as echoing some of the formulations of Adler and Horney.

Sidis' influence on White had been considerable, dating from their collaborative study of mental dissociation (19, p. 156). It would appear that his contacts with Sidis contributed both to White's receptivity to psychoanalysis and to his persistent eclecticism. The same can also be said of the influence emanating from his deep friendship with Jelliffe.

Both White and Sullivan also gave great weight to the role of the environment in shaping personality. They were as concerned with social and cultural influences as with instinctual drives. They sought and established active communication and collaboration with a wide range of social scientists, including sociologists, anthropologists, linguists, and social psychologists.

Viewed in the perspective of the history of ideas, Sullivan's "interpersonal psychiatry" was paralleled by several distinct similar developments within orthodox psychoanalysis. Among these have been the shift from id psychology to ego psychology (A. Freud, Hartmann, Kris, and Lowenstein), recognition of the crucial importance of the mother-child relationship and preoedipal experience (Spitz, Bowlby, Mahler, Benedek, and Winnicott), emphasis on adaptation to the environment (Hartmann), stages of psychosocial development (Erikson), object relations theories (M. Klein, Fairbairn, Balint, Jacobson), and the treatment of narcissistic disorders (Kohut, Kernberg).

Several of these developments were foreshadowed and drew impetus from Ferenczi and his intellectual and psychoanalytic descendants, among whom Sullivan must be counted as one. Sullivan had been favorably impressed by Ferenczi's lectures in the United States during his 1926-27 visit. When Clara Thompson decided to journey to Europe for personal analysis, Sullivan recommended that she go to Ferenczi. Later, Sullivan briefly became a psychoanalytic patient of Thompson. Lewis Hill was another of the early Washington-Baltimore leaders who received direct training from Ferenczi, though it was cut short by Ferenczi's terminal illness and death in 1933. Hill had earlier been in personal analysis with Clara Thompson before her move to New York.

From his early years at Worcester State Hospital through his two periods of service at Sheppard-Pratt Hospital, Hill maintained his keen interest in the treatment of schizophrenia. His book *Psychotherapeutic*

Intervention in Schizophrenia (23) remains today one of the clearest and most sensibly practical discussions of the topic available. His return to Sheppard-Pratt in 1950 coincided approximately with the dividing of the Washington-Baltimore Society and of the Institute. Subsequently, Hill was not as active in psychoanalytic education as previously, though he remained a respected member of the separate Baltimore Society and, in fact, was its first president and was elected an honorary member of the Washington Society.

From some viewpoints one might have expected Hill to have joined the Washington group when the division occurred. His remaining with the Baltimore group can probably be taken as evidence of how splits are complicated by factors of geography, ideology, genealogy, and personal friendship. They are not reducible to neat, clear-cut lines of cleavage nor to single principles of classification.

Another case in point was Alfred Stanton. On the one hand, Stanton was closely affiliated with Sullivan and Fromm-Reichmann, taught an important course in the Washington School of Psychiatry, and was a senior psychiatrist on the Staff of Chestnut Lodge, where he carried out pioneering collaborative research with a sociologist on the social psychology of the mental hospital and the effect of the social milieu upon schizophrenic patients. Yet, on the other hand, his personal analyst had been Lucile Dooley, who had traveled to Vienna for analysis with Ruth Mack-Brunswick and tutorial sessions with Robert Waelder.

For a time, between the division of the Society in 1947 and of the Institute in 1952, Dooley and Stanton joined with Waelder-Hall and six others in an attempt to form a third Society, presumably intended to be more orthodox and more "Viennese" than either the Washington or the Baltimore Society and to preserve classical analysis from destruction.

Application was made to the American Psychoanalytic Association for official approval of this embryonic third Society, which was named the Maryland-District of Columbia Psychoanalytic Society. After action on this application was deferred, the group led by Waelder-Hall, evidently decided that its goals could be attained by joining the existing Baltimore Society, so plans for a separate third Society were dropped. Stanton, to whom friends had commented, "You seem to be trying to ride two horses that are headed in opposite directions," moved on to Boston to become Medical Director of McLean Hospital.

The position of the American Psychoanalytic Association toward splits of psychoanalytic societies and institutes has always been touchy and complex, probably even more so today than in the days of Brill's domination of the organization. Then his judgment alone might determine which group would receive accreditation, as when Karpman was somehow excluded in the founding of the Washington-Baltimore Society in 1930. Today the structure of the American Psychoanalytic Association, or simply "the American," as it is usually referred to, comprises an array, one might even say a maze, of committees and sub-committees. Some of these committees are concerned with accreditation functions; they formulate standards for psychoanalytic training and conduct inspections of institutes to determine whether these standards are being met. Other committees perform a quasi-certification function and judge whether individual applicants for membership in "the American" are qualified as adequately knowledgeable and skilled in psychoanalytic principles and technique to merit election to membership. Thus, acceptance by the membership committee is analogous, and partially equivalent, to passing a medical specialty board examination.

In carrying out the functions of accreditation of training institutes and of the quasi-certification of individual graduates of institutes "the American" is a powerful force. Obviously, institutes and their graduates are eager to pass both forms of examination conducted by "the American." The desire for approval from the central organization is exacerbated if, within a particular institute, there are sub-groups or individuals who are dissatisfied with the institute's present policies and wish to gain official sanction, if not active support, for a different program.

When this situation arises "the American" finds itself in a delicate position, wherein it must attempt to reach impartial judgment as to which and how many groups in a particular region should be accredited to conduct psychoanalytic training. It may be difficult to resist intense pressures to choose sides, and the judgment rendered may be akin to Solomon's in the case of the two mothers.

The question can be raised as to whether the splitting of societies and institutes ultimately strengthens, or weakens, psychoanalysis, both as a discipline and as an organization. How one answers this question would depend in considerable part on one's view of whether psychoanalysis would be best served by orthodoxy or by diversity and eclecticism. The impetus for the splits of psychoanalytic groups in America has come sometimes from the side of orthodoxy, at other times from the eclectics. However, one might assume that almost by definition those of eclectic leanings might be more content with a relatively large diverse group, including perhaps "professors and mental hospital superintendents," while the orthodox would favor a smaller, more select group. In any event, it seems fair to say that the tension between these two points of view usually continues in some form or other within the new groups even after splits have occurred. In this respect, as in others, I believe that the history of psychoanalysis in Washington-Baltimore provides an illuminating case example.

REFERENCES

1. Adler, A., *The Neurotic Constitution; Outlines of a Comparative Individualistic Psychology and Psychotherapy*, trans. by B. S. Glueck and J. E. Lind. New York: Moffat, Yard, 1917 (1912).

2. Burnham, D., Discussion of Dr. Robert Kvarnes' "The Founding of the William Alanson White Psychiatric Foundation," in A. D'Amore (Ed.), *William Alanson White, The Washington Years*. DHEW Publication, No. (ADM) 76-298, 1976.

3. Burnham, J. C., Psychoanalysis and American Medicine, 1894-1918: Medicine, Science, and Culture. *Psychological Issues*, Monograph 20. New York: International Universities Press, 1967.

4. Burrow, T., Permutations Within the Sphere of Consciousness, or the Factor of Repression and Its Influence upon Education. *J. Abnormal Psychol.*, 1916, 11:178-188.

5. ———, The Group Method of Analysis. *Psychoanalytic Review*, 1927, 14:268-280.

6. Campbell, C. M., Psychological Mechanisms with Special Reference to Wish-Fulfillment. *New York State Hospital Bulletin*, 1908, 2:12-26.

7. ———, The Form and Content of the Psychosis; The Role of Psychoanalysis in Psychiatry. *New York State Hospital Bulletin*, 1910, 3:3-21.

8. ———, The Application of Psychoanalysis to Insanity. *New York Medical Journal*, 1912, 95:1079-1081.

9. ———, The Roots of Mental Disorders in Childhood. *State Hospital Bull.* 1915, 8:8-11.

10. Dejerine, J., and Gauckler, E., *The Psychoneuroses and their Treatment*, trans. by S. E. Jelliffe. Philadelphia: Lippincott, 1913 (1911).

11. Dooley, L., Outline of a Series of Talks on Psychoanalysis. *Psychoanalytic Review*, 1919, 6:214-225.

12. Dubois, P., *The Psychic Treatment of Nervous Disorders*, ed. and trans. by S. E. Jelliffe and W. A. White. New York: Funk & Wagnalls, 1905 (1901).

13. Freud, S., On the History of the Psychoanalytic Movement (1914). *S. E.*, XIV.

14. Glueck, B., The God-Man or Jehovah Complex. *New York Medical Journal*, 1915, 102:496-499.

15. ———, *Studies in Forensic Psychiatry*. Boston: Little, Brown, 1916.

16. ———, Reflections and Comments. In: *Centennial Papers, Saint Elizabeths Hospital, 1855-1955*. Baltimore: Waverly Press, 1956.

17. Green, M. R., Her Life. In: *Interpersonal Psychoanalysis: The Selected Papers of Clara M. Thompson*, M. R. Green (Ed.). New York: Basic Books, 1964.

18. Hadley, E., Psychoanalysis, Its History and Development in the Washington, D.C. and Baltimore, Md. Vicinity. Unpublished, 1951.

19. Hale, N. G., Jr., *Freud and the Americans, The Beginnings of Psychoanalysis in the United States, 1876-1917*. New York: Oxford University Press, 1971.

20. Hale, N. G., Jr., *James Jackson Putnam and Psychoanalysis*, Cambridge: Harvard University Press, 1971.

21. Hassall, J. C., The Role of the Sexual Complex in Dementia Praecox. *Psychoanalytic Review*, 1915, 2:260-276.

22. Hendrick, I., *Facts and Theories of Psychoanalysis*. New York: Knopf, 1939 (1934).

23. Hill, L. B., *Psychotherapeutic Intervention in Schizophrenia*. Chicago: University of Chicago Press, 1955.

24. Jung, C. G., *The Psychology of Dementia Praecox*. New York: Journal of Nervous and Mental Disease Publishing Co., 1909 (1907).

25. Jung, C. G., *The Theory of Psychoanalysis*. New York: Journal of Nervous and Mental Disease Publishing Co., 1915.

26. Kempf, D. C., and Burnham, J. C. (Eds.), *Edward J. Kempf, Selected Papers*. Bloomington: Indiana University Press, 1974.

27. Kempf, E. J., The Social and Sexual Behavior of Infrahuman Primates, with Some Comparable Facts in Human Behavior. *Psychoanalytic Review*, 1917, 4:127-154.

28. Kempf, E. J., *Psychopathology*. St. Louis: Mosby, 1920.

29. Lewis, N. D. C., The Psychoanalytic Approach to the Problems of Children Under Twelve Years of Age. *Psychoanalytic Review*, 1926, 13:424-443.

30. MacCurdy, J. T., The Productions in a Manic-Like State Illustrating Freudian Mechanisms. *J. Abnormal Psychol.*, 1914, 7:361-375.

31. Meyer, A., The Dynamic Interpretation of Dementia Praecox. *Amer. J. Psychol.*, 1910, 21:385-403.

32. ———, A Discussion of Some Fundamental Issues in Freud's Psychoanalysis. *State Hospital Bull.*, 1910, 2:827-848.

33. Moore, T. V., *Dynamic Psychology*. Philadelphia: Lippincott, 1924.

34. Noble, D., and Burnham, D. L., History of the Washington Psychoanalytic Society and the Washington Psychoanalytic Institute, 1969.

35. Oberndorf, C. P., *A History of Psychoanalysis in America*. New York: Grune & Stratton, 1953.

36. Shakow, D., and Rapaport, D., *The Influence of Freud on American Psychology*. Cleveland: World Publishing Co., 1968.

37. Silberer, H. *Problems of Mysticism and Its Symbolism*, trans. by S. E. Jelliffe. New York: Moffat, Yard, 1917 (1914).

38. Sullivan, H. S., Erogenous Maturation. *Psychoanalytic Review*, 1926, 13:1-15.

39. Thompson, C. M., Unpublished "History of the William Alanson White Institute," presented before the Harry Stack Sullivan Society on March 15, 1955.

40. White, W. A., *Outlines of Psychiatry*, 1st edition. New York: Nervous and Mental Disease Monograph Publishing Co., 1907.

41. ———, *Outlines of Psychiatry*, 2nd edition. New York: Nervous and Mental Disease Monograph Publishing Co., 1909.

42. ———, *Mental Mechanisms*. New York: Nervous and Mental Disease Monograph Publishing Co., 1911.

43. ———, Dreams. *Reference Handbook of the Medical Sciences* (3rd ed.), 1914, pp. 688-95.

44. ———, The Unconscious. *Psychoanalytic Review*, 1915, 2:12-28.

45. ———, Symbolism. *Psychoanalytic Review*, 3:1-25.

46. ———, Professor Freud's Seventy-Fifth Birthday. *Psychoanalytic Review*, 1931, 18:237-240.

CHAPTER 7

The Chicago Institute for Psychoanalysis from 1932 to the Present

George H. Pollock, M.D., Ph.D.

PSYCHOANALYSTS ARE NOT in the vanguard of revolution, but in the field of theory and clinical practice of psychiatry and psychoanalysis they were the founder-members of a far-reaching movement that has influenced the Western world in profound ways. In more recent years we have found a conservatism that frequently follows the innovative phase of a new field. Perhaps we will soon see a renaissance with new breakthroughs—already the seeds of such changes may be detected but as yet they have not fully taken root and obviously have not flowered. In the future, I can foresee a greater emphasis on prediction, prevention, and early intervention. I can foresee applications to and from other fields, especially the social, political, and humanistic disciplines. I can foresee a greater emphasis on the study of all phases of the life cycle and their deviations. I can foresee a new alignment of specialties, health care facilities, and an increasing emphasis on quality-of-life issues. I can foresee different educational models and paths. I can foresee alternative therapeutic applications and treatment modalities where there is the simultaneous combination and

Presented on June 3, 1976. Also published in Volume V, *The Annual of Psycho-analysis*. George H. Pollock is Director of the Chicago Institute for Psychoanalysis, Chicago, Illinois.

application of different therapies, and can see a greater understanding and integration of biological and sociological approaches and data with those of psychoanalysis. The existing approaches of sociobiology are not antithetical to and they may add dimensions to the fundamental theories of psychoanalysis.

With this preamble of what may be in the future for psychoanalysis let me switch and return to the theme of this series. However, let me first quote Marcus Aurelius, who noted: "What keeps the whole world in being is change: not merely change of the basic elements, but also change of the larger formations they compose" (Meditations, Book Two, Number 3). Marcus Aurelius indicates the effect of Heraclitus, who taught that the essence of Being is Becoming, that is, the incessant movement of change, by which one aspect of a thing is always leading on to another. We need not fear change or the future and we should not forget the past from which we come.

It is difficult enough to capture the essence of a single individual at any given moment, let alone his development, functioning, past difficulties and triumphs, even if that person has provided us with all possible data and we have ample time. The nuances of living, the vicissitudes of past interactions, and the chance events which either facilitated or inhibited growth in one or another direction are not easily recaptured and are most difficult to describe. The autobiographers make valiant attempts, the biographers with distance and perspective add dimensions to the story, and the psychoanalysts, who can be witness to the past unfolding in the present, all contribute to the picture of the individual.

To be autobiographer, biographer, and historian of an institution is a complex but not impossible task, even though the institution is and was a relatively small one and one that had specific goals and objectives. The institution I am talking about is the Chicago Institute for Psychoanalysis, one that has been of great importance to me for over twenty-five years—and I plan to discuss the Institute's *philosophy*, some pivotal *people*, some *places* where the Chicago Institute sponsored initial training, some *programs* (research and educational), and some *projections* for the future. Our Institute has had its difficulties, its differences and divisions, but we have never split and throughout our almost forty-five year history, have remained cohesive and institutionally united. I believe we are a viable institution today and one dedicated to psychoanalytic education, research, service, and scholarship. While remaining classical in clinical education, the Institute has been innovative throughout its history. It has espoused psychoanalysis as a science as well as a profession and has encouraged younger people with new ideas to carefully test them out either alone or as part of a research team.

In 1964, not long after Franz Alexander's sudden death, both the Chicago Institute for Psychoanalysis and the Chicago Psychoanalytic Society convened special meetings to honor the founder of their organizations. The tributes offered by Alexander's colleagues and students were privately published, and in them one learns much about this vital man, who seemed forever growing and youthful, incomplete and always searching for new horizons and new ideas. He was creative and colorful, productive and provocative, courageous and controversial, pioneering and proper. Much could be said of this man of contrasts—he was a psychoanalyst, a researcher, an educator, a teacher. From boyhood on, he wanted an academic career, yet he spent much of his professional life actively committed to private work with patients. Identified with the goals and ideals of his father, who was a professor of philosophy, and exposed to the culture and ideas of the nineteenth century in his home, in his schools, and in his social environment, he nevertheless chose medicine as a career, and early studied and worked in physiology, biochemistry, and bacteriology. This background of humanistic-philosophical concerns and rigorous scientific testing and theory building made him an early participant in the "two cultures" polarity currently being debated. Another paradox refers to Alexander the conformist, the political conservative, yet the rebel of sorts. Alexander could be a follower (throughout his life he had many heroes, the chief ones being his father and Freud) and he often spoke admiringly of others who influenced him— among them Abraham, Eitingon, Sachs, and Ferenczi. On the other hand, he was a charismatic leader who inspired others to creative work. He could work alone, or with a single collaborator such as Hugo Staub, William Healy, Thomas French, Helen Ross, or with teams of research colleagues who were stimulating to and stimulated by him. From the beginning Alexander always saw to it that there was an almost equal mix of men and women at the Institute—for example, he brought Karen Horney, Therese Benedek and Helen Ross to Chicago, and he involved Helen McLean, Margaret Gerard, Catherine Bacon, Adelaide Johnson, Lucia Tower, Charlotte Babcock, Irene Josselyn, and many other outstanding women in the psychoanalytic Institute community. If I were to mention the outstanding men he found or brought to Chicago, it would be a roll of leaders in American analysis. I shall speak of Thomas French in a few minutes, but there are many others—for example, Maurice Levine, George Mohr, Leon Saul, Karl and William Menninger, Leo Bartemeier, and Lionel Blitzsten.

Alexander, though a powerful man, respected independence and freedom. This provided the milieu in which students and associates could work in their own directions or in congress with each other. Because of this ability to tolerate differences, and because he insisted from the start on separating the psychoanalytic institute from the psychoanalytic society, Chicago remained united, even though disruptions and break-ups threatened.

Alexander was born in Budapest in January 1891. His father was professor of the history of philosophy at the University of Budapest. As a young medical student in Göttingen, he worked in physiology, returning to Budapest to complete his medical training and research in physiology and biochemistry. He received his medical degree in 1912, worked in bacteriology in 1913, and in 1914 became a military physician. He served on various battlefronts, including a section of the Italian front, where in 1918 he was head of a bacteriological field laboratory and in charge of malaria prophylaxis. After the war he returned home to work in brain physiology in the Neuropsychiatric Clinic of the University of Budapest.

Although he had read Freud's *Interpretation of Dreams* as a medical student, its relevance and applicability to clinical matters first became clear to Alexander during this period in the psychiatric department. In 1919, skeptical but increasingly convinced that the various examinations and tests then employed in psychiatric evaluation and study were meaningless in comparison with the vital and centrally aimed approach of psychoanalysis, Alexander went to Berlin, where he became the first student in the recently founded Berlin Psychoanalytic Institute. Alexander completed his personal analysis with Hanns Sachs and became an assistant in the Psychoanalytic Institute. In 1921 he won a prize awarded by Freud for research in psychoanalysis, and in 1924 and 1925 he gave a series of lectures at the Berlin Institute which formed the basis of his book, *The Psychoanalysis of the Total Personality*. Developing his ideas on the superego presented in this volume, Alexander began to work with Hugo Staub, a lawyer, and together in 1929 they published what is now a classic book on the understanding and diagnosis of criminal personalities—*The Criminal, The Judge, and The Public*. As a result of this book and largely through the efforts of William Healy, Alexander was invited in 1930 to the First International Congress for Mental Health in Washington, D. C. (1).

While in Washington, Alexander received a telegram from Robert Hutchins, the newly installed President of the University of Chicago and the former Dean of the Yale Law School, inviting him to visit Chicago and discuss an appointment in the University's medical school. President Hutchins offered Alexander a visiting professorship in psychiatry for one year in order to introduce psychiatry into the medical curriculum. Alexander suggested instead the title "Visiting Professor of Psychoanalysis." President Hutchins and Dr. Franklin McLean, then the Director of the University Clinics, agreed and the world's first university chair in psychoanalysis came into being (2). Freud appreciated Alexander's insistence on being called Professor of Psychoanalysis, but foresaw that this might increase the difficulties of being accepted by the University. And Alexander's first year in Chicago did indeed seem to confirm Freud's predictions as to the non-acceptability of psychoanalysis by American medicine. At the University of Chicago, the social scientists, philosophers, and lawyers were far more interested in the new field than were the physicians. The exceptions included Franklin McLean (whose wife Helen subsequently became an analyst and an esteemed member of the Chicago Institute's Faculty), and a handful of internists who became involved in work on the psychological aspects of medicine. Alexander suffered formal defeat during that year, but left Chicago convinced that the psychological approach to the study and treatment of disease would soon become an important consideration in medical education, research, and patient care. These predictions have been fully confirmed.

Following the Chicago experience, Alexander spent a year in Boston working collaboratively with William Healy, Director of the Judge Baker Foundation, on problems of delinquency. The Rosenwald Fund financed this research, which derived data from the actual psychoanalyses of offenders and which resulted in the publication of *Roots of Crime* by Alexander and Healy.

The imprint of Alexander's Midwestern visit remained, and during the Boston year a group of interested people joined to ask him to return to Chicago to organize a psychoanalytic institute. This he did in 1932 (3). Although the Institute was in part modeled after the Berlin Institute from which Alexander came and of which he was the first graduate, the model was also that of the academic research institutes in Germany— where scholars, teachers, and researchers could gather, exchange, debate, and live in harmonious collaboration. To a large extent this was the original organizing philosophy of the Chicago Institute and it continues to be a guiding principle today. Many Faculty members have their private offices in the Institute's quarters, where the classrooms are also located, as well as the library and information services, administrative offices, dining room and kitchen, and offices of such auxiliary programs as Child Therapy and Teacher Education. There are weekly research meetings plus many smaller ongoing research workshops.

To staff the new Institute, Alexander brought new people to Chicago and invited analysts already on the scene to collaborate in training and research activities (4). To finance it, he secured the assistance of the Rockefeller Foundation, the Rosenwald Foundation, the Macy Foundation, and a number of other granting agencies. To insure its independence, he established the Chicago Institute as separate from the Chicago Psychoanalytic Society and all other academic organizations.

From the beginning, Alexander emphasized the psychosomatic "specificity" research that became a hallmark of the Chicago Institute and an area of major interest to him and many who have been associated with the Institute. Alexander introduced the idea of team research in psychoanalysis. He brought Therese Benedek to Chicago and encouraged her in her classic research contributions.

In 1956 Alexander left Chicago to become a Fellow at the then recently established Center for the Advanced Study of the Behavioral Sciences in Palo Alto. He then decided to begin with a new venture in the Los Angeles area, and assembled new groups at the Mt. Sinai Hospital and the Southern California Psychoanalytic Institute. He was constantly moving into new fields, but the legacy he left our Institute included: a philosophy; a group of exciting and venturesome teachers and researchers; an academic-research institution with officers equivalent to those in academic institutions and who now have a tenure of such length as to allow program development and follow through; a research orientation; a "lay" Board of Trustees who assumed legal and fiscal responsibility for the Institute thereby leaving administrative and educational responsibility to the professionals; an informal relationship with medical schools, hospitals, psychiatric facilities, business schools, hospitals, psychiatric facilities, business schools, law schools, the social science and humanities departments; and a number of people who either favored him or found him unacceptable.

I am aware of the personal nature of these statements and that others might see Alexander and his contributions differently—but as the third Director of the Chicago Institute, as a student of Alexander, Benedek, Fleming, French, Kohut, Piers, and the many other analysts who have played an intimate role in the development of the Institute, I have a perspective based on direct contact and personal communication, as well as seeing later developments.

Since this essay is an attempt to tell the story of an institution, however, let me close this section by pointing out that after Alexander left Chicago, the Institute continued to grow and develop under the able leadership of Gerhart Piers, the second Director, and Joan Fleming, the Dean. It was Piers' initiative that led to the establishment of a graduate clinic, at the time one of the few psychoanalytic clinics in the country serving "low-fee" patients. During the years of Piers' directorship, the Child Therapy Training Program came into being. This program has helped to substantially raise the level of child psychotherapy in social agencies and clinics through its training of practitioners and supervisors. Piers had a direct impact on the dissemination of psychoanalysis through his great efforts in extending and practically implementing the activities of geographic facilities, namely St. Louis and Denver. He also broadened the base of the Institute's lay governing board so as to make it representative of more varied segments of the Chicago population. The fact that the Institute could survive a transition by retaining much of what had proven successful while moving in new directions, and by continuing to develop a corps of younger analysts who could and did become contributors to analysis and the Chicago Institute later on, seems to be reflective of Alexander's influence and impact.

While in Berlin, Alexander analyzed many who later became international leaders in psychoanalysis, for example Bertram Lewin. Helen Ross, a school teacher from Independence, Missouri, had wished to be analyzed by Alexander. He suggested that she instead go to Vienna where she worked with Helene Deutsch, Anna Freud, and others, later returning to Chicago to become the Chicago Institute's Administrative Director (5). She remained in Chicago until she was asked by the American Psychoanalytic Association to become involved with surveying the state of psychoanalytic education with Bertram Lewin, who himself had been an Alexander analysand.

Thomas French, also an Alexander analysand in Berlin in the late 1920s, came to Chicago and became Alexander's Associate Director at the Chicago Institute in 1932. French and Alexander collaborated on many projects. Outstanding was their work in psychosomatic medicine and their studies on the controversial "brief psychotherapy."

French, originally an engineer by training, went to Cornell Medical School and received his M.D. in 1920. Then, finding himself bored with private practice, he became a psychiatrist. Like Alexander, he was fascinated by Freud's *Interpretation of Dreams* and resolved to get psychoanalytic training. He became a house officer at the Westchester Division of the New York Hospital and while there was awarded a fellowship in 1926 to the Berlin Institute, where he went into analysis with Alexander. When Alexander came to Chicago, French joined him and a lifelong collaboration began. Only a few months ago, French died in Chicago. Although these two pioneers had different temperaments and styles, they worked together while each pursued his individual research at the Institute. French had his own students who worked with him in his dream studies and in his integrative investigations of the psychoanalytic process. When Alexander left for the West, French remained in Chicago to continue his productive work with new teams of young collaborators.

Therese Benedek was invited to join the staff of the Chicago Institute in 1936. Benedek, a pioneer in psychoanalytic research, continues to write, teach and carry out investigations even today at age eighty-four. Though trained as a pediatrician, she very early began her psychoanalytic training with an analysis with Ferenczi. She was a student at the Berlin Institute and began to train younger colleagues in Leipzig, where she remained until coming to Chicago to join the staff at the Chicago Institute. Her pediatric background provided Benedek with the interest and experience that are reflected in her later research on the mother-child unit, confidence, the female sexual cycle, and the psychology of women. She later began her collaboration with Joan Fleming on psychoanalytic education, supervision, and selection. Always a stimulating teacher with a fertile imagination and a great reservoir of energy, Benedek easily fitted into the scholarly, academic, and research atmosphere of the Chicago Institute, where she has been an inspiration to her students, colleagues, and patients.

During the Alexandrian years, younger and older colleagues flocked to Chicago. Some came from Europe to escape from the Hitler terrors, and some came from other centers in the United States to join the vital researchers and teachers at the Chicago Institute.

In 1956 with the departure of Alexander for California and of Helen Ross to the survey and the American Psychoanalytic Association, a new team took over the administration of the Chicago Institute. Gerhart Piers became the Director; Joan Fleming became the Dean of Education; Thomas French, Director of Research; and George Mohr, Director of Child Analysis. Kate Rosenthal Ollendorff, formerly Helen Ross's assistant, took over as Administrative Director. New committees were appointed and greater delegation of responsibility occurred. The Clinic became more formally organized and a Graduate Clinic, providing more low cost analysis to the community through the involvement of recent graduates, was established. Graduate research workshops came into being. Candidates continued to come to Chicago from Cincinnati, Denver, St. Louis, Detroit, Indianapolis, Rochester (New York and Minnesota), Syracuse, Oklahoma City, Milwaukee, Dallas, New Orleans, and Dayton. The Institute's teaching continued to be organized around a weekend schedule. The Clinic began to investigate analyzability and follow-up studies. A research on selection of psychoanalytic candidates was undertaken. As the number of geographic candidates and faculty increased, Dr. Louis Shapiro was appointed Geographic Liaison Coordinator, and meetings of faculty members in and outside of Chicago were held regularly. New teachers were appointed and a research department was established. This department was responsible for the training of research fellows, research training of regular candidates, and arranging regular research meetings which occurred every Wednesday afternoon. In 1961, the Institute's librarian, Jeremiah O'Mara, left to become librarian of the American Psychiatric Association, and later the Institute librarian at the University of Pittsburgh. He was succeeded by Glenn Miller, also a professional librarian. The original Child Care Program for social workers, nurses, pediatricians, etc., was reorganized into a Child Therapy Program for social workers, and in 1965 the Teacher Education Program was established. In 1971, Piers left the Directorship and in 1969 Fleming retired as Dean and moved to Denver, where she became affiliated with the newly established Denver Psychoanalytic Institute and the University of Colorado. Louis Shapiro succeeded her as Dean, and I became the third Director of the Institute.

With my assumption of the Directorship, various administrative changes took place. The Director was now appointed by the Board of Trustees to a five-year term. On July 1, 1976, I begin my second term as Director. The staff, to which one had previously been appointed for life, voted itself out of existence, and a Psychoanalytic Education Council, to which members are elected from and by the Faculty of the Institute, became the major decision-making body of the Institute. Every graduate of five years who is a member of the American Psychoanalytic Association is automatically considered for appointment as training and supervising analyst, following the successful completion of a year of consultation on an analytic case with a member of the Training Analysis Committee. A uniform payment scale was introduced and everyone is compensated for his or her time, be it in teaching, administration, committee work, or interviewing prospective candidates for selection, matriculation or progression. Many teachers and researchers came into prominence—for example Michael Basch, John Gedo, Arnold Goldberg, Heinz Kohut. When Louis Shapiro left the Deanship, he was succeeded by Henry Seidenberg, and younger people became involved with administrative matters. During my first term, candidate representation on most committees became a reality. The library expanded, the Chicago Psychoanalytic Literature Index began publication, the Gitelson Film Library came into being, and videotape interviews with psychoanalytic pioneers commenced. The library was named The Helen and Franklin McLean Library in honor of two distinguished colleagues and friends. In 1973, *The Annual of Psychoanalysis* began publication. Thus far four volumes have appeared, the fifth is in press, and the sixth is being assembled. Denver, Cincinnati, and St. Louis have become independent institutes and candidates now commute from Minneapolis-St. Paul, Madison, Milwaukee, and Montreal.

As noted before, in 1973 the Chicago Institute was authorized by the State of Illinois to award the degree Doctor of Psychoanalysis. There are two candidates in training for this degree, and another application for this program has been received. The Institute's adult clinical program was accredited by the Joint Commission on Accreditation of Hospitals in 1976.

A great many visiting teachers have come to the Chicago Institute either to participate in the "Wednesday research meetings," to teach in extension programs, or as speakers at such special events as the Alexander, Ross, Benedek, and Neisser Lectures. Among these visitors have been Anna Freud, Jean Piaget, René Spitz, Edith Jacobson, Konrad Lorenz, Richard Sterba, Ludwig Von Bertalanffy, James Anthony, Roy Schafer, Abraham Zaleznik, Phyllis Greenacre, Rudolf Ekstein, and others.

The Institute moved to its present quarters in December 1966 and we are constantly expanding as additional space is required, for example for the new Barr-Harris Center for Prevention and the recently inaugurated Continuing Education Program.

The Institute continues to operate under the general guidance of a lay Board of Trustees, a system that has worked very well for over four decades. In addition, a volunteer Women's Committee is actively involved in fund raising and community education projects. The Institute conducts a continuing public relations program which has resulted in many favorable stories about psychoanalysis and its applications in medical, parental, educational, and general areas. Successful appearances by various faculty members have been arranged on radio and television.

The budget of the Institute in 1933-1934 was $62,000; in 1960-1961 it was over $311,000; and it will be over $760,000 for 1976-1977. Institute funds come from tuition and fees, grants and contributions. The low-fee out-patient clinic continues to provide diagnostic, referral, and therapeutic services for over 30,000 hours every year.

Research continues at the Institute. There are many continuing investigations by individuals and groups of faculty members and graduates. There are a dozen workshops, some including candidates, and some carried out under the co-sponsorship of the Institute and the nearby Center for Psychosocial Studies. From these research activities have come many publications and scientific presentations. Investigations in such areas as narcissism, the psychology of the self, the mourning process, psychosomatic problems of children, and creativity, have already appeared and other works are in progress. Heinz Kohut's germinal research on narcissism and the self already is classic even though it is still ongoing.

The Child Therapy Training Program, the Teacher Education Program, the Continuing Education Program, the Business Executives Program, the new Barr-Harris Prevention Center, are either continuing or newly launched projects.

The Erikson Institute for Early Childhood Education and the Center for Psychosocial Studies, though independent, have been intimately involved with the Chicago Institute. It is hoped that a newly established Group for the Study of Biology and Social Behavior, and the Group for the Study of the Adaptations in the Second Half of Life, will also provide the Institute with new ideas, research projects, and personnel.

A student loan fund started at the Chicago Institute in 1943 has grown in size and has become a major source of transitional aid for students in their psychoanalytic educational progression. This fund, now the Irving and Neison Harris Student Loan Fund, will continue to be available to Institute students.

Several outstanding psychoanalysts have moved to Chicago in recent years, for example Merton Gill and Philip Holzman. They have contributed to the Institute and have added to the "gene pool" of Chicago analysis. The danger of recessive gene dominance as a result of in-breeding is not only relevant to physical disease, but also applicable to institutional and disciplinary in-breeding. Chicago has benefited from the influx of people and ideas from the outside and this should continue if it is to have ongoing vitality.

Before closing this whirlwind historical account, it is important to note that the Chicago Institute maintains excellent contacts and relationships with many institutions nationally and also within the Chicago area. Its graduates are leaders in psychiatry and psychoanalysis—Roy Grinker, David Hamburg, Melvin Sabshin, Karl Menninger, Leo Bartemeier, Jules Masserman, Henry Brosin, Milton Rosenbaum, John Spiegel, Thomas Szasz, Marc Hollender, George Engel, Herbert Gaskill, Donald Langsley, Louis Gottschalk, Leon Saul, Joan Fleming, Heinz Kohut, and many others. There are now about three hundred graduates from the core program and over forty graduates from the child analysis program. Many of the Institute's graduates have left Chicago to settle and work elsewhere. Some who are deceased, like Max Gitelson and Maurice Levine, were outstanding leaders in psychoanalysis and psychiatry.

It is difficult to make accurate predictions about the future of psychoanalysis and psychiatry in a world that is constantly changing and where traditional professional distinctions are less clear than before. The Chicago Institute, though autonomous and having its own path of development, is linked to the fate of psychoanalysis. My own personal point of view is that the Chicago Institute will continue to grow and develop—perhaps not at the same rate as before, perhaps in directions that are as yet uncharted, perhaps with ideas from other disciplines, and undoubtedly with problems, pressures, dilemmas and decisions. If we can strike a balance between the ideal and the practical, the desired and the necessary, the pleasure and the reality, we will continue what began modestly over forty years ago and has grown into something of which we are very proud.

DISCUSSION AND ADDENDA

Following the presentation of the above essay, several questions were asked of the author which warranted further elaboration or extension of what was presented in somewhat condensed fashion. Answers have been combined and are now included as an addendum to the above report. The author is grateful to those unnamed members of the audience for their stimulating queries.

I

The Chicago Institute for Psychoanalysis was modeled after the organization of the Berlin Psychoanalytic Institute, where Franz Alexander received his psychoanalytic education. Bertram Lewin and Helen Ross (6) have reported on the history of the Berlin Institute, which was organized in 1920 by Karl Abraham, Max Eitingon, and Ernst Simmel (7). It was founded as part of a low-cost ambulatory Poliklinik. The Poliklinik was officially opened on February 14, 1920, and on March 5, 1920, Karl Abraham gave the first lecture of a course on the elements of psychoanalysis. The initial emphasis in Berlin was on the clinic and public service; the actual word "institute" was first used at a meeting of the Berlin Psychoanalytic Society on February 20, 1922. Simmel referred to the Berlin Psychoanalytic Institute at the international congress in Salzburg in April 1924. After that date this designation was used in official correspondence and courses of instruction were offered by the Institute.

Lecture courses were open to anyone who wished to attend. There was no distinction between professional courses and extension courses. There were no special prerequisites or enrollments. General lectures were attended by "all sorts of persons" and were held in the evening. "Many of the Berliners were more interested in the clinic than in the teaching, and . . . the group went on for some time thinking of itself as a society with an attached outpatient clinic" (6, p. 5). As in Berlin, the Vienna Psychoanalytic Society opened its institute in 1925 after many years of rather informal "society teaching." The Vienna Institute, similar to Berlin, was closely related and connected to the ambulatory clinic, which opened officially on May 22, 1922, and to which a child guidance center had been added in 1924. Once again we note that formal psychoanalytic education was directly derived from the clinical setting.

In the pre-institute era, "lecture courses and a complete curriculum were not always available to the student" (6, p. 29). The analytic "candidate" depended on reading and loosely organized literary and case seminars. A formal curriculum following the model of the Berlin Institute was organized with the founding of Institutes. The New York, Chicago, and Boston Institutes used Berlin as their model. Following the historic 1925 report by Eitingon at the Bad Hamburg Congress, an International Training Commission was organized and the education committee system came into being. The "admission to training" system was inaugurated and analytic societies were asked to provide a curriculum of lectures and seminars as well as opportunities for supervised clinical work. The Berlin-Vienna plan became the model used in other places.

Sandor Rado at the Berlin Institute presumably was the first one to initiate the clinical case conference, where there was the presentation of a case at each conference.

Siegfried Bernfeld, a Berlin Institute student, has written that "Hanns Sachs was invited to move from Vienna to Berlin to specialize in the analysis of psychoanalysts, established ones as well as beginners" (8, p. 464). He thus became the first training analyst. Although the Berlin Psychoanalytic Society was founded by Karl Abraham on August 27, 1908, it was in late 1923 or early 1924 that "the training committee of the Berlin Society decided to streamline its activities. It prepared to offer a complete training course to those psychiatrists who accepted, among others, the following terms: the committee to admit or reject the candidate irrevocably according to the impression gained in three preliminary interviews with him; the candidate to undergo first a personal analysis of at least six months duration: the training analyst to be designated by the committee; the committee—on advice of the training analyst—to decide when the analysis was sufficiently advanced for the candidate to participate in further stages of training; and further to decide when his personal analysis could be considered completed. The candidate was to promise in writing that he would not call himself a psychoanalyst before his formal admission to the society" (8, pp. 464-465). It is interesting to note that this procedure is still followed in one form or another and with some modification by many American institutes today.

In a volume entitled *Psychoanalytic Pioneers* edited by Alexander, Eisenstein, and Grotjahn (9), various historical facts are presented about the Berlin Institute and some of its trainees. Although of historical interest, the great impact of this germinal institution on psychoanalytic education is matched by the influence its students and faculty have had continuously on psychoanalysis. I will briefly note but a few of these illustrious (albeit at times controversial) contributors to psychoanalysis.

Karl Abraham, Max Eitingon, and Ernst Simmel were vital forces in the development of the Berlin psychoanalytic clinic. Eitingon developed and directed the supervised analyses and clinical case seminars at the Berlin Institute. In 1926, he established his psychoanalytic sanitorium on the outskirts of Berlin and thus pioneered the development of the hospital care of patients utilizing psychoanalytic principles.

In 1922, Sandor Rado came to Berlin to be analyzed by Abraham. He quickly joined the faculty of the Berlin Institute and taught there from 1922 to 1931, when he left for New York to organize the psychoanalytic institute there on the model of the Berlin Institute. Subsequently he founded the Columbia Psychoanalytic Clinic and Institute, again using Berlin as the model.

Helene Deutsch left the Berlin Institute in 1924 to return to Vienna and assist in creating the psychoanalytic institute there, again along Berlin lines. The Vienna Psychoanalytic Institute was founded in 1925 and Helene Deutsch was its director for ten years until she departed for the United States. She and Hanns Sachs came to Boston and actively worked in the Boston Psychoanalytic Institute, another facility influenced by the Berlin model.

Georg Groddeck was a member of the Berlin Psychoanalytic Society in the 1920s.

Melanie Klein was invited to practice in Berlin where she worked from 1921 to 1926, when she moved to London.

Karen Horney did her psychoanalytic work in Berlin from 1919 to 1932, when she came to Chicago. She was analyzed by Karl Abraham and Hanns Sachs, and was an active faculty member of the Berlin Institute.

Other psychoanalytic pioneers who worked, taught, or were trained at the Berlin Institute include Wilhelm Reich, Annie Reich, Erich Fromm, Freida Fromm-Reichmann, Edward Glover, Hugo Staub, Otto Fenichel, Berta Bornstein, Edith Jacobson, Bertram Lewin, Carl Müller-Braunschweig, Jeno Harnik, Felix Boehm, Therese Benedek, and Gregory Zilboorg.

The Berlin Institute and its teachers, students and members were truly an unusual group and it may be an important study to try and ascertain why so many neo-Freudians had their origins there.

The historical development of psychoanalysis had its origins in Vienna centering around Freud and his early students. Soon other small groups appeared in Berlin, Zurich, and elsewhere. These groups, usually starting with one or two leaders, shared their insights, discussed their observations, debated the germinal papers, and speculated about theory. As the groups consolidated, students came for training in the new and exciting field of psychoanalysis. Soon educational institutions were established and the psychoanalytic movement became organized. Unlike the highly personal, private and individual nature of the clinical analytic relationship, the group activity had a definite effect on the mood, nature, and choice of interests of the individual members. The theoretical focus, the method of thought, the choice of areas of interest and research, were frequently influenced by the charismatic leaders and core members of the group. The challenge of questions, the interplay of provisional hypotheses, the encouragement or discouragement of particular lines of inquiry reflected the ambience provided by minds focused on the new science. The great analytic centers of Europe such as Vienna and Berlin exercised their influence on the development of psychoanalysis and psychoanalytic institutions in the rest of Europe and subsequently in the United States and Latin America. In the United States the imprints of Berlin and Vienna are still in evidence even though subsequent developments and extensions are reflective of more unique, autonomous, and progressive unfolding.

The Chicago Institute is grateful for the pioneering and stimulating heritage it received from Vienna and Berlin. It is proud of its further continuity and extension to newer psychoanalytic institutes that it sponsored in Topeka, Detroit, Cincinnati, Denver, and St. Louis.

II

The Chicago Institute for Psychoanalysis has remained intact in the more than forty years of its existence despite theoretical, clinical, and at times personal differences. Many have asked why, unlike many other analytic institutes the world over where splits have occurred, the Chicago Institute has remained unified. Many possibilities have been considered. My own personal point of view relates to the separation from the beginning of the Chicago Psychoanalytic Society and the Chicago Institute for Psychoanalysis. Alexander, who founded both of these institutions, decided that it would be better to have two completely separated entities. Thus both Institute and Society are completely autonomous—financially, structurally, administratively. Analysts belong to the Society, pay dues, and hold elective and appointive offices. The Institute has a faculty, is organized as an educational institution, pays everyone who performs a service for it—teaching, committee work, administration, etc.—and has elected and appointed administrators for specific terms of office, and also has a tenured faculty system along with mandatory retirement.

The Institute has as its purview education, research, the clinic, the library and information services, the extension program. The Society is an organization of professionals. It has political, scientific, or professional responsibilities which rarely overlap with those of the Institute. In troubled times of the past, the Society has served as a forum to criticize and debate theoretical and clinical issues where differences occurred. Sometimes these involved Institute faculty members and on other occasions were primarily limited to intra-society individuals. The opportunity to express and communicate differences is essential if there is to be a unity to the institution, even though individual feelings were less than universally cohesive.

NOTES AND REFERENCES

1. Incidentally, the paper which he presented, though critically discussed by Karl Menninger, must have made an impact because Menninger not long afterward came to Chicago for analysis with Alexander and for analytic training, and he became the first graduate of the Chicago Institute for Psychoanalysis. Later Robert Knight and William Menninger also came to Chicago for psychoanalytic work and both graduated from the Chicago Institute in the mid-thirties.

The Topeka Institute was the first "geographic" psychoanalytic institute sponsored by the Chicago Institute. In subsequent years the Detroit, Cincinnati, Denver, and St. Louis Institutes had similar sponsorship and students still commute from many other cities.

2. It is of interest that only recently the State of Illinois has authorized the Chicago Institute to award the degree Doctor of Psychoanalysis. This is the first time such a degree has been authorized and the Chicago Institute was the first and I believe still the only institution that can grant this degree.

3. Although Alexander also "founded" the Chicago Psychoanalytic Society in 1931, he never was President of this Society, probably because he felt the Director of the Institute should not occupy both positions. The Institute opened its doors on Monday, October 3, 1932. The first staff consisted of Franz Alexander, Karen Horney, Thomas French, Helen McLean, and Catherine Bacon. Soon Leon Saul from Boston and George Wilson from Detroit joined this group.

4. Karen Horney came from Berlin to join Alexander as Associate Director. She resigned in January 1934 and went to New York.

5. Helen Ross was appointed Administrative Director in 1942. In this year, three analysts graduated from the child analytic program. The three child analytic faculty members had all been trained in Vienna with Anna Freud. They were Margaret Gerald, Helen Ross, and George Mohr. Helen Ross began the Child Care Program

which later evolved into the Child Therapy Training Program. She also established a solid funding structure and firm relations with community organizations for the Institute.

6. Lewin, D., and Ross, H., *Psychoanalytic Education in the United States*. New York: Norton, 1960.

7. The Berlin Psychoanalytic Society was founded by Abraham in 1908. The first meeting took place on August 27, 1908. The first members were Magnus Hirschfeld, Ivan Bloch, Otto Juliusburger, and Heinrich Körber.

8. Bernfeld, S., "On Psychoanalytic Training," *Psychoanalytic Quarterly*, 1962, 31, 453-482.

9. Alexander, F., Eisenstein, S., and Grotjahn, M. (Eds.), *Psychoanalytic Pioneers*. New York: Basic Books, 1966.

CHAPTER 8

Historical Reflections on the Organizational History of Psychoanalysis in America

Arcangelo R. T. D'Amore, M.D.

WHEN I WAS APPOINTED Chairman of the Committee on History and Archives of the American Psychoanalytic Association in 1973, one of my first acts was to go to the Central Office of the Association and examine what records were kept there for the period from its founding on May 9, 1911, in Baltimore up to the time of the establishment of the Central Office in New York in 1948. I found that one notebook contained all that existed from the period 1911-1937. The period from 1911 to 1919 was not represented at all—Clarence P. Oberndorf's reports and minutes for meetings only began in 1919. For several years thereafter Oberndorf and Adolf Stern of New York recorded the meetings until Ernest E. Hadley of Washington took over for the period from 1930 to 1937.

There has not been an official historian of the American Psychoanalytic Association. Oberndorf comes the closest to being one beginning with 1919. His reports of the activities of the Association in the early years appeared in the *International Journal of Psycho-Analysis* and in the *Psychoanalytic Review*. His paper on the "History of the Psychoanalytic

Presented September 30, 1976. Arcangelo R. T. D'Amore is Chairman, Committee on History and Archives, American Psychoanalytic Association, Washington, D.C.

127

Movement in America," presented at the 1925 meeting of the Association, was published in the *Psychoanalytic Review* (8). His book, *A History of Psychoanalysis in America,* was published in 1953 (9). He is relied upon as a primary source, and is often quoted in the literature. Unfortunately, he was poorly informed as to the history of the Association before 1919 and his book is unreliable for that period.

What I have to contribute to the history of psychoanalysis between the two World Wars is drawn from two sources: several dozen oral history tape recordings I have made of interviews with senior colleagues, and personal correspondence I have researched during the last five years. The personal correspondence of William Alanson White, now in the National Archives, became available for historical research in 1972 and is a rich lode of information. I have also been privileged to be the first to study the close to 10,000 letters in the personal correspondence of Smith Ely Jelliffe before they were donated to the Library of Congress by Nolan D. C. Lewis. In addition, I have studied the Brill papers at the Library of Congress and the Ernest Jones papers in London. Brill, Jelliffe, Jones, and White—from a composite picture of their correspondence emerges a clearer view of the early history of the Association.

It started with the meeting each year in a city on the East Coast of a small friendly coterie of male colleagues interested in psychoanalysis—a diverse and eclectic group who were scattered geographically. A number of the meetings were held in conjunction with the American Psychopathological Association. By 1919, however, its leadership was decimated. Ernest Jones, the leader in its founding, had returned to England in 1913. James J. Putnam, the first President, died in 1918. August Hoch, the second President, died in 1919. G. Stanley Hall, the fourth President (1917-1919), was a very old man who was not present to chair the 1919 meeting. In 1919 White (third President, 1915-1917) was the only former President still active in the Association. This vacuum in leadership, and debility in ranks, made the Association vulnerable to dissolution or takeover.

As Oberndorf records it, Jelliffe substituted for Hall as presiding officer with only six persons present. Brill was elected President of the Association in 1919. In effect, Brill—who had founded the New York Psychoanalytic Society on February 12, 1911, three months before Ernest Jones had founded the Association—and his New York colleagues became the dominant force in Association politics for the next decade and more. With his New York colleagues Frink and Oberndorf, Brill decided to hold the 1920 meeting of the Association in New York and he sent the notice out on New York Psychoanalytic Society stationery. White's differing wishes were overridden, and White and Jelliffe were denied their proposal that Jelliffe's protegé, Louise Brink, become a member of the Association. Brill suspected White of losing the only copy of the Constitution rather than let Brill have the satisfaction of proving that women were not permitted to become members.

Oberndorf incorrectly states in his history (9, pp. 135-136) that White was present at the 1919 meeting. Actually White was elected Secretary-Treasurer *in absentia*. Oberndorf attributes to White the statement, "the time has come to free American psychiatry from the domination of the Pope at Vienna." In his minutes for the 1920 and 1921 meetings Oberndorf stated that several influential members wanted to disband the Association and make it a branch of the American Psychopathological Association.

In his book Oberndorf states: "After a fiery and prolonged discussion Dr. Adolf Meyer rose and stroking his beard, a characteristic mannerism of his when in deep thought, said in his quiet voice: 'I think that the contributions of psychoanalysis to the understanding of psychiatry have been sufficiently great that there should be some organization in this country to guide its destinies.' The weight of his opinion swayed the vote for the continuation of the Association. I believe, however, that had the vote gone the other way, Brill, Frink and I would have immediately formed a new national society" (9, p. 136).

Oberndorf makes Adolf Meyer into the good guy and William A. White into the bad guy. What must be remembered about Oberndorf as a historian of this event is that he states in his autobiographical sketch that in his senior year in medical school in 1905 he listened to ten lectures by Adolf Meyer of which he said:

When Dr. Meyer entered the lecture hall for the first time, his resemblance to my own father was so great as to startle me. As I later realized, the strong attachment which I had retained for my father immediately was unconsciously transferred to Dr. Meyer. It may also have been extended to the subject which Meyer taught. Thus at the time of graduation from medical school two powerful influences may have impelled me toward specialization in psychiatry —an awareness of a certain faculty which I possessed in making contact with patients and the emotional identification of Meyer with my own father (10, p. 14).

As we know, during their lifetimes Meyer and White were unofficial rivals as to which one was the best psychiatrist. I believe Oberndorf showed his partiality in this regard, as some others have in the other direction. It is interesting to note that in extensive articles on "The Nervous Breakdown" and "Sanitariums" in *Fortune* magazine (April 1935) there are pictures of White and Meyer. The caption for White reads: "If a No. 1 U.S. *practicing* psychiatrist can be named, he is probably Dr. William Alanson White. . . ." For Meyer it reads: "The No. 1 U.S. *research* psychiatrist is unquestionably Swiss-born Adolf Meyer. . . ."

Reliance on Brill and Oberndorf as historians of the Association proved to be disillusioning to Lawrence S. Kubie. As Secretary he was charged with the task of producing Volume I of the *Bulletin*, the first publication of the Association, in 1937. He considered it appropriate to start off with a history of the Association. In late 1938 and in March 1939 he contacted several senior colleagues, noting the loss of the early records of the Association, and asking for help as to the list of founders and other early historical data. He asked for a quick reply because it was holding up publication of the *Bulletin*. Brill told Kubie that he suspected White of losing all the documents of the early period because Jelliffe and White disputed with Brill that the Constitution excluded women members. He gave Kubie other information, some of which proved to be erroneous. Oberndorf gave Kubie dismally inaccurate information as to former officers and meeting places of the Association for the period before 1920, and the same errors appear in the appendix of Oberndorf's book. Adolf Meyer, although he was in actuality a founder, wrote that he had no clear memory of the conferences, except that Ernest Jones included him and that he would be interested in hearing what the investigations showed.

The *Bulletin* went into print stating that "Drs. Brill and Jones arranged the first meeting of an American Psychoanalytic Association in Washington, D. C." (p. 14). This elevation of Brill's role is not surprising since in his Introduction to the *Basic Writings of Sigmund Freud* he states, "Very soon after the New York Psychoanalytic Society was formed, we organized the American Psychoanalytic Association, with Dr. James J. Putnam as President and Dr. Ernest Jones as Secretary. The membership of this organization was made up of those who, living in various parts of the country, had no opportunity to belong to the New York Society" (1, p. 30). He then proceeds to list erroneously the charter members.

Notice that he used "we" whereas there was really considerable rivalry between Brill and Jones. Brill was not a founder of the Association. Also, in Brill's view, the Association was a second-best organization for those who could not belong to New York. Furthermore, the Association was founded in Baltimore, not Washington.

A copy of the *Bulletin* made it across the Atlantic Ocean to Ernest Jones in London. When he had been elected to Honorary Membership in the Association in 1931 Jones had replied, "The American Psychoanalytic Association has naturally always been a pet child of mine, it being my first-born." Small wonder that he sent Kubie two pages of historical comments on the *Bulletin* history. He questioned how anyone could say that the records were lost without asking him, its Secretary for the first three years. After some other corrections he stated in re page 14: "The reference to Drs. Brill and Jones in the first line is hardly accurate. Brill was scarcely concerned with the founding of the American Psychoanalytic Association, though of course he was consulted and approved of it. The reason for this is simply that the first purpose of the Association was to serve as a rallying point for psycho-analysts who could not belong to the New York Society, not being resident there; hence the name Association, not Society, for members scattered over the Continent. It gave them an opportunity to belong to the International Association which they could not otherwise have had. The idea of it was mine and I promptly approached Putnam about it who cordially agreed." Jones then cited the publication in which the charter members were correctly listed and corrected other errors.

In the Jones papers in London I found a letter from Oberndorf dated May 3, 1954, in which he told Jones that several persons—notably Ives Hendrick and Franz Alexander—had written to him to complain that he had given insufficient space in his book to the achievements of the Chicago Institute, and to the Boston Society after its reorganization. Not mentioned was the criticism of Ernest E. Hadley who, in writing the history of the Washington-Baltimore Psychoanalytic Institute, noted Oberndorf's failure to mention the existence of the original Washington Psychoanalytic Society founded on July 6, 1914, at Saint Elizabeths Hospital.

Oberndorf died in 1954; to my knowledge his book was never revised. We are indebted to him for his records of the history of the Association, but we must realize that not only did Brill, Oberndorf, and their New York colleagues take over the American Psychoanalytic Association—they rewrote its early history from the point of view frequently attributed to New Yorkers, that anything outside of THE city is derived from and dependent on New York.

Ernest Jones was made Honorary President of the Association in 1956 in connection with his visit to New York and Chicago to give the Freud Centenary Lectures. It would be interesting to speculate as to what would have been the history of psychoanalysis in America if Ernest Jones had stayed in Toronto, or, heaven forbid, moved to New York!

New York was the hub of psychoanalysis in America in the 1920s. Half of the members of the Association were in New York. It was also a magnet. Over the years, from the Washington-Baltimore area alone, it drew Bernard Glueck, Edward J. Kempf, Harry Stack Sullivan, Clara Thompson, William Silverberg, and others. The New York Psychoanalytic Society was the base and the battleground for issues and decisions on increasing professionalization of psychoanalysis; restricting its practice to the medical profession; distinguishing it from deviant forms; objecting to the training of Americans in Europe without prior approval, especially lay analysts who then returned to the United States to practice; setting up the first training program in America; and other manifestations of "growing pains."

In addition to what has been recorded by Brill and Oberndorf, we have other sources to draw upon for the history of this era. Sandor Lorand, who came to New York from Budapest in 1925, has written about the development of psychoanalysis in New York. He noted upon his arrival that ". . . in New York many were ready to listen to analysts and a sizeable segment of the lay public seemed eager to learn about psychoanalysis. There was, to be sure, no lack of criticism and resistance to the Freudian theories among the more conservative members of professional and lay groups, but the general atmosphere was far different from the rigid antagonism prevalent in Europe" (6, p. 589). In 1965, Lorand was appointed Chairman of the newly-established Archives Committee of the American Psychoanalytic Association. When I became Chairman of the Committee on History and Archives in 1973 he agreed to be a Consultant. He has rendered invaluable service which I deeply appreciate.

In 1921-22 the President of the Association was Cornelius C. Wholey of Pittsburgh, a psychiatrist who was not trained in and did not practice psychoanalysis. During the 1920s a transition took place. While the eclectic, psychoanalytically oriented but not psychoanalytically trained older colleagues remained members under the grandfather clause, the Constitution of the Association was changed to to admit as members only physicians, and later, only physicians with exposure to psychoanalytic training. In another development, Marion Kenworthy of New York and Lucile Dooley of Washington became in 1926 the first women members of the Association.

Another shift that took place was initiated by William Alanson White when he became President of the American Psychiatric Association in 1924. The 1925 meeting of the Psychoanalytic was held in conjunction with the Psychiatric in Richmond, Virginia, in the spring. This arrangement lasted for fifty years, until 1974, when the Psychiatric met in Detroit and the Psychoanalytic in Denver. A second meeting of the Psychoanalytic in New York City in December, initiated in 1923, became a regular event.

The Psychoanalytic now had one foot in the much larger Psychiatric Association, and the other where its core membership resided. Brill, Oberndorf, White, and others were very pleased with the exposure psychoanalysis got among the psychiatrists. However, when some colleagues, on their own, developed psychoanalytic programs for the psychiatric meeting, it was decided to control the situation by petitioning to form a Section on Psychoanalysis of the American Psychiatric Association. Brill, Oberndorf, and Sullivan led this move, which became a reality in May 1934.

Brill and Oberndorf also wanted to see the American Psychopathological Association die from neglect, thus reinforcing the preeminence of the Psychoanalytic. It is interesting to note that when a new journal was announced on October 23, 1931, the name was "Psychopathology: A Psychoanalytic Quarterly." However, it was quickly changed to *The Psychoanalytic Quarterly*. The separation-individuation anxieties felt concerning psychoanalysis—whether it should stand alone, or be closely allied to a more general psychopathology and eclectic psychiatry—were a distinct part of the evolution and development of psychoanalysis in the 1920s and 1930s.

The meeting of greatest significance to the history of psychoanalysis in two decades was the First International Congress on Mental Hygiene in May 1930, in Washington. The fruition of Clifford Beers' dream and the years of hard work by the National Committee on Mental Hygiene, the Congress brought together over 3,000 persons from 40 countries, among them an impressive array of the leaders in psychiatry, psychoanalysis, and mental hygiene. The program of the Congress was prepared in close cooperation with the program committees of the American Psychiatric and the American Psychoanalytic Associations, and of the American Association for the Study of the Feeble-Minded. William Alanson White was President of the Congress.

Among those coming from Europe was Helene Deutsch, who described her experience in her book *Confrontations with Myself* (4, pp. 172-73). It prepared her for her returning and settling in Boston in 1935. Franz Alexander came, and it was while he was in Washington that Robert Hutchins, President of the University of Chicago, invited him to visit there and discuss an appointment in the University's medical school. Karl A. Menninger and Leo H. Bartemeier, who became friends and fellow-candidates at the Chicago Institute, met each other for the first time at the 1930 Congress.

The meeting of the American Psychoanalytic Association, held along with the Congress, was attended by so many prominent psychoanalysts that it could be compared to Freud, Jung, and Ferenczi at Clark University in 1909. Certainly nothing like it had taken place between 1909 and 1930. It ushered in a decade of rapid growth for psychoanalysis in America.

At the meeting Ernest E. Hadley of Washington discussed with Brill the formation of a new psychoanalytic society in Washington that would have the approval of the International Psychoanalytic Association. Within the month, plans that had been nursed along for some time resulted in a meeting at Hadley's office on May 31, with Harry Stack Sullivan, then Vice-President of the American Psychoanalytic, presiding. The Washington-Baltimore Psychoanalytic Society was created, with Clara Thompson elected President, and William V. Silverberg, Secretary-Treasurer (7, pp. 21-24).

Similar developments took place in Chicago and Boston in the early thirties as analysts settled there who had gone to Europe for training, or who started training in the budding institutes in the United States. Brill, who followed White as President of the Association in 1929 and served until 1936, recognized that organizational changes were in order. He announced that at the joint meeting of the Association with the New York Psychoanalytic Society on December 29, 1931, in New York, a special meeting would be held to formulate a *modus operandi* to reorganize the American into an American Federation of Psychoanalytic Societies. This plan was implemented in due course. Boston, Chicago,

Washington-Baltimore and, later, other societies became equal partners with New York.

The era of the American pioneer analysts came to an end when Isador H. Coriat of Boston completed his Presidency in 1938. White had died in 1937, and others associated with psychoanalysis by interest but without personal analysis and training faded away. The organizational politics of psychoanalysis was now in the hands of men with analytic training and experience, and decision-making involved colleagues in several cities, not just New York.

Swelling the ranks of psychoanalysts in America were the refugees from the scourge of Nazism in Europe. Emergency committees were established to assist them to become relocated. The economic depression of the thirties made it difficult to find positions and patients for analysis, and there was some concern that too many would settle in New York. Stories have been told of New York analysts who described to the emigrés the advantages of moving on to Cleveland, Cincinnati, or St. Louis.

Although World War II restricted the organizational activities of psychoanalysis, it spread the contact and influence of psychoanalysts in wartime psychiatry, led by William C. Menninger for the Army, and John M. Murray for the Air Force, contributing to the surge of interest in psychoanalytic training after the war was over. Educational benefits for veterans helped pay for analytic training.

In the post-war years the American Psychoanalytic Association was reorganized to accommodate its growth. The Central Office was established in New York, a Journal was launched, and new affiliate societies and approved institutes proliferated. The joint meetings with the American Psychiatric Association in the spring and the separate winter meetings in New York City were attended by ever-increasing numbers as membership grew. The affairs of the Association required more and more committees, and the reports in the *Bulletin,* now a part of the *Journal,* chronicle these organizational developments. The Association became old enough to become interested in preserving its own history.

For this overview of the organizational history of psychoanalysis in America up to the end of World War II—an era I did not know from firsthand knowledge—I have drawn upon archival research and oral history interviews. The last part of my presentation, focused on the splitting and splintering in the organizational structure in the post-war era, is based on my personal experiences and observations.

A brief review is in order. The decade following Freud's visit to

Clark University in 1909 was an American age of innocence. Jelliffe and White were shocked to find how intense the conflicts were in Vienna and Zurich when they founded the *Psychoanalytic Review* in 1913. I have referred to Freud's critical letter to White concerning the *Psychoanalytic Review* in the proceedings of the White Symposium (2, pp. 88-89). Americans interested in psychoanalysis were too few, too busy, and too separated from Europe by the war to quarrel.

During the 1920s the distinctions and differences among European analysts became clearer to Americans. Organizationally, however, the problems were those of developing structure, specialization, and training requirements which were being formulated for the first time.

It was in the 1930s that the stage was set in America for factional splitting. The leaders of the 1920s and early 1930s—Brill, Oberndorf, White, and Hadley, in particular—were pragmatists who maintained strong ties to medicine and psychiatry. With the increase in numbers of those who had gone to Europe for training, and the arrival of European emigrés, a shift took place toward more stress on autonomy, purity, and control over who was qualified and what was called psychoanalysis.

Brill, Oberndorf, and Sullivan were the proposers for a Section on Psychoanalysis of the American Psychiatric Association in a circular letter dated May 2, 1933. Aside from a personal attack on Brill by Zilboorg, there were others who accepted the move but raised important questions. Franz Alexander, in a letter to the Secretary of the Section on December 7, 1937, stressed that the requirements for membership in the Section must not be construed as qualifications for being a psychoanalyst. Alexander stated: "Psychoanalysis today is practiced as a specialty, and as it is today there is only one official or semi-official method of being recognized as a qualified psychoanalyst, and that is membership in the American Psychoanalytic Association." Six months later he took over from Isador Coriat, the last of the original coterie of untrained American analysts, as the first of the trained European analysts to become President of the American Psychoanalytic Association.

Karen Horney had been brought to the Chicago Institute by Alexander, but had resigned in 1934 and moved to New York. In 1941 she was the central figure in a dramatic break with the New York Psychoanalytic Institute and the American Psychoanalytic Association. This event and the position statement by Horney, Clara Thompson, and others have been described by Maurice Green (5, pp. 361-366). It led to the formation of the American Association for the Advancement of Psychoanalysis, the first significant new organization outside the American Psychoanalytic Association. It is not surprising that New York, the largest psychoanalytic community, was the first to have a split in the ranks. World War II followed immediately thereafter, and there was little time and energy for organizational politics. In fact, the American Psychoanalytic Association did not hold an Annual Meeting in the spring of 1945 because there were too few colleagues around to plan for or attend one.

When I arrived in Washington from overseas in 1946, I became acquainted with the psychoanalytic community there. I had not heard of Harry Stack Sullivan before coming to Washington, having been attracted to the city by its beauty, by the opportunity to work at St. Elizabeths Hospital, and by the knowledge that advanced training would be available. I enrolled in the Washington School of Psychiatry and in the Washington-Baltimore Psychoanalytic Institute. At that time it was hard to tell the difference, as several courses were given in the name of both the School and the Institute. I got considerable exposure to Sullivan in course work before he died in 1949. After that time the distinction between School and Institute became clearer.

The Washington School of Psychiatry, as I think of it, was not really a split or splinter group from psychoanalysis. It evolved in the 1930s in a nativistic way reflecting the ambitions and hopes of Hadley, Sullivan, and others, and influenced by the broad interests of William Alanson White for whom the parent foundation was named. I am sure that if Hadley and Sullivan had received the kind of financial backing the Chicago Institute got in the 1930s, the Washington School would have grown and manifested a creative American quality, as contrasted to institutes elsewhere with imported European directors and imported unresolved feuding.

Clara Thompson came to Washington from New York regularly to lecture and to supervise. I came to know her well during the period from 1947 to 1952 when I took her courses and she supervised a couple of my cases. In addition, my wife, who was executive assistant to David Rioch, the Executive Director of the Washington School of Psychiatry, had known Clara Thompson in the 1930s through Janet Rioch. A pattern developed in which, after Thompson finished teaching in the evening, we would take her to Union Station and have a nightcap together before she took the overnight sleeper back to New York. Much was revealed and discussed during those late evening encounters that stretched over a period of years.

Clara Thompson was troubled. She felt concern for her William Alanson White Institute in New York, and especially for the students. What could they join after they finished their training? Not the American Psychoanalytic Association, where admission to membership was the equivalent of a specialty board certificate. She wanted her graduates to have recognition at a national level. She did not want to feel that they had been handicapped by having trained in her Institute. Yet, at the same time, she did not want to make the changes in the Institute itself which she had been told by the powers-that-be in the American Psychoanalytic Association would result in approval by the Board on Professional Standards. Such changes would make a mockery of what she had stood for and fought for over the years.

As time went on these late evening encounters evolved into a talent scout search for psychoanalytic colleagues outside of New York City, who would take the initiative to form a new national association which her graduates could join. She would ask us for names. She would ask for our reaction to names given to her. The names that others had given her were of colleagues who had not fared well with the analytic training clique in control in Washington; ones who were bypassed in the appointment of new training analysts—for example, a colleague who claimed that he had decided for himself that his training was completed and terminated his relationship with the psychoanalytic institute, whereas others said he had been bounced.

Although I felt compassion for Clara Thompson, found her to be a genuine person, and respected her all the more for not wanting her graduates to suffer for having trained in her Institute, I was only a candidate in training myself and was not about to be saddled with involvement in such a cause. I wondered if, unconsciously, the William Alanson White Institute vs. the American Psychoanalytic Association was her reenactment of her own analysis—of Sandor Ferenczi's position in relation to Sigmund Freud at the time that she saw him in Budapest. My contact with her became minimal after 1952.

The American Academy of Psychoanalysis came into being and began to serve the purpose Clara Thompson had felt was necessary. Now, graduates of her institute, of Karen Horney's institute, and of other institutes not approved by the American Psychoanalytic Association had a national psychoanalytic organization to join. Membership was available to graduates of the approved institutes as well. Its first meeting, significantly, was held in 1956, the centenary of Freud's birth. It has served as an alternate to joining the American Psychoanalytic Association, but I do not think it is comparable. The Association remains much larger and more influential.

The Academy at times has made trouble for the Association. In May 1965, the American Psychiatric Association met at the Americana Hotel in New York. Jules Masserman, very active in Academy affairs and one of its Presidents, was program chairman for the Psychiatric. He used his position to usurp the privilege of the program committee of the American Psychoanalytic Association to determine the content of its joint meeting with the Psychiatric. Erik Erikson spoke on "Psychoanalysis and Ongoing History" as desired by the American Psychoanalytic. Masserman selected Roy R. Grinker, Sr., as the other speaker and his paper on "Fields, Fences and Riders" was discussed by Judd Marmor. Both Grinker and Marmor were Presidents of the Academy of Psychoanalysis. At the meeting, Erikson made a public disavowal of the legitimacy of the other half of the program. Masserman's defense was that Grinker and Marmor were members of the American Psychoanalytic Association. Since then the Academy has established separate joint meetings with the American Psychiatric Association.

Of more lasting significance has been the impact of the existence of the Academy of Psychoanalysis upon matters of certification in psychoanalysis; positions taken in relation to governmental affairs; insurance, etc. Neither the American Medical Association nor the American Psychiatric Association has the contention from another organization in their specialties that the American Psychoanalytic Association has in its field. I understand the historical development of the Academy, and appreciate the value of the forum it has provided for its members, but I wonder whether such a small specialized field as psychoanalysis, which is not continuing to gain in size as it has in the past in relation to psychiatry and medicine, can give proper attention to, and convey its position on, what are called guild issues under these circumstances.

In this American Revolution Bicentennial year both the American Psychoanalytic Association and the American Academy of Psychoanalysis have held special historical programs during their May meetings. The Association celebrated its 65th anniversary by returning to the site of its founding in Baltimore, Maryland, where an exhibit was mounted, a bronze historical marker was dedicated, and a panel on history and an oral history workshop were held. The Academy celebrated its 20th anniversary in Miami Beach, Florida, with an historical program of its own.

With such consciousness and appreciation for history we should be able to profit from studying the organizational history of psychoanalysis in America in order to maintain constructive leadership in our present organizations, and preserve the good in psychoanalysis for those in need of its beneficial effects.

REFERENCES

1. Brill, A. A., Ed., *The Basic Writings of Sigmund Freud*, New York: Modern Library, Random House, 1938.

2. D'Amore, A. R. T., Ed., *William Alanson White: The Washington Years 1903-1937*, Washington, D.C.: U.S. Government Printing Office, 1976.

3. D'Amore, A. R. T., *William Alanson White: Contributions to Psychoanalysis in America.* Presented at the annual meeting of the American Psychoanalytic Association, Baltimore, Md., May 9, 1976.

4. Deutsch, H., *Confrontations with Myself: An Epilogue*, New York: Norton, 1973.

5. Green, M. R., Ed., *Interpersonal Psychoanalysis: The Selected Papers of Clara M. Thompson*, New York: Basic Books, 1964.

6. Lorand, S., Reflections on the Development of Psychoanalysis in New York from 1925, *International J. Psycho-Analysis*, 1969, 50, 589-595.

7. Noble, D., and Burnham, D. L., *History of the Washington Psychoanalytic Society and the Washington Psychoanalytic Institute*, Washington, D.C.: Washington Psychoanalytic Society, 1969.

8. Oberndorf, C. P., History of the Psychoanalytic Movement in America, *Psychoanalytic Review*, 1927, 14, 281-297.

9. Oberndorf, C. P., *A History of Psychoanalysis in America*, New York: Grune & Stratton, 1953.

10. Oberndorf, C. P., *An Autobiographical Sketch*, Ithaca, N.Y., 1958.

CHAPTER 9

Organizational Schisms in American Psychoanalysis

Marianne Horney Eckardt, M.D.

THIS PRESENTATION will be limited to the four major schisms which erupted in the 1940s and the context in which they took place: the exodus from the New York Psychoanalytic Society of Karen Horney, Clara Thompson, Sarah Kelman, Saul Ephron, and Bernard Robbins, when the Society withdrew teaching privileges from Horney; the breaking away of two separate groups from the newly formed Association for the Advancement of Psychoanalysis, leading to the foundation of the William Alanson White Society and Institute and the creation of the Comprehensive Course in Psychoanalysis at the New York Medical College; and the events which led to the formation of the Association for Psychoanalytic Medicine and the Columbia Psychoanalytic Clinic. I will conclude with a brief description of the formation of the American Academy of Psychoanalysis, as its origins are closely related to these schisms.

Organizational schisms are characteristic of psychoanalytic organizations the world over. They are symptomatic of what one might call a constitutional or genetic factor inherent in the discipline of psycho-

Presented November 11, 1976. Marianne Horney Eckardt is Associate Clinical Professor in the Department of Psychiatry, Division of Psychoanalysis, New York Medical College, New York, New York.

141

analysis. The European schisms in Germany, Austria, France, Sweden, and Norway, with which I have some acquaintance, basically resemble the events in this country, though with local variations.

Henri F. Ellenberger, in his magnificent book *The Discovery of the Unconscious*, states: "Freud's most striking novelty was probably the founding of a 'school' according to a pattern that has no parallel in modern times but is a revival of the old philosophical schools of Greco-Roman antiquity. Almost from the beginning Freud made psychoanalysis a movement, with its own organization and publishing house, its strict rules of membership, and its official doctrine, namely, the psychoanalytic theory" (3).

The founding of a "school" was certainly the outcome, but it had not been Freud's explicit intent. Freud's influence had many facets. There existed Freud the scientist, who speculated on the many possible dynamic interconnections of the clinical facts he observed. He used the word meta-psychology as defined in the dictionary, a theory that aims to supplement the facts and empirical laws of psychology by speculations on the connection of mental and physical processes. He stressed over and over again the process of searching for the structure underlying the empirical data. First they have to be divined, then gradually formulated with increasing clarity. Progressively modified, these concepts become widely applicable and at the same time logically consistent. Then it may be time to immure them in definitions. "The progress of science, however," he stated, "demands a certain elasticity even in these definitions. The science of physics furnishes an excellent illustration of the way in which even those basal concepts that are firmly established in the form of definitions are constantly being altered in their content" (4).

But there also existed Freud the autocrat, who did not give his followers the license to divine and formulate their vision of the connecting links of the empirical data observed. He became hurt, called dissenters immature, and pointed to their unresolved oedipal rivalry with him. They were subdued or expelled from the legitimate circle. Thus Freud the scientist was at odds with Freud the person, who did in fact promote a "school" in the manner described by Ellenberger. When psychoanalysis became organized, this schism between psychoanalysis as a young, growing, and changing science and psychoanalysis as confined by doctrinal limits continued to plague the discipline.

Freud's heritage thus contains a double bind which continues to entrap our modes of organization. The repercussions of this entrapment are particularly evident in two areas: in our use of language and in our use of technique. Freud was a scientist and a poet. He was at home in the world of mythology and the world of science. His language belonged to both worlds at the same time: the literal and the metaphorical. I believe that it was the metaphorical potential of Freud's language which gave it the flexibility to survive needed change. But clarity of concept was bound to suffer, as, with use, each analytic term became imbued with new meaning, though still retaining its original cast.

The repercussions in the area of technique again contain an irony of faith. Freud was extraordinarily creative and ingenious in his experimentation with technique. Yet in the course of his development and that of psychoanalytic organization, technique became a symbol and thus a servant of theory rather than a servant of the patient. Techniques have to be mastered so that they can be used according to one's best clinical judgment and discrimination. A freedom to modify techniques is necessary, as new results or observations will pose new conceptual challenges.

The practice of psychoanalysis, though, has suffered less from these limitations than one might assume. Theory and practice have always been at variance, a trend encouraged by the privacy of the practitioner's therapeutic setting. This variance has been explored time and time again ever since Edward Glover's first questionnaire in 1939. The results were disturbing to the purists and reassuring to those who believe in the primacy of the good clinician.

These very general remarks must suffice as context for the recurrent phenomenon of schisms in psychoanalytic organizations. When we examine specific schisms, as I will be doing presently, many factors interact in each recurrent drama. The most obvious are:

1. Organizational vulnerabilities or rigidities in the parent organization.

2. Deviations from accepted doctrine if the standard terminology is discarded and a new one created. Conceptual modifications which adapt the standard language do not offend even though conceptual alterations may be substantial.

3. Changes brought by the passage of half a century in basic scientific assumptions and in socio-cultural milieus.

4. Influences exerted by outstanding personalities. I have purposely listed personal influence last, though the events will show the powerful

effects of personal rivalries, polarizing charismatic leaders, or specific personal attributes. I list them in fourth place because I strongly believe that interpersonal friction flourishes when structural tensions or organizational faults exist.

Now a brief account of my perspective on these events. I was one of the first group of candidates in the newly formed American Institute of Psychoanalysis. Karen Horney, my mother, was its dean. I graduated in the spring of 1944, having witnessed the two schisms of this organization. I was elected student representative to the faculty council for 1943-1944 and heard some of the pertinent faculty discussions leading to the second split. Upon entering as a candidate, I was given credit for my already completed didactic analysis with Erich Fromm. This fact saved me much conflict and embarrassment when, at the time of the first split, Fromm and Horney became antagonists. My memories of these occurrences are unpleasant. I took no active part and remained an observer. Being young and idealistic, I felt disillusioned. I experienced the events as an outcome of personal rivalries and clashes, and I agreed with those who later emphasized that the so-called issues were red herrings. When I was invited to speak about these schisms my initial response was decidedly negative. I preferred to forget rather than to remember. Then I concluded that I might gain something from this undertaking. I accepted, and I have not regretted the decision.

Psychoanalytic institutes in America had existed for a decade when the first schism occurred. On April 29, 1941, at a business meeting of the New York Psychoanalytic Society, Karen Horney was disqualified as an instructor and training analyst on the grounds that she was disturbing the students. The vote was 24 to 7, with 29 abstaining. Following the vote, Horney and four colleagues walked out in silence. Among them was Clara Thompson, who describes the group's jubilant spirits as they marched down the street singing "Go down, Moses, let my people go," the spiritual celebrating the liberation of the Jews from the tyranny of the pharaoh.

The following day, April 30, letters of resignation were drafted by Karen Horney, Clara Thompson, Bernard Robbins, Sarah Kelman, and Saul Ephron and sent to the New York Society and the American Psychoanalytic Association. An excerpt from the letter to the Society reads: "For the last few years, it has become gradually apparent that the scientific integrity of the New York Psychoanalytic Society has steadily deteriorated. Reverence for dogma has replaced free inquiry; academic freedom has been abrogated; students have been intimidated; scientific sessions have degenerated into political machinations. . . . We are interested only in the scientific advancement of psychoanalysis in keeping with the courageous spirit of its founder, Sigmund Freud" (5). The letter to the American Psychoanalytic Association uses stronger language in its attack on the New York Society. "The Society has become a hotbed of political intrigue; a religious fervor has replaced free inquiry, and dogma has firmly established itself under the guise of science. The major disaster implicit in this situation has fallen upon the students . . ." (6). Fourteen candidates resigned at the same time as the five members. These students had met with difficulties. Their presentations and their tests were considered unacceptable, and they were unable to graduate.

The secession was not quite as spontaneous as has often been told. There were preparations, as I will presently describe, and the decision to withdraw Horney's teaching privileges created the dramatic moment of action. Yet the preliminary discussions, the revolution, the formation of the new Association for the Advancement of Psychoanalysis and its Institute, the American Institute of Psychoanalysis, evolved in a very short period of time. It appears to have been just a matter of a few months. This speed of action was to have its consequences.

These were the stages of this schism. Meetings of concerned psychoanalysts began in the spring of 1941. On April 4, twenty-five days prior to the exodus, sixteen members of the New York Society met at the home of Bernard Robbins to discuss matters of resignation, the formation of a new society and its name, and the founding of a new institute. A committee was chosen to work on a preliminary constitution. A follow-up meeting on April 15 concerned negotiations already in progress with the New School for Social Research with respect to teaching facilities. April 29, 1941, saw the dramatic walk-out, linked to the Society's decision to disqualify Horney. The following day, April 30, the new organization was formed, the name Association for the Advancement of Psychoanalysis accepted, and a pro-tem constitution adopted. On May 15 officers of the Association were elected. May 27 was devoted to the constitution of the new institute, the American Institute of Psychoanalysis. In June, Horney was elected Dean of the Institute, and its faculty, council, and committees were formed.

Dr. William Silverberg, who had remained a member of the Washington-Baltimore Society even after his move to New York in 1933, joined the new Association. Candidates who had finished their requirements, but who as yet had not received sanction for graduation, were graduated and became members. Thus the Association counted 15 charter members. Harry Stack Sullivan and Erich Fromm became honorary members. Among the candidates were analysands of Abram Kardiner and Sandor Rado, acting in the belief that Kardiner and Rado would be among the seceding members. Thus it appears that Kardiner and Rado had participated in the early discussions, seriously entertained the idea of leaving the New York Society, but then bided their time.

The new association intended to become a second national psychoanalytic association, hoping to rally discontented members from other cities. In 1942 the roster of the Association for the Advancement of Psychoanalysis showed a membership of 34, with 8 members residing in Chicago, Detroit, and Greater Washington, D. C. A letter of explanation and invitation was sent immediately by the five rebels to all members of the American Psychoanalytic Association. This letter profoundly reflects the sentiments of this group and also the larger group of members of the New York Society who were becoming restive.

Before quoting passages from this letter, I will interpolate some background atmosphere which may permit some understanding of the ferment of thinking in the thirties which influenced most of the events to come.

The easiest way is to select and mention the so-called Zodiac group—seminal thinkers Harry Stack Sullivan, Karen Horney, Clara Thompson, William Silverberg, and later Erich Fromm. They met informally and enjoyed exchanging their ideas. Their influence on each other was profound, creating an atmosphere of free inquiry, stimulating their creative thinking, exposing them to new ideas, and affirming their dissatisfactions. This was an outstanding group of people drawing on many disciplines. Sullivan's interest in Sapir and Cooley is well known. Fromm was equally at home in sociology and psychoanalysis; all of them were friendly with Ralph Linton, Ruth Benedict, and other anthropologists. Clara Thompson writes about this group: "We were a very stimulating group, and we had some very good ideas. Anyway, the things we started talking about then became more and more organized into Sullivan's thinking" (16). It would be fair to assume that what was talked about also became more and more organized into Fromm's and Horney's thinking, each in his/her own way.

Thus an atmosphere of independent thinking was established. In addition, Sullivan, Horney, and Fromm were temperamentally inclined to be independent mavericks. A close observer once wrote about Karen Horney: "Karen Horney was an intelligent and gifted woman. The influence of Erich Fromm and Sullivan combined with her own clinical experience to move her into the category of psychoanalysts who felt that Freud had underestimated the influence of social and cultural factors in the etiology of mental disorders and in personal development in general. She was, unlike Sullivan, primarily an analyst, and her position made her a maverick among the analysts. She was, to say the least, an extremely independent woman. Some people found her arrogant. In any case, Horney was not temperamentally suited to a subordinate position in any organization. She had . . . many traits that attracted attention and won partisan allegiance . . ." (personal communication).

Judd Marmor, who was one of the resigning candidates in 1941, has this to say in retrospect (1973). "The revolt within the New York Psychoanalytic Institute that took place in 1941 must be seen in the perspective of the ferment that was taking place in American psychoanalysis in the late thirties, particularly around the contributions of Sullivan, Sandor Rado, Abram Kardiner, Karen Horney, and Erich Fromm. The emerging emphasis on ego psychology began to shake the foundation of classical instinct theory, and as always in such ideological struggles much heat and hostility were generated.

"The appearance," Marmor continues, "in 1939 of Horney's openly polemic book *New Ways in Psychoanalysis* aroused particular irritation in conservative psychoanalytic circles. What Horney said does not seem as revolutionary today as it did then. In retrospect, I strongly suspect that it was not just the content of her book but the tone in which it was written that caused so much resentment. Horney wrote as though there were only two protagonists in the psychoanalytic movement, Freud and herself, and made no effort to place her views in an historical context that would have given due credit to some of the prior works that had prepared the soil for her ideas, e.g., Freud's *The Problem of Anxiety,* Anna Freud's *The Ego and the Mechanisms of Defense,* Wilhelm Reich's *Character Analysis,* to say nothing of the contributions of Sullivan, Rado, Kardiner, Fromm and others" (10).

Now back to the letter of explanation and invitation sent by the five resigning members to their colleagues. This letter well reflects the conflict of young science versus dogma which I mentioned before. "The resignations are a response to a situation which constitutes a crisis in psychoanalytic education. Psychoanalysis is a young science, still in an experimental stage of its development, full of uncertainties, full of problems to which anything approaching final and conclusive answers is still to be sought. As in all sciences, the solution of these problems is directly dependent upon more voluminous and keener observations, as well as upon further weighing and consideration of observations already made.

"Education in any field consists in a passing on from an older to a younger generation of the truth that the older generation believes it has learned, as well as a bequeathing to the younger generation of the problems left unsolved by their elders. In psychoanalysis as it is today, we cannot afford to subject the younger generation to any dogmatism, we should not mislead it with the illusion of certainty where none actually exists . . ." (7).

The American Institute of Psychoanalysis gave their courses at the Post Graduate School of the New York Medical College, facilitated by Dr. Stephen Jewett, head of its Department of Psychiatry and also a member of the Association, and at the New School for Social Research. The New School for Social Research had already played a significant part in the total scenario. Clara Meyer, Dean of the New School, was instrumental in 1935 in offering Horney the opportunity to teach at the school. Unencumbered there, she felt free to formulate her concepts in her own words. Horney's first course was titled "Culture and Neurosis," laying the work for her first book, *The Neurotic Personality of Our Time* (1937). Her second course, "Open Questions in Psychoanalysis," paved the way for the book which so offended, *New Ways in Psychoanalysis*, published in 1939.

The new group appeared to be flourishing when, in April 1943, two years after its inception, a storm shook the Association, centering on the teaching priviliges of Erich Fromm.When the storm had subsided, twelve members had resigned, among them Fromm, Thompson, Janet Rioch, and Sullivan.

On April 7, 1943, Fromm resigned when his privileges as training analyst were withdrawn on the basis that the American Institute of Psychoanalysis did not want to jeopardize its relationship to the New York Medical College by introducing the issue of lay analysis. The arguments presented at the time by Horney, Robbins, and Silverberg fail to convince, even on rereading, that lay analysis was the sole issue. Fromm had been only an honorary member of the Association because it desired from the start to be a medical organization. Fromm had not raised the issue of lay analysis. He had asked to be given all the privileges of a training analyst or none. Dr. Jewett had only stated that he did not accept lay therapists on his faculty but had not objected to Fromm being on the faculty of the Institute. Fromm could have been accommodated in the same way as other institutes accommodated outstanding lay analysts from Europe, without compromising the basic medical stance.

Retrospective discussions reveal two currents which fed into the storm. A polarization of two groups had formed in the Association, one around Horney and one around Fromm and Thompson. The Horney group, so Clara Thompson later describes (16), had more power, and Thompson and Fromm felt an increasing current of discrimination. Judd Marmor vividly recalls (11) that Horney seemed to resent Fromm's growing popularity and used the spurious issue of the inadvisability of having a non-medical person as training analyst to insist that Fromm be removed from his position.

Another view is opened by retrospective remarks made by Janet Rioch (14). Rioch places Sullivan in the background of these events. She had been close to Sullivan, as Clara Thompson had been. Rioch reports that Sullivan, who had returned from New York to Bethesda, Maryland, in 1939, had maintained an interest in the Association for the Advancement of Psychoanalysis. Sullivan was present at the crucial meeting of the Association which withdrew Fromm's teaching privileges. The meeting was held in Rioch's apartment. She writes: "By no accident Harry had been present on the sidelines. The meeting broke up. Clara, Fromm, and Sullivan remained. Harry Stack was happy about the turn of events; he was now able to realize his dream of a New York Branch of the Washington School of Psychiatry." Plans were made right away for a meeting in Maryland with other members of the Washington School there. The meeting was held that spring and included Frieda Fromm-Reichman, David Rioch, Ralph Crowley, and others. Washington and New York, so they planned, would share their analysts, who would commute to do the teaching. Janet Rioch describes: "Travel between New York and Washington under wartime conditions was not easy, but Clara, Frieda, and Harry Stack expended themselves beyond the call of duty. Through these formative years Clara maintained a tireless jovial optimistic attitude that kept us buoyed up and working together. With the end of the war and the return of many men who had interrupted their psychoanalytic training, the New York Branch became much more substantial. The immediate reason for getting a separate charter from the New York Board of Regents was to qualify for the G.I. Bill of Rights. . . . This was no schism. It was decided that we should adopt our own distinguished name, and Clara's choice, with which we all agreed, was to name our school after Dr. William Alanson White of St. Elizabeths. Thus the start of the William Alanson White Institute" (14).

Clara Thompson, looking back on the formation of the American Association for the Advancement of Psychoanalysis and the subsequent split remarked: "The funny thing about this new society (the Association) was that it was very much like the Allies in World War II. We were against the same enemy, but we were not all the same thing. . . . But we were starting out with high hopes" (16).

Now I will trace the events of the third schism, which was the second one to occur in the American Association for the Advancement of Psychoanalysis. The American Institute of Psychoanalysis had continued to give courses at the two colleges mentioned. Beginning in the fall of 1943 Dr. Jewett was making plans to enlarge his Department of Psychiatry. He initiated discussions with the Institute probing the possibilities of its affiliation with the New York Medical College. The minutes of the Executive Council on December 1, 1943, show the discussion to be amiable but clearly polarized. There was unanimity about retaining the Institute even when affiliated. Details had been worked out. Horney, Harry Kelman, and Muriel Ivimey raised doubts. Horney felt the College had only to gain, while the Institute could lose prestige and was taking a great risk. She felt strongly that the group should negotiate as a group and avoid informal individual discussions with Dr. Jewett. On the other side, Silverberg, Robbins, and Marmor saw the affiliation as an opportunity to establish psychoanalysis within a department of psychiatry and believed the risk to be worth taking. The next step was to be a joint meeting of the Council with Dr. Jewett, and precise points for discussion were prepared. This meeting apparently did take place, but without resolution. On February 18, 1944, a letter from Dr. Jewett was received by the Secretary of the Association stating his decision to make arrangements for his department independent of an already existing organization. He stated: "There is nothing further in the nature of a blueprint than the proposed plan I already outlined at the last meeting. This was to lay the groundwork for a comprehensive program of post-graduate teaching in psychiatry leading to the degree of Doctor of Medical Science and to provide for special certification in psychoanalysis and other subjects within the field of psychiatry.

"As I indicated in my last letter, the difficulty seems to be in working out satisfactory arrangements with a group as a whole which is already organized into an institute. Upon further careful reflection it seems wise that I follow my original inclination and develop the plan independent of an already existing organization. This would provide for my dealing directly with any individual" (8).

This letter was dated February 18. The following day, six members resigned from the Association—as reported by the Secretary—without having previously given any indication of their intention, and without giving reasons for their decisions. The six were Silverberg, Robbins, Marmor, Ephron, Frances Arkin, and Isabel Beaumont. All candidates but one followed their analysts.

The six members had been invited to found a three-year training course in psychoanalysis at the College. They had accepted and immediately set about organizing the Comprehensive Course in Psychoanalysis. Much care was given to organizational matters, aiming at arrangements which would avoid ideological fights. Every instructor was to be free to teach in his/her own conceptual mode. A formula was devised to maintain some balance between Freudians and so-called Culturalists. The formula was applied loosely, and basically represented an expression of intent not to become a "school of thought." A principle of rotation was established for the terms of offices and the chairmanships of committees.

In this schism, as in the previous one, we again read of the existence of two currents, as described by Judd Marmor in a retrospective review. "There again arose a growing concern on the part of a number of members that the Association seemed to be becoming a 'Horney Group' rather than what had been originally envisioned: an institute and a society in which varying points of view would have free expression and would be freely taught.

"Consequently, when Stephen Jewett suggested that the New York Medical College might be willing to sponsor a full psychoanalytic training program within the framework of the department of psychiatry, a number of us were extremely interested. It appeared to present a significant and historic opportunity to bring psychoanalysis into the framework of organized medical education. Not only would we be reaffirming the roots of psychoanalysis in medical practice, but also we would be bringing it into a university setting, where academic freedom was a long established and hallowed principle. . . . Horney's great reluctance seemed to confirm fears of some that what Horney wanted to do, consciously or unconsciously, was to perpetuate her own particular school of thought rather than sponsor an open system of psychoanalytic training. Although most of us admired her tremendously, we did not wish to be her disciples or anyone else's" (12).

In 1947 this group organized the Society of Medical Psychoanalysts and elected Silverberg its first president. Silverberg's reflections on the beginning of the Society suggest his ever-present yearning to see a narrowing of the political gap in the field of psychoanalysis. He wrote: "This society came of age, as it were, in 1950, when it offered its first Symposium on Feminine Psychology. It was intended as a kind of Agape or Feast of Love whereby, it was hoped, many political antagonisms within the field of psychoanalysis would be dissolved by the antagonists finding they had a common ground in discussion of scientific matters. Though the Symposium was participated in by many at great geographic as well as orientational distance from ourselves, it cannot be said that it resulted in any political intra-psychoanalytic miracles of love . . ." (15).

The pruned Association for the Advancement of Psychoanalysis and its Institute survived well. All institutes saw an increase in enrollment once the men returned from the war. The Institute became officially identified with Karen Horney's teaching. A great step in its future development was the founding of the Karen Horney Clinic in 1953, providing added training facilities for the students and services for the community.

My source material for the fourth schism is chiefly George Daniels' impressive *History of the Association for Psychoanalytic Medicine and the Columbia Clinic,* which documents the events by quoting original resolutions and letters of negotiation (1). The story of the origins and the development of the Association and the Clinic stands in refreshing contrast to the schisms previously mentioned. Patience, political wisdom, and determination to see the new society and institute accepted under the umbrella of the American Psychoanalytic Association were rewarded after four years of negotiation. The chief obstacle to their goals was the one-unit rule of the American Psychoanalytic Association, which permitted only one society and one institute in any one geographical area.

To effect a change of this rule was thus essential and required a change of the constitution.

The same disillusionment with the atmosphere of the New York Psychoanalytic Society which led to the April 30, 1941, resignation of the Horney group was experienced by other members of the Society. Informal discussions about options for change became more frequent, and plans of action began to be formulated. Jack Millet, one of the most respected and cherished members of our psychoanalytic community—we still mourn his recent passing—described the emerging dissonances in an essay he wrote in 1962. "As more and more of the refugee analysts became qualified as members of local societies and joined the faculties of the training centers, the influence of their authoritarian approach to training became more and more apparent. Regulations as to qualifications for training analysts, minimum duration of training analyses, frequency of analytic sessions, number and frequency of supervisory sessions, etc., became more numerous, more exacting, and spread over more areas of the training process. By the time the United States entered the war a new pattern of administrative policies was emerging in which the influence of the European group and their American pupils was paramount. The number of analysts whose training had been secured in local institutes was too small for them to pit their experience and ideas successfully against the strength in numbers, reputation, and experience of their elders. The accolade of knighthood in the order of traditional conceptualists had already been given to a handful of American leaders either in Vienna or in Berlin. Their acceptance of the authority vested in Freud and handed down through the International Association was sustained, fortified, and crystallized through reunion with their exiled colleagues . . ." (13).

On June 12, 1942, the following members of the New York Psychoanalytic Society met for an organizational meeting to found the Association for Psychoanalytic and Psychosomatic Medicine. They were Carl Binger, George Daniels, Richard Frank, Phyllis Greenacre, Abram Kardiner, David Levy, Max Meyer, John Millet, Bela Mittleman, M. L. Oberholzer, and Sandor Rado. Carl Binger, acting for the group, addressed a letter to the president of the New York Psychoanalytic Society, Dr. Leonard Blumgart. An excerpt reads: "For several years there has been an atmosphere of bickering, slander, and gossip [in the Society] in which none of us felt that we could function profitably either to the

Society or to ourselves. For this reason, it is our declared intention to withdraw from the activities though not to resign from it" (1).

Because of the provisions and by-laws of the American Psychoanalytic Association, which did not permit more than one society in a locality, the existence of the new association was not advertised. Informal discussions were immediately initiated with Dr. Karl Menninger, the incoming president of the American Psychoanalytic Association, concerning the group's plan for a graduate psychoanalytic training school. The unofficial nature of this exchange was continuously emphasized. These informal contacts had a great deal to do with the final success. Initially the group aimed only at recognition of a second training institute. The idea of a separate society would not be countenanced at that time by the American.

A formal application to the American was made for the establishment of the new training center. Dr. Menninger agreed to nominate a committee on professional training to study and report on the application. Dr. Menninger's attitude throughout was friendly and helpful. On May 9, 1943, the Executive Council of the American rejected an amendment to permit multiple institutes in one locality. Yet that same day, in another joint meeting of the Executive Council and the Council on Professional Training, a new start was made. Dr. Menninger initiated a general discussion and called first on Franz Alexander. Alexander gave an impassioned speech, in which he urged: "It is time that we finally explicitly recognize a fundamental principle of teaching which is accepted in all fields of academic life, I mean the autonomy of teaching institutes. Whenever this principle has been violated in the past in any field of science, teaching deteriorated. Whenever the teaching in universities has been unduly exposed to the control and influence of outside factors such as influence of state politics, party politics, business interest, or even religious groups, academic teaching ceased to fulfill its purpose: transmission of knowledge. This is the reason why universities have always so jealously defended their autonomy. An organization of practicing specialists, too, is unsuited to control and direct teaching institutions. In a society of practitioners, like the American Psychoanalytic Association, the policies change from year to year according to elections. . . . An academic institution must develop its own tradition, the teaching staff should have a permanence, and its policies should be determined exclusively by its own faculty. Of course, the American Psychoanalytic Association should reserve the right to judge these institutions and to classify them, to recognize them or to withdraw recognition from them. But here its function in relation to the institutes should stop.

"It would be even more disastrous for the development of our field if the American Psychoanalytic Association should insist upon retaining its right to allow or to forbid the foundation of new teaching and research institutes. Our field is a new one, still very much in the stage of pioneering. We need the enterprising spirit and initiative of groups which independently undertake the organization of new teaching and research institutions. The American Psychoanalytic Association should have again the right to judge and evaluate, on the basis of their performance, these new institutes, to recognize them or not. However, a monopolistic central organization must be avoided. What we need is not conformity, but free development of divergent points of view and emphases. We must avoid suppressive attempts to standardize our new field by enforcing conformity of opinion. Therefore, I am pleading for a thorough re-orientation of our policies concerning teaching and research, our policies concerning new and old institutes. Instead of trying to control, centralize, and standardize teaching we should encourage free development of teaching, and research centers by well qualified analysts who will group together according to a common point of view and interests which they share with each other. Only such a policy will lead to raising of standards and further development of our vital but still so young field" (1).

Karl Menninger, in summing up the discussion, stated: "We have arrived nowhere in our discussion of the matter. Perhaps Dr. Rado's group should go ahead and start an institution of their own" (1). This encouraging suggestion implied that such a challenge could reopen the issue in a more effective way.

Dr. Rado's group did proceed. A small committee began meeting at David Levy's apartment to work out the details of the new training institute. Dr. Alvin Johnson, Dean of the New School for Social Research, and Dr. Nolan D. C. Lewis, Director of the Department of Psychiatry at Columbia University, participated in these discussions. Plans with Nolan Lewis consolidated rapidly towards a possible integration of the new institute and clinic into the College of Physicians and Surgeons, Columbia University. In September 1943 Rado submitted a memorandum outlining the plan for the new school.

The Association for Psychoanalytic and Psychosomatic Medicine continued its informal meetings and in June 1944 began working on a constitution and on matters of incorporation.

The task of mobilizing the American Psychoanalytic Association into action still lay ahead. Unexpected help came in the form of Dr. Silverberg's announcement of the plan to establish a psychoanalytic training center in the department of psychiatry of the New York Medical College. The Council of Professional Training of the American was aroused. Sandor Rado's patience was wearing thin, and he was inclined to take more militant action. He drafted a sharp note. The group's leaning to friendly diplomacy won out, and the draft was shelved. An active correspondence was resumed with Leo Bartemeier and then Bertram Lewin, the successive Presidents of the American Psychoanalytic Association.

On May 20, 1945, a joint resolution was passed by the Executive Council and the Council on Professional Training of the American Psychoanalytic Association expressing a desire to maintain cordial professional relationships with the group represented by Drs. Daniels and Rado, and referring the question of inclusion of a new society within the framework of the American to a newly appointed committee on reorganization, which was reevaluating the relationships of the American Association to local societies and institutes. The foundation was laid. Feverish correspondence continued in order to assure proper wording of constitutional changes in preparation. On December 24, 1945, the Executive Council passed a resolution expressing its favorable inclination to accept the Association for Psychoanalytic Medicine and the teaching institution at Columbia into its organization. In 1946 the changes in the constitution and by-laws of the American were made, and the new society and training center were finally accepted as affiliated society and institute of the American Psychoanalytic Association. George Daniels writes in his history that a debt of gratitude goes to Dr. Lewin for his sympathetic steering of negotiations and bringing them to a successful termination. Obviously much credit also goes to the unusual skill in negotiation shown by the Columbia group.

The birth of the American Academy of Psychoanalysis in Chicago on April 29, 1956, belongs to this sector of history, as the following partial list of its presidents shows: Janet Rioch, Jules Masserman, William Silverberg, John Millet, Frances Arkin, Roy Grinker, Sandor Rado, Franz Alexander, Judd Marmor. Again this was a story of good timing and good preparation. The wish and the idea for a new national psychoanalytic organization occurred simultaneously in many places beginning in 1951. Gradually a network of informal discussions developed. Clara Thompson, who had harbored the dream of a new kind of national organization for a long time, was a key figure in the active planning of what was to be a scientific forum for a free exchange of ideas. Rado, Masserman, Alexander, Kardiner, and many others were receptive to the idea of such a forum. Clara convened a meeting at the Croyden Hotel in October 1955, which prepared for a larger organizing meeting to be held in New York in December at the same time as the winter meeting of the American Psychoanalytic Association. The auditorium of the New York Medical College held a large and enthusiastic crowd. Janet Rioch defined the purpose of the organization, emphasizing that there was no thought or intent to start a rival organization to the American Psycho-analytic Association. The organization was to stand on its merits as a scientific forum. A provisional constitution was drafted with much care to avoid the establishment of hierarchical leadership or continuing control of committees. The Academy was to have no function of licensing, authorizing, or supervising methods of instruction and training in psychoanalytic institutes.

An essential aspect of the concept of a scientific forum was to promote interchange with scientists in related fields. The category of Scientific Associate was established to permit these scientists to become an integral part of the organization. The membership was open to any psychiatrist who graduated from what was loosely defined as a bona fide psychoanalytic institute. The organization invited international membership, but was to be distinctly an American-based organization. Having been a charter member of the Academy and having had my turn as trustee and president, I have been deeply gratified by the unwavering devotion of the American Academy to its original commitment and its superb atmosphere of congeniality and mutual respect.

In conclusion: Schisms in psychoanalytic organizations are a particularly active and apparent manifestation of a spirit of conflict or dissension pervasively present in these organizations. The dissensions, whether over issues or ideologies, generate quite typically a high degree of personal animosities. Each decade in addition has had factors of its own influencing the currents of motivational energy. The forties were a period of trial and error in a period of transition. One aspect of this transition is worth noting. Horney, Sullivan, and also Rado were the last of the unitary system builders in psychoanalysis. They saw Freud to be in error in certain of his premises, but they, too, believed in a potentially unitary system. They were making efforts towards a better, corrected system. They believed in the rightness of their own contribution, in their mission, and thus in the idea of a school of their own. There was no more system building after 1950. The principles of General System Theory, knowingly or unknowingly, were influencing our scientific thinking.

Let me return to the theme of schisms as a character trait, or as a symptom of a malady in psychoanalysis. The theme of malaise about our organizational dysfunction is heard over and over again, within and outside the fold. Listen to these words by Robert Knight, spoken in his presidential address "The Present Status of Organized Psychoanalysis in the United States" in 1952 to the American Psychoanalytic Association. Referring to the trends of dissensions, he states: "The spectacle . . . of a national association of physicians and scientists feuding with each other over training standards and practices . . . calling each other orthodox or deviant . . . is not an attractive one to say the least. Such terms belong to religious or to fanatical political movements and not to science and medicine. . . . Perhaps we are still standing too much in the shadow of that giant Sigmund Freud to permit ourselves to view psychoanalysis as a science of the mind rather than as the doctrine of its founder. . . . In the physical sciences one does not squelch an Einstein by quoting passages from Newton. . . . On the other hand, one does not cease teaching Newton just because Einstein has gone further, for from the student's standpoint, Einstein cannot be understood until one has a thorough grasp of Newton. . . . Our minds must be constantly open to new observations, new conceptions, revisions of hypotheses, and testing and retesting of the revisions. We have no time to waste in building a stockade around sacred ground, erecting a statue of worship, and then conducting loyalty investigations within the stockade." Ontogenetically, Knight said, psychoanalysis might be regarded as an overgrown adolescent, and he hoped to see a greater maturity in another decade from then (9).

This was in 1952. In 1966 Jack Millet, saddened by the same difficulties, again referred to adolescent behavior of the discipline, feeling optimistic that with the passing of the old guard, it will mature.

Almost a quarter of a century has passed since Knight spoke, and we can no more tie our hopes to a diagnosis of adolescence. As I mentioned in the beginning, I believe that our malaise is built in. We have had many an outstanding leader with sound perspective. Just to name the few that appeared in this history: Karl Menninger, Bertram Lewin,

Robert Knight, Franz Alexander, George Daniels, Sandor Rado, and many others; but they were unable to affect the basic structural model. I am neither optimistic nor pessimistic. We will continue to live with our areas of inborn organizational illogic. Time and creative thinking cannot be stopped. The avalanches of interdisciplinary contributions in the field have had liberalizing opening effects. Psychiatry has absorbed the best of psychoanalysis, simply marches on, and cares little about the internal knots of the psychoanalytic discipline. The graduating candidates of the various psychoanalytic institutes are less in awe of their teachers and feel free to benefit from the stimuli of new therapeutic or conceptual endeavors. Time will be a force for change and integration.

One more comment. My mother, Karen Horney, seems to have played the role first of sparking a revolution and later that of a bête noire. Her creative world always had been her work: first her studies, later her writing and teaching. She was not a leader in an organizational sense. She was charismatic because of a charm of personality, her lucidity of ideas and expression, her marvelous clinical observations, and a gift for organizing her concepts. She believed in her mission. She lacked interest in organizational matters and thus brushed aside rules, which facilitate organizational work. She delegated these organizational tasks but, though in leadership position, took no responsibility for them. She was as admirably human as anyone else; a remarkable person from childhood on. She was shy rather than combative; but the combination of intellectual leadership combined with an obliviousness to organizational matters tends generally to promote friction. In contrast, Rado and Alexander, both openly temperamental, knew the value of proper organization and created less personal animosity.

I will finally end on a lighter note. After her death we discovered an absolutely delightful diary my mother wrote off and on from age thirteen to twenty-four. The diary was her friend, her confidant, and a person to dialogue with. I will quote an age fourteen entry which shows her early spirit of inquiry and intensity of thought. Her Protestant upbringing was strict, imposed with an obvious excess of zeal by her father. Thus, the first questions she posed were religious ones. At age fourteen she writes: "Berndt [her older brother] really is a good fellow. Yesterday he enlightened me again on several issues which were not clear to me. The least clear to me up to now has been the personality of Christ. Although Herr Schulze [her teacher] did teach me about this, it seems to make no sense to me that Jesus should be God's son. Berndt told me:

'Christ is and always will be the greatest among all men, because the divine element, which is embedded in every human being, was much stronger in him, and so he stood nearest to God.' With this explanation something like a stone fell from my heart, for I could not imagine, could not love, such a mixture of God and man. Now Jesus has become much dearer to me.

Three days later this clarification gets her into trouble with her beloved Herr Schulze. "Something dreadful happened today. I'm afraid my adored Herr Schulze is angry with me. It happened this way: we were going through the fifteenth chapter of I Corinthians and also the (so-called) proofs Paul cites of Christ's resurrection, namely, that he appeared to various people and also to Paul. I dared express the view that Paul had been in an overwrought nervous condition and so imagined he saw this luminous vision. I implied that this was really no proof of Christ's resurrection. I don't know whether he misunderstood me, or what, but, in short, he got quite excited and said, slapping his Bible shut, that in that case we could just as well go on to something else . . . and delivered a sermon to me. If I were not still totally dumbfounded, I should long ago have despaired, for the awareness or the feeling that he is angry with me is terrible to me. I think I shall be very much embarrassed at his next lessons, for I cannot overcome this so easily" (2). She was a passionate and independent thinker and in this sense she was a disciple of Freud.

REFERENCES

1. Daniels, G. E., "History of the Association for Psychoanalytic Medicine and the Columbia Clinic," sent to Dr. John Weber, President, the Association for Psychoanalytic Medicine, January 29, 1969. Unpublished.

2. Eckardt, M. H., Life Is a Juggling Act: Our Concepts of "Normal" Development— Myth or Reality? *American Journal of Psychoanalysis*, 1975, 35:103.

3. Ellenberger, H. F., *The Discovery of the Unconscious*. New York: Basic Books, 1970, p. 550.

4. Freud, S., Instincts and Their Vicissitudes (1915). *Collected Papers*. London: Hogarth, p. 60.

5. Horney, K., et al., Letter of resignation to the Educational Committee, New York Psychoanalytic Society, May 1, 1941.

6. Horney, K., et al., Letter of resignation to the Secretary of the American Psychoanalytic Association, May 1, 1941.

7. Horney, K., et al., Letter of explanation sent to the membership of the American Psychoanalytic Association. *American Journal of Psychoanalysis*, Vol. 1, 1941.

8. Jewett, S. P., Letter to the Secretary of the Association for the Advancement of Psychoanalysis, February 18, 1944.

9. Knight, R. P., Present Status of Organized Psychoanalysis in the United States. *Journal of the American Psychoanalytic Association*, Vol. 1, 1953, p. 197.

10. Marmor, J., *WAWI Newsletter*, 1973, Vol. VIII, No. 1.

11. Marmor, J., *WAWI Newsletter*, 1968, Vol. III, No. 1.

12. Marmor, J., *Newsletter*, Society of Medical Psychoanalysts, September 1964.

13. Millett, J. A. P., Changing Faces of Psychoanalytic Training. In: L. Salzman and J. H. Masserman, Eds., *Modern Concepts of Psychoanalysis*. New York: Philosophical Library, 1962.

14. Rioch, J. B., *WAWI Newsletter*, Spring 1969.

15. Silverberg, W. V., *Newsletter*, Society of Medical Psychoanalysts, 1962, Vol. 1, No. 1.

16. Thompson, C., The History of the William Alanson White Institute, March 15, 1955. Unpublished.

CHAPTER 10

Ego Psychology: Its Relation to Sullivan, Erikson, and Object Relations Theory

Roger L. Shapiro, M.D.

IN HIS 1923 MONOGRAPH, *The Ego and the Id* (14), Freud proposed new formulations of the mental apparatus in the structural theory, which conceptualized a mental organization of differentiated functions frequently in conflict, the id, the ego and the superego. This theory constituted a radical departure from prior conceptualizations in psychoanalysis which simply equated the unconscious with the instinctual drives and their vicissitudes. In the structural theory the ego and the superego, too, had unconscious and preconscious aspects in addition to conscious aspects and the pychology of the unconscious was no longer limited to the vicissitudes of the instinctual drives in the id. These concepts of unconscious ego and superego, determined in part by reality relationships, were an important step in establishing psychoanalysis as a developmental psychology. They provided conceptual means for focusing upon processes of internalization of object relations in the development of mental structure. Freud's conceptualization was expanded and modified in the work

Presented February 17, 1977. Roger L. Shapiro is Clinical Professor, Department of Psychiatry and Behavioral Sciences, George Washington University School of Medicine, Washington, D. C., and member of the faculty, Washington Psychoanalytic Institute.

of Anna Freud (8), Hartmann (17, 18), Hartmann, Kris, Loewenstein (19), and others, in the constructs of ego psychology.

Concurrently, the work of Sullivan (29), Erikson (3), and the Object Relations Theorists (6, 22, 23, 24, 25, 31, 32) constituted important new contributions to psychoanalytic developmental theory. These investigators all attempt to comprehend the relation of the individual to reality, through understanding and conceptualizing his developmental experience and its persistence and state of organization in both conscious and unconscious mental processes. The theories differ in their ways of conceptualizing the forces and contents of the unconscious. They differ in the assumptions about the nature of biological givens and the links between biological dispositions and experience; and they differ in the constructs they hypothesize linking the content and forces of the unconscious with conscious mental activity. These differences have been one focus for much of the dissension within psychoanalysis since 1923.

Elements in common in the framework of these investigators are frequently not attended to in the controversy over their differences. They are all concerned with the framework of a developmental psychology rooted in the individual's biological nature. They all attempt to conceptualize the individual's internalization of experience, and the relation of biological and experiential variables to unconscious mental activity. Consideration of similarities as well as areas of differences between the theories is frequently not done with objectivity and careful attention to evidence.

It is occasionally noted (30, 34) that apparent significant differences between psychoanalytic personality theories may not alter in a fundamental way the therapeutic method. The differences in theory, although they are much emphasized, may well not outweigh the similarities in the framework in which psychoanalysis is done by therapists of different theoretical persuasions. The psychoanalytic process depends upon utilization of a method involving the creation of a situation in which the technical work, broadly stated, is interpretation of transference and resistance. This was Freud's original definition (9), and it still provides the framework in which interpretative work is done within different constructs of personality theory. This complicates the use of the clinical situation to verify alternate theories, as the method utilizing interpretation of transference for increasing self understanding appears to survive much inexact interpretation and still be effective. It is important, in the debates over differences in theory, to weigh carefully the evidence that these differences have significant consequences for technique of therapy. These consequences are frequently overstated.

Differences in theory frequently become part of a political struggle rather than a scientific investigation within psychoanalysis. Psychoanalysis as a science does not lend itself easily to the formulations of clear alternative hypotheses within a common overall framework which can be explored carefully in an effort to weigh evidence or to determine consequences for therapeutic application. Responsibility for the divisiveness of new ideas in psychoanalysis resides not only with the psychoanalytic authority structure but also with those who develop new theory, frequently making little effort to relate the concepts and language they develop to the concepts of Freud and the classical theory despite obvious and important links between the theories. This usually makes assessment of new theory difficult. For example, Sullivan makes no attempt to relate his theory of anxiety to Freud's, although it is parallel in many ways to Freud's final anxiety theory and central to both of their conceptualizations of psychopathology. In fact, Sullivan makes only the most general statement about Freud's work in his *The Interpersonal Theory of Psychiatry* (29); beyond acknowledging that the Interpersonal Theory rests upon the discoveries of Freud, Sullivan does not spell out what his theory uses from Freud and what it discards.

Erikson links his work much more directly and explicitly to the work of Freud. Erikson's epigenetic theory of development is rooted in concepts of ego epigenesis which are related to Freud's conceptualization of drive epigenesis (3). Rapaport contributes much detailed explication of the connections between Erikson's work and ego psychology (26).

Object Relations Theory is very closely linked to Freud's final drive theory in the work of Melanie Klein (22, 23) and her followers (24, 25). However, such theorists as Fairbairn (6) and Winnicott (31, 32), although they base their personality theories on the decisive importance of early object relations, have different concepts from Klein and her followers of the nature and relation of instinctual drives to early object relations.

Psychoanalytic theory is intricate and complex. It is difficult to assimilate existing theory and work with it in the clinical situation. In addition, serious limitations of the structure of psychoanalytic theory, its metapsychology, have been apparent as developmental theory has become central in clinical work and in research. The work of Sullivan, Erikson, and Object Relations Theory may each be viewed as commentary on a variety of problems that developmental theory poses for classical Freudian theory and metapsychology. The following discussion of the relation of Ego Psychology to Sullivan, Erikson, and Object Relations Theory will attempt to characterize some aspects of this commentary and some continuing problems of psychoanalysis as a developmental psychology.

I

Freud's structural theory is the foundation from which later developments in ego psychology, as well as the theories of Sullivan, Erikson, and the Kleinians grew. A number of clinical and theoretical considerations led to Freud's formulations of the structural theory. One set of factors were clinical observations which required a conceptualization of unconscious ego (and superego) as well as id, thereby effecting a major revision on the older topographic theory. In particular, concepts of unconscious defenses became necessary to understand observations of resistances in analysis and negative therapeutic reaction (14). Clinical observations of unconscious guilt were the evidence which led to constructs of identification with lost objects in *Mourning and Melancholia* (12). The theory of identification was further elaborated in *Group Psychology and the Analysis of the Ego* (13); and in *The Ego and the Id,* superego formation was conceptualized as finally determined by oedipal identifications. The concept superego (earlier called ego ideal) also had an earlier source in Freud's 1914 paper *On Narcissism* (11). Here the ego ideal was characterized as the individual's earliest internalizations of the critical influence of his parents, now invested with libido which was originally invested in the individual's own primary narcissism. Freud related the ego ideal to an even earlier structural precursor, the dream censor.

In addition to being stimulated by clinical observations, the new structural concepts were also provoked by theoretical controversies. Much of the impetus for the formulations in *On Narcissism* appears to be Freud's response to Jung's and Adler's differences with him over libido theory. This is explicit in the paper, and is elaborated more fully in Freud's *On the History of the Psycho-analytic Movement* (10), which he was writing more or less simultaneously. It is clear that important developments in psychoanalytic theory have been stimulated not only by new clinical observations but in response to the challenge of the ideas of other investigators. These challenges are too frequently seen as destructive, and their value for the stimulation of scientific dialogue is not acknowledged.

Freud's structural theory replaced his previous major emphasis on instinctual drives with a more balanced formulation of instincts in relation to control mechanisms, specifically defenses. Furthermore, Freud defined the ego as the portion of the id modified by reality, providing conceptual means for formulating the consequences of reality relation for personality formation. Anna Freud's (8) and Heinz Hartmann's (17, 18) extensions of Freud's structural theory into Ego Psychiatry go far beyond Freud's formulations, yet are so firmly rooted in Freud's metapsychology that their differences from Freud are frequently minimized. In *The Ego and the Mechanism of Defense* (8), Anna Freud expanded the concept of defense. While previously the ego's defenses were considered chiefly as resistances to therapy, she showed that the defenses were in fact highly adaptive in their origins. Then, in his monograph *Ego Psychology and the Problem of Adaptation* (17), Hartmann made adaptation a central principle in his work, a shift away from Freud's central preoccupation with conflict.

In an important discussion of the work of Hartmann, Yankelovitch and Barrett (33) argue that Hartmann accomplished a radical reorientation of Freud's theory. In their words, "Freud stresses the ego's conflict ridden limitations while Hartmann's work stresses the ego's conflict free achievements." Freud's ego starts as a weaker force than the instincts and borrows its energies from them. The ego grows out of the id as a secondary development; the id, the seat of the drives, is primary. They emphasize Freud's view of the ego as devoid of goals or purposes of its own, regarding the ego as the servant of the id and the superego. Thus, they say that for Freud the pleasure principle, the regulatory principle of the id, remained the fundamental law of psychic life, and the ego serves the id by striving after pleasure and seeking to avoid pain. For Freud, they say, the past carries more weight than the present, and biological heritage represented by the id is far stronger than the effect of individual learning and experience represented by the ego.

In arguing that others minimize Hartmann's differences with Freud, Yankelovitch and Barrett in turn minimize the shift in Freud's own thinking about the strength of the ego implicit in the new concept of ego in the structural theory. This is already clear in the introductory chapter to *Group Psychology and the Analysis of the Ego,* where Freud wrote (p. 69): "Individual psychology is concerned with the individual man and explores the paths by which he seeks to find satisfaction for his instinctual impulses; but only rarely and under certain exceptional conditions is individual psychology in a position to disregard the relations of the individual to others. In the individual's mental life someone else is invariably involved as a model, as an object, as a helper, as an opponent; and so from the very first, individual psychology, in this extended but entirely justifiable sense of the word, as at the same time social psychology." Two years later, in *The Ego and the Id,* Freud's structural formulations provided new concepts for the internalizations of social experience in personality formation. Although Freud continued to emphasize the power of the instincts, Yankelovitch and Barrett minimize the important developments in his theory of identification and object relations which give increasing power to reality determinants of personality formation in the superego and the ego. These aspects of Freud's thought were carried much further in the work of Hartmann and were the areas of major new theorizing in the work of Sullivan, Erikson, and Object Relations Theory.

Yankelovitch and Barrett point out that by developing the notion of the ego as autonomous, Hartmann placed strength and forces at its disposal which he insisted must be more than a developmental by-product of the influence of reality on the instinctual drives. Hartmann's ego does not develop solely as a result of learning and experience; it follows its own timetable of inborn processes analogous to the development of physiological process. Hartmann postulated that there are functions of the ego which develop independently of the drives; that the ego has biological roots of its own and that some ego functions that developed out of conflict come to have autonomy. In consequence, the Freudian concept of a weak ego has been changed to the Hartmann concept of a potentially strong and autonomous ego, although its autonomy is vulnerable to threat not only from within but from changed environmental conditions. Hartmann insisted that the changes he introduced were logical extensions and refinements of Freud's thought. He integrated his theories of a strong ego with Freud's metapsychology and the intrapsychic systems of id, ego, and superego and concepts of psychic energy. Yankelovitch and Barrett state that in the interest of maintaining continuity with Freud, Hartmann retained all the conceptual awkwardness of the old metapsychology. They believe his concepts were incompatible with it. In particular they are arguing about Hartmann's use of the concept of neutralized energy.

In their view, Hartmann had the choice of grounding his new concepts on empirical evidence or forcing them to fit metapsychology by a logical adjustment; i.e., by using units of neutralized energies to account for the transition from a weak to a strong ego. Unfortunately, they say, he chose the latter course which they feel helped to create some of the problems which plague psychoanalysis today. Hartmann accounts for the differences between strong versus weak ego metapsychologically by positing increments of neutralized energy. However, the evidence upon which this theory is based is the clinical experience of psychoanalysts which suggests that the development of a strong versus a weak ego is primarily determined by early experience. Yankelovitch and Barrett point out that, increasingly, clinicians place great emphasis on the individual's early object relations. The analyses of early mother-child relationships are used as evidence within psychoanalysis in support of Hartmann's concept of autonomous ego. Yankelovitch and Barrett argue that Hartmann's proposals are inferences which have only an indirect relationship to this evidence. Ego strength does not seem to depend on the apparatuses of primary autonomy such as perception, memory, or motility. These serve a strong or weak ego apparently indifferently. It is not always clear that ego strength depends on apparatuses of secondary autonomy, although here the evidence can be argued either way. Yankelovitch and Barrett conclude that clinical observations which suggest that ego strength depends primarily on the quality of the child's early human relationships are not explained by metapsychological concepts of primary and secondary autonomy or autonomous apparatuses. It is not clear how to use metapsychology to clarify how the mother-child relationship helps to create a strong ego. Hartmann's defense for these metapsychological concepts is that they are compatible with clinical evidence. But Yankelovitch and Barrett point out that while Hartmann's concepts of neutralized energy do not directly contradict the clinical data, neither do they explain or add understanding to the data. New observations on the relation of early experience to ego development and ego strength are not explained through concepts of neutralization of energy.

New efforts to conceptualize developmental data and the importance of early object relations for personality functioning led to the theories of Sullivan, Erikson, and Object Relations Theory.

II

The developmental findings of clinical psychoanalysis and research in child development led Hartmann to modify Freud's concept of the ego. The theories of Sullivan, Erikson, and Object Relations Theory are all conceptualizations of development which derive their data from the same areas of clinical exploration which led to Hartmann's formulations. Psychoanalytic explanations of characteristics of the ego's strength were based increasingly on the quality of the child's early object relationships. The development of child analysis was an important impetus in this theory building. It pushed the developmental emphasis in the work of Anna Freud (7, 8), Erikson (3), and Melanie Klein (21, 22, 23). Continuing psychoanalytic work with borderline and psychotic patients was another source of new theory. It was the clinical experience out of which Sullivan formulated his interpersonal theory (29), and Kleinian analysts found evidence in adults for their constructions of the earliest phases of childhood which originally came from child analysis.

These theories each conceptualized developmental data in a different way. They all represent efforts to move beyond the limitations of classical metapsychology for reasons similar to those which motivated Hartmann in his Ego Psychology. The evidence of clinical psychoanalysis and of child development has required theory which addresses itself to the impact of the child's early relationships on his personality formation. This requirement is not adequately met by the propositions about the psychic apparatus in metapsychloogy, which conceptualizes behavior abstractly in terms of quantity of drive and degrees of neutralization of energy. This is not a suitable language for conceptualization of the quality of relationships.

However, metapsychology has been extremely valuable in meeting another requirement central to the methods and findings of clinical psychoanalysis: the requirement for conceptualization of unconscious determinants of behavior which, to a significant extent, reflect and represent infantile and childhood experiences. Sullivan, Erikson and Object Relations Theory each differ in the means they employ to conceptualize the logic and the language of unconscious determinants of behavior, the relations of the unconscious to instincts, and the importance of innate disposition versus experience.

Much of the controversy over these theories concerns the adequacy of their conceptualizations of the unconscious and the degree to which they integrate their developmental emphasis with an adequate theory of unconscious mental functioning.

Sullivan's theory is an interesting contrast to the theory of Hartmann. Hartmann is occupied with constructions of intrapsychic organization, both of structural components of the mind and of the nature of the drive energies which determine mental functioning. Sullivan's attention is to the universe of external relationships which affect a relatively unformulated mental organization (the self system) from infancy onward. He is interested in the relation of psychopathology to disturbances in interpersonal relationships. He conceptualizes the area of relationships between people to formulate a theory of development.

Erikson's theory is concerned with important elements of the areas of interest both of Hartmann and of Sullivan. His theory is consistent in its utilization of Freudian intrapsychic constructs, and he advances epigenetic propositions of intrapsychic development. It is above all a developmental theory, and its focus is on the relation of epigenetic intrapsychic development to the interpersonal and social relations which meet new maturational needs of the individual in each developmental phase and become part of his personality organization and his capacity to achieve a new developmental level. Erikson has worked most extensively on the phase of adolescence and on new formulations of the identity crisis which characterizes that phase (3, 4).

Object relations theory is occupied with the earliest phases of development. It began in the work of Klein with constructs of intrapsychic drives and structural organization in infancy. Klein's interest is largely intrapsychic and conceptualizes structural consequences of life and death instincts in relation to introjection and projection of objects of the drives as they are experienced in early or late phases of infantile development. Her use of drive theory focuses upon the relation of the quality of the drive to the quality of fantasy content, and defensive structures which are mobilized in relation to those contents. In contrast, Hartmann's use of drive theory is far more focused as an effort to conceptualize degrees of neutralization and of independence of function of the ego, not on contents of fantasies.

Later Object Relations Theorists such as Fairbairn (6) and Winnicott (31, 32) were much more interested in the quality of the object relations themselves and the consequences of the nature of the object relationships for the nature of internalizations. In this sense, they were much closer to the area of Sullivan's interest than Klein was.

It is interesting to consider the emphasis in Object Relations Theory on the earliest developmental phase in the context of Erikson's theory of the life cycle. Without regard for the correctness of the details of Object Relations Theory or indeed the fact that there are conflicting theories within it, it is an example of a serious body of work conceptualizing a maturing mental apparatus in relation to developmental experience in the earliest phase of life, comparable to Erikson's efforts to conceptualize similar elements throughout the life cycle, particularly exemplified in his construct of adolescent identity formation.

III

The theory of Sullivan has as its conceptual center the nature of interpersonal relations of the child and their consequences for adult mental functioning, beginning with the infant-mother relationship (29). Sullivan does not much concern himself with the biological substrate of human personality; he takes it for granted, and he considers the concept of instinct extremely misleading. He holds that the human is the product of interaction with other human beings; that it is out of personal and social forces acting upon one from the day of birth that the personality emerges. The human being is concerned with two inclusive goals, the pursuit of satisfaction and the pursuit of security. He does conceptualize dynamisms of vaguely defined impulses and drives which are relatively enduring configurations manifesting themselves in numerous ways in human situations.

In a discussion of Sullivan's theory, Guntrip (16) says that Sullivan comes close to Object Relations Theory when he says personality is a function of the kinds of interpersonal situations a person integrates with others, whether real persons or fantastic personifications. If Sullivan's fantastic personifications were recognized more fundamentally as Melanie Klein's internal psychic objects; and if the theory of impulses, as cohering in dynamisms or relatively enduring configurations of energy, were seen to imply Fairbairn's theory of impulses as reactions of dynamic ego structures to objects, then Guntrip says Sullivan would have transcended a purely "culture-pattern" type of thoery. In Guntrip's view, he does not, however, take the step, but proceeds to outline only the process of acculturation of the conscious and pre-conscious ego in relationships with external objects.

Sullivan's theory is weak in its conceptualization of internalization processes and of epigenetic aspects of development. Hence his theory is inadequate in its conceptualization of the unconscious registration of interpersonal experience. He ignores classical drive theory, which ego psychology relies upon to conceptualize unconscious processes, but does not replace it, which impoverishes his theory of the unconscious. Guntrip argues that Sullivan fails to supply a theory of the unconscious in terms of internalized object relationships, and without this he feels his entire "culture-pattern" theory is a structure without a foundation. However much the growing child encounters a changing world without, Guntrip points out, the child and adult remain tied to an unconscious and relatively unchanging environment within himself. It is this fact that gives great power to the original developmental pattern of the ego. In Guntrip's view the "culture-pattern" theorists such as Sullivan, Adler (1), Horney (20), and Fromm (15) are in the predicament of having discarded orthodox instinct theory (which did make it possible to describe the dynamic unconscious in some approach to structural terms), while they have not yet formulated its true alternative, which in his view is internal object theory. Thus, they have no concepts capable of accounting for the unconscious in the dynamic sense which is demanded by so many clinical facts. Their study of the molding pressure of the cultural milieu is valuable, he believes, and an important corrective to biological theory. But their theory is psychologically superficial and, in his view, Sullivan goes no further than the study of the Freudian ego and superego and has no real theory of the unconscious.

IV

In his 1946 essay "Ego Development and Historical Change" (2), Erikson observes that while it was a step of great importance when Freud applied contemporaneous concepts of physical energy to psychology, the resultant theory that instinctual energy is transferred, displaced, transformed in analogy to the conservation of energy in physics no longer suffices to help us manage psychoanalytic data. It is here, he says, "that ego concepts must close the gap and we must find a nexus of social images and organismic forces. . . . More than this, the mutual complementation of ethos and ego, of group identity and ego identity, puts a greater common potential at the disposal of both ego synthesis and social organization."

Erikson's theory (3) is rooted in developmental concepts of epigenesis of the ego as well as the drives. Rapaport (26) points out that whereas Hartmann postulates pre-adaptedness to an average expectable environment in his concept of autonomous ego development, Erikson postulates an epigenetic maturation in the ego and the id to a whole sequence of average expectable environments. Erikson's theory outlines a sequence of phases of psychosocial development and relates these phases to psychosexual epigenesis, laying the groundwork for the study of ego epigenesis.

Each phase of the life cycle is characterized by a phase-specific developmental task which must be solved in it, although the solution is prepared in the previous phases and is worked out further in subsequent ones. Erikson's concept of mutuality specifies a crucial coordination between the developing individual and his human (social) environment. Rapaport argues that the crucial characteristic of Erikson's psychosocial theory of ego development and of Hartmann's adaptation theory, in contrast to culturalist theories such as Sullivan's, is that they offer a conceptual explanation of the individual's social development by tracing the unfolding of the genetically social character of the human individual in the course of his encounters with the social environment at *each* phase of his epigenesis. Thus it is not assumed that societal norms are grafted upon the genetically asocial individual by "disciplines" and "socialization," but that the society into which the individual is born makes him its member by influencing the manner in which he solves the tasks posed by each phase of his epigenetic development. Erikson introduces the concepts of organ mode and mode epigenesis and thereby specifies a major mechanism by which society influences the solution of phase-specific developmental tasks. These constitute specific instances of Hartmann's concept of change of function.

Erikson therefore specifies the requirement in personality formation for significant human responses to the id and ego epigenesis of each developmental phase. These experiences are internalized and become unconscious as well as conscious determinants of preparation for the next phase. Erikson's theory is an elegant conceptualization of the relation of psychosocial experience to development within the framework of drive theory and a theory of the unconscious. However, he does not involve himself in the complexities Hartmann is concerned with in his efforts to comprehend ego development and, as Rapaport points out, he relates his theory, explicitly, mainly to the drive concepts of Freud's id psychology, less to the concepts of Freud's ego psychology, and only slightly to Hartmann's theory.

Yankelovitch and Barrett (33) state that Erikson has gone beyond Hartmann's theory to the point where clear incompatibilities in psychoanalytic theory are seen. They argue that man does not first exist in a world of Freudian forces, energies, and cathexes and then search for meaning. This, they believe, is the paradox encountered in attempting to make Freud and Erikson compatible. Erikson describes identity as a structure of meanings, and epigenesis as a series of crises and transformations. They state: "In the formation of ego identity a person does not change because he imitates a model but because the encounter with some living fellow creatures serves as a catalyst that enables the person to transform himself and shape his own self. The difference is critical: the former process might be explained in metapsychological terms, the latter cannot possibly be. In his search for a more viable philosophy for psychoanalysis than metapsychology, Erikson affords us the curious picture of a prominent psychoanalytic theorist who ignores four-fifths of Freud's metapsychology, and uses the remainder idiosyncratically. Erikson almost never discusses his materials in terms of the topographical or the dynamic or the economic or the structural points of view although he utilizes and accepts the basic distinctions between id and ego. He has evolved his own version of the genetic point of view."

In his paper "The Nature of Clinical Evidence," Erikson says (5) "the points of view introduced into psychiatry and psychology by Freud are subject to a strange fate. . . . Since on their medical home ground they were based on physical facts such as organs that function, in the study of the mind they sooner or later served as improper reifications, as though libido, or the death instinct, or the ego really existed. Freud was sovereignly aware of this danger, but he was always willing to learn by giving a mode of thought free rein to see to what useful model it might lead. He also had the courage, the authority and the inner consistency to reverse such a direction when it became useless or absurd. Generations of clinical practitioners cannot be expected to be equally detached or authoritative. Thus, it cannot be denied that in much clinical literature, the clinical evidence secured with the help of inferences based on Freud's theories has been increasingly used and slanted to verify the theories. This, in turn, could only lead to a gradual estrangement between theory and clinical observations."

Yankelovitch and Barrett point to Erikson's own estrangement from metapsychology, stating that he implicitly depends on a philosophy at odds with the scientific materialism that underlies classical metapsychology, but that he has not himself developed a scientific philosophy explicitly to the point where he can lean on it for support. They add that in departing from metapsychology Erikson on the surface appears to be less faithful than Hartmann to the Freudian heritage because he abandons most of Freud's theoretical machinery. But they say a strong case could be made that, in ignoring metapsychology, Erikson has kept faith with the deepest elements in Freud—the biological thrust of his thought.

Far more than Hartmann, Erikson returns again and again to early sexual origins as the grounds of human development, although he treats these early facts of biological-cultural development in other than a mechanical and reductionist fashion.

V

Object Relations Theory began with the work of Melanie Klein in child analysis (21, 22). The observations she made led her to major reformulations of early ego development. Hanna Segal summarizes Klein's thought as follows (28): "Freud's definition of the ego included the statement that it was the precipitate of abandoned object cathexes; Klein conceptualized this precipitate as introjected objects. The first of such objects described by Freud was the superego. Klein's analysis of early projective and introjective object relationships revealed evidence for fantasies of objects introjected into the ego from earliest infancy, starting with introjection of the ideal and persecutory breasts. To begin with part objects are introjected, like the breast, and later whole objects like mother and father. The earlier the introjection the more fantastic the objects introjected, and the more distorted by what is projected into them. As development proceeds and the reality sense operates more fully, the internal object approximates more closely to real people in the external world.

"With some of these objects, the ego identifies through introjective identification. They become assimilated in the ego and contribute to its growth and characteristics. Others remain as separate internal objects and the ego maintains a relationship to them. The internal objects are also felt to be in relationship with one another; for instance, the internal precursors are experienced as attacking the ideal object as well as the ego. Thus a complex inner world is built up. The structure of the personality is largely determined by the more permanent of the fantasies which the ego has about itself and the objects that it contains."

Melanie Klein's theory is built upon Freud's theory of the instinctual drives. In Klein's view unconscious fantasy is the mental expression of life and death instincts, and therefore, like these, exists from the beginning of life. Instincts, by definition, are object seeking and the experience of an instinct is connected with the fantasy of an object appropriate to the instinct.

Much of the controversy about Klein's theory has to do with her detailed conceptions about infantile fantasies about objects, and their persistence into later childhood and adulthood. Much of her innovation in theory has to do with her conceptions of the paranoid-schizoid position and the depressive position, phases of development which are subdivisions of the oral stage. The paranoid-schizoid position occupies the first three or four months and is characterized by the infant's unawareness of persons, his relationships being to part objects, and by the prevalence of splitting mechanisms and paranoid anxiety. The depressive position, roughly the last half of the first year, is marked by the recognition of the mother as a whole object and is characterized by a relationship to whole objects and by evidence of integration, ambivalence, and depressive anxiety and guilt. Klein chose the term position to emphasize the fact that the phenomena she was describing were not simply a passing stage or phase. This emphasis is similar to Erikson's concept of sequential phases of psychosocial development. Her term implies a specific configuration of object relations, anxieties, and defenses which persist throughout life. The depressive position never fully supersedes the paranoid-schizoid position; the integration achieved is never complete, and defenses against the depressive conflict bring about regression to paranoid-schizoid phenomena so that the individual at all times may oscillate between the two. Klein believes that the way in which object relations are integrated in the depressive position remains the basis of personality structure. What happens in later development is that depressive anxieties are modified and become gradually less severe.

Some paranoid and depressive anxieties always remain active within the personality, but when the ego is sufficiently integrated and has established a relatively secure relationship to reality during the working through of the depressive position, neurotic mechanisms gradually take over from psychotic ones. Thus, in Klein's view, infantile neurosis is a defense against underlying paranoid and depressive anxieties, a way of binding and working them through. As integrative processes initiated in the depressive position continue, anxiety lessens and reparation, sublimation, and creativity largely replace both psychotic and neurotic mechanisms of defense.

Melanie Klein's main concepts relate to the earliest phases of mental life. Much controversy has arisen over her application of Freud's hypothesis of life and death instincts to findings in young infants. There is also disagreement over her postulating primitive mental mechanisms such as splitting and projection in infants similar to mechanisms in psychotic disorders, and about the nature of their persistence into childhood and later life. She postulates an ego which has some rudiments of cohesion and integration from the beginning in contrast to Hartmann's undifferentiated phase. She also postulates the presence of conflict before ego development is much advanced and before the power to integrate mental processes is established at all fully. These hypotheses, as well as her conceptualization of the coexistence of object relations with the classical narcissistic phase of development, continue to be disputed today.

These differences exist not only between Kleinian theory and Ego Psychology. Other Object Relations theorists such as Fairbairn (6) also dispute important aspects of Klein's theory. For example, Fairbairn builds his object relations theory without assuming an innate destructive drive. In his view, structural differentiation in the ego originates under the disturbing impact of experience of bad object relations in reality, in contrast to Klein's view that the good and bad objects are split in order to preserve the good object from the disintegrating impact of a primary destructive instinct.

In Object Relations Theory, as in other schools of psychoanalytic theory, there are thus continuing differences in view between postulates of innate instincts and innate dispositions, and experiential determinants of characteristics of internalized objects. There are differing views of the determinants of structural differentiation of the ego and the relation of these to the nature of actual early object relationships.

VI

In his book, *A New Language for Psychoanalysis* (27), Schafer points out that Freudian psychoanalysts have been steadily, if not always graciously, assimilating what is best in Object Relations Theory, Sullivan and the Culturalists, and the Existential analysts. Assimilation of insights into preoedipal fantasy life and object relations, the constitutive influence of the social environment, and the importance of discovering each person's experiential-representational life themes, make up a large part of current Freudian ego psychology.

In this essay, I hope I have made it clear that I agree with Schafer's statement. I have attempted to elucidate the important common themes, some of the common conceptual problems, and some of the differences in major contributions to psychoanalysis as a developmental theory since Freud. The theories of Sullivan, Erikson, and Object Relations have resulted in scientific growth in the realm of ego psychology, as well as continued controversy, during the period of the development of psychoanalysis in America.

REFERENCES

1. Adler, A., *The Neurotic Constitution.* New York, 1916 (1912).
2. Erikson, E., Ego Development and Historical Change. In *Psychological Issues,* 1 (1), New York: International Universities Press, 1959 (1946).
3. Erikson, E., *Childhood and Society.* New York: Norton, 1950.
4. Erikson, E., The Problem of Ego Identity. *Journal Amer. Psychoanalytic Assoc.,* 1956, 14, 451-474.
5. Erikson, E., The Nature of Clinical Evidence. In: *Insight and Responsibility,* New York: Norton, 1964 (1958).
6. Fairbairn, R., *An Object Relations Theory of Personality.* New York: Basic Books, 1954 (1952).
7. Freud, A., Lectures on Child Analysis. In: *The Writings of Anna Freud,* Vol. I, New York: International Universities Press, 1974 (1927).
8. Freud, A., The Ego and the Mechanisms of Defense. In: *The Writings of Anna Freud,* Vol. II, New York: International Universities Press, 1971 (1936).
9. Freud, S., Papers on Technique. *Standard Edition,* Vol. XII, pp. 89-171, London: Hogarth Press, 1958 (1911-15).
10. Freud, S., On the History of the Psycho-Analytic Movement. *Standard Edition,* Vol. XIV, pp. 7-66, London: Hogarth Press, 1957 (1914).
11. Freud, S. On Narcissism. *Standard Edition,* Vol. XIV, pp. 67-104, London: Hogarth Press, 1957 (1914).
12. Freud, S., Mourning and Melancholia. *Standard Edition,* Vol. XIV, pp. 237-258, London: Hogarth Press, 1957 (1917).
13. Freud, S., Group Psychology and the Analysis of the Ego. *Standard Edition,* Vol. XVIII, pp. 69-144. London: Hogarth Press, 1955 (1921).
14. Freud, S., The Ego and the Id. *Standard Edition,* Vol. XIX, pp. 12-68. London: Hogarth Press, 1961 (1923).
15. Fromm, E., *Escape from Freedom.* New York: Holt, Rinehart & Winston, 1942.
16. Guntrip, H., *Personality Structure and Human Interaction.* New York: International Universities Press, 1961.
17. Hartmann, H., *Ego Psychology and the Problem of Adaptation.* New York: International Universities Press, 1958 (1939).
18. Hartmann, H., *Essays on Ego Psychology.* New York: International Universities Press, 1964.
19. Hartmann, H., Kris, E., Loewenstein, R., Papers on Psychoanalytic Psychology. In: *Psychological Issues* IV (2). New York: International Universities Press, 1964.
20. Horney, K., *The Neurotic Personality of Our Time.* New York: Norton, 1937.
21. Klein, M., *The Psychoanalysis of Children.* London: Hogarth Press, 1949 (1932).
22. Klein, M., *Love, Guilt and Reparation and Other Works.* London: Hogarth Press, 1975 (1921-45).
23. Klein, M., *Envy and Gratitude and Other Works.* London: Hogarth Press, 1975 (1946-63).
24. Klein, M., Heimann, P., Isaacs, S., and Riviere, J., *Developments in Psychoanalysis.* London: Hogarth Press, 1973 (1952).
25. Klein, M., Heimann, P., and Money-Kyrle, R. (Eds.), *New Directions in Psychoanalysis.* New York: Basic Books, 1957.

26. Rapaport, D., Historical Introduction to Identity and the Life Cycle: Selected Papers of Erikson. *Psychological Issues,* 1 (1) , 1959.

27. Schafer, R., *A New Language for Psychoanalysis.* New York: Yale University Press, 1976.

28. Segal, H., *Introduction to the Works of Melanie Klein.* London: Heinemann, 1964.

29. Sullivan, H. S., *The Interpersonal Theory of Psychiatry.* New York: Norton, 1953.

30. Sutherland, J., Object Relations Theory and the Conceptual Model of Psychoanalysis. *Brit. J. Med. Psychol.,* 1963, 36, 109.

31. Winnicott, D. *Through Paediatrics to Psychoanalysis.* New York: Basic Books, 1975 (1931-1956) .

32. Winnicott, D. *The Maturational Processes and the Facilitating Environment.* London: Hogarth Press, 1965 (1957-1964) .

33. Yankelovitch, D., and Barrett, W., *Ego and Instinct.* New York: Random House, 1970.

34. Zetzel, E., Recent British Approaches to Problems of Early Mental Development. *J. Amer. Psychoanal. Assoc.,* 1955, 3, 534-543.

CHAPTER 11

The Future of Psychoanalysis

Earl G. Witenberg, M.D.

PREDICTING THE FUTURE in any area of human experience is hazardous; predicting the future of psychoanalysis is impossible. There are so many factors outside the field that will determine its relative importance, its influence, and its popularity. Issues such as the social significance of individualism, ethnicity, orthodoxy, the rise of health insurance plans, and the importance placed on self-reflection will determine its future position in the culture as much as will any factor in its internal development. And yet, standing on the shoulders of the present we may attempt to see the future.

My comments are limited to what I see for psychoanalysis in the United States. Psychoanalysis has enjoyed a great deal of popularity and popularization. The power of its ideas was particularly evident in the 1950s and 1960s. The ideas permeated the culture. The awesome character of World War II capped by the nuclear explosions terrified many of us and led us to look for a way to deal with these man-made horrors. Religion had lost its appeal. Technology was rampant. And psychoanalysts and psychoanalysis offered a way of understanding. Probably never before has such a small group offered explanations for so many phenomena, from child-rearing to the creative arts, as did the first generation of American psychoanalysts. And their ideas were powerful

Presented March 17, 1977. Earl G. Witenberg is Director, William Alanson White Institute, New York, New York.

enough to influence a whole generation, particularly the intellectuals. The belief in individual freedom and development so popular then was indeed fertile atmosphere for the expansion of the post-World War II years. In addition, the founding of many divisions of clinical psychology as well as post-doctoral programs mandated an intensified interest in psychoanalysis.

In order for psychoanalysis to flourish, certain criteria have to be met, and post-World War II America met these criteria. It was restoring a liberal United States—after the restrictions necessitated by the war effort. There was increased emphasis on individual advancement—for psychoanalysis needs people who believe that they can better themselves by understanding themselves. Also, in America everyone is an immigrant and mobile. Where one belongs is ambiguous and the precise meaning of "having arrived" is unclear. This being in the periphery enhances the attractiveness of analysis. The American obsession with physical health was joined by a notion of "psychological health." Couple with that another of our national obsessions, self-study, and its ubiquitous companion, self-criticism. In addition, we have a middle class for whom self-disclosure, empathy, articulation of feelings are all considered virtues. So how do I see the future? In discussing psychoanalysis and its future, I would like to break the discussion down into three parts—education, theory, and practice.

EDUCATION

Education to become a psychoanalyst is usually done under a tripartite system—classes, supervision, and personal psychoanalysis. Beyond that specification, there is no unanimity of agreement about who is to be trained and the level of entry, that is, what prior training is necessary. In America, one organization has historically stood for organized psychoanalysis—the American Psychoanalytic Association. It has essentially limited the front doors of its institutes to M.D.s, psychiatrists all. The back doors of the institutes have admitted droves of non-M.D.s who have received essentially the same training. As fewer M.D. psychiatrists sought training in institutes of the American, they somehow managed to take in more non-M.D.s. At present, more M.D.s are seeking training than in the past decade.

Outside of the American Psychoanalytic Association, there are numerous institutions and organizations that offer training in psychoanalysis. A few of them are vintage institutions—in existence since the early

1940s. The vast majority have proliferated in the last twenty to twenty-five years. In the city of New York, for example, there are currently three member institutes of the American Psychoanalytic Association—Columbia Psychoanalytic, Downstate, and New York Psychoanalytic. There are four additional institutions whose M.D. graduates are eligible for membership in the American Academy of Psychoanalysis—New York Medical College, the American Institute of Psychoanalysis, the Post-Graduate Center Division of Medical Psychoanalysis, and the William Alanson White Institute. In addition, there are to my knowledge thirteen other institutions in New York City offering training in psychoanalysis. Nationwide, there are twice as many institutions for training in psychoanalysis as there are within the American Psychoanalytic Association and probably three times as many practitioners from these institutes as from the American. It is idle to speculate about whether adequate training is furnished by these institutions, but they do exist and they are flourishing. Many of them have symposia; a number have journals. A reading of their bulletins indicates that for some, all that is required for admission is being a patient.

This raises multiple questions; the one I wish to address now is who should be permitted to be trained as a psychoanalyst, what should the training consist of, and in what kind of institution. The American Psychoanalytic Association and the American Academy of Psychoanalysis have put themselves four-square behind the M.D.-psychiatrist as the source of psychoanalyst practitioners. They have stated, in effect, that they are depending upon the medical schools to furnish the right kind of person to practice psychoanalysis. Is this necessarily true? Will the criteria used for selection for medical school be close enough to those personal qualifications that are necessary for being a resourceful psychoanalyst? Are the personal requirements for a prolonged intimate relationship based on cooperation and collaboration, on the belief that one person can help another—that the human relationship is the strongest force for growth or inhibition of development—are they or will they be compatible with the qualities sought for in medical school applicants? There is, in addition, the factor that in the last thirty years the psychologists, particularly the clinical psychologists, have developed intensive programs with emphasis on psychotherapy.

Under the existing system(s) there is also the fact that, by and large, psychoanalytic training is the training of someone in a technique. Psychoanalysts tend to be by and large technicians. For psychoanalysis to grow as a profession it is going to be necessary to expand the curricula to include such areas as research methodology, biology, the so-called social sciences, and literature. Psychoanalytic institutes should become Institutes of Man or of the Human Sciences. This would be truly an opportunity to develop experts in human behavior and relationships. It would also afford an opportunity to develop a theory which would approach the entire elephant rather than the parts mistaken for the whole as is the situation today.

I would also like to draw a distinction between two kinds of institutes, because this distinction has implications for the future. There are those that are run by societies, which are basically the alumni of the institutes. These are essentially guild operations. The educational activities at the institutes are subject to the stresses and strains within the societies. These institutes are subject to essentially no external controls. They are chartered in the State of New York as membership corporations—much as any professional society is. There is another institute model, of which the William Alanson White Institute is an example. The White Institute is an educational corporation chartered by the State Board of Regents rather than being a membership organization as in the case of the other autonomous institutes. This means there is a lay board of trustees representing the community. The White Institute and the similarly structured Chicago Institute have been less subject than the society institutes to the violent internal explosions so typical of psychoanalysis. A report of the recent intra-institute battle in Los Angeles reveals problems similar to those arising when civil war erupts in a society. By contrast, there have been two occasions in the history of the White Institute when the will of the majority of the Society would have been contrary to the administration, but the Institute, because of its structure, was able to introduce innovations that were forward-looking and have contributed to its continuing vigor. Similarly, the Chicago Institute has taken constructive steps on issues that would probably have caused a break-up in the politics of a society. The beginning there of a program leading to a doctorate in psychoanalysis is an example of what is possible under a structure such as I have outlined. In essence, instead of a medically-based program, there ought to be a unique training for psychoanalysis with the training done by psychoanalytic educators. It also has become increasingly evident that any psychoanalyst must become versed in all psychotherapeutic theories.

The domain of psychoanalysis lies between the purely biological (chemical) and genetic and the purely social-cultural. A psychoanalyst must be aware that the brain and the psyche are not identical. Toward the end of his career, the great neurosurgeon Wilder Penfield realized this. Psychoanalysts cannot be crypto-Pavlovians as some seem to be. The recent work in neuropharmacology and in neurophysiology is of great interest to the analyst, but not determinant. Also, the analyst must be aware that certain entities, schizophrenia for example, have not been proven to be solely organic in nature. Recurrently over the years, the organic basis for psychological illnesses has been hypothecated. Recently the micro-techniques applied to biological systems have become overwhelming both in the rapidity of their development and in the volume of data with which we have been inundated. But at least in our lifetimes I doubt if the soul of man will be found in a molecule. Keeping informed of these matters is essential for the analyst, but at present it has no direct bearing on his work. The institutes integrated into universities and medical schools appear to me to have failed to use the other disciplines to help them and vice versa.

THEORY

It would follow from the above that the future of psychoanalysis rests squarely upon the teaching of many theories. Ignorance thrives in isolation. Unchallenged assumptions become dogma in absence of critical evaluations. Also, the ceaseless repetition of the same theoretical concepts reifies them. In light of this, it is interesting to note that there is what has been called by Wolstein an evolving "American School" of psychoanalysis. This is a school started in the late thirties by ego psychologists, people interested in interpersonal relationships and in cultural perpectives. This "American School of Psychoanalysis" is a heuristic term applied to a group of analysts that undercuts the hard and fast connection Freud had made between metapsychology and the psychology of unconscious experience.

It is represented by Hartmann (5), Kris (7), Lowenstein (10), and Rapaport (12). They all delineated functions of the ego without requiring any inherent connections between such functions and the original function of the id. Fromm-Reichmann (4) may be included because of her emphasis on the theme of experience rather than interpretation as the therapeutic agent in psychoanalytic inquiry. Sullivan (20) may also be included here because of his intensive study of parataxic distortions free of any commitment to libido metaphor or to id metapsychology. Horney (6) and Thompson (22) saw that the problems of women derive from cultural rather than id-biological pressures. All these findings have been refined and expanded in the past twenty-five years by many authors, but more particularly by those connected with the White Institute. Examples are found in the writings of Arieti (1), Chrzanowski (2), Levenson (9), Moulton (11), Schecter (14), Schimel (15), E. Singer (17), J. L. Singer (18), Spiegel (19), Tauber (21), and Wolstein (23). Others could be included.

Recently the philosophy of language has intrigued analysts in an effort to extend and supersede Freud's earlier biological and later sociological models. The linguistics of DeSaussure has been used by Lacan (8), the approach of Ryle by Schafer (13), and that of Chomsky by Edelson (3). These approaches have separated experience from interpretation, but the psyche cannot be reduced to language. The next step is to combine experience with meaning.

All a priori parameters attributed to the psychoanalytic procedure are abstractions. The caveat set forth by Freud about the so-called narcissistic neurosis was destroyed from the 1930s onward by Fromm-Reichmann, Sullivan, and Thompson, among others. They had no need for the id-metaphor or libido. Recently Kohut and Kernberg have joined the ego psychologists, object relationists, and Kleinians (all of whom retain the id-metaphor) to face the therapeutic realities introduced by Fromm-Reichmann, Sullivan, and Thompson. They continue to hold the id perspective inviolate. They still maintain the conservative point of view— the doctor-patient relationship is still considered as the parent-child. Direct deeply personal, spontaneous aspects of the experience of transference, countertransference, and so on are still not openly acknowledged, nor jointly worked out. Biological metapsychology and the psychology of the unconscious experience are still connected in these works. They have introduced the concept of the self which is an interpersonal concept in its formulation and used heavily by the American School.

The works of J. Bruner and Piaget have also introduced into psychoanalytic thinking the stages of cognitive development. This has introduced a new dimension to theory and practice.

So I would predict the future of psychoanalytic theorizing will go in two directions. One is the structural linguistic-cognitive trend. Structuralism in the U.S. is considered under general systems theory. The other is emphasis on the shared two-way experience of processes and patterns appearing within its field of therapy. Theories in psychoanalysis have heuristic value, they express a philosophy about what happens in treatment—they organize data, they serve to keep the analyst anchored so that he can see patterns and not be transformed by the patient; they also serve to facilitate communication with colleagues. They never cured anyone (9).

PRACTICE

But what about practice and its future? Of course, the future probably lies in the hands of the bureaucrats with National Health Insurance somewhere in the wings. Bureaucrats love to measure and standardize procedures, so they obviously must opt for pills and time-limited procedures. And with the renascence in this decade of a preference for a biological approach (after approximately twenty years of humanistic renascence) the practice of psychoanalysis (or the talking therapies, if you will) will diminish for a decade or so until the cycle reasserts itself.

In the interim one might consider certain figures. In a survey of the utilization of governmental insurance programs (finances therefore not being a factor), Sharfstein et al. (16) show that one percent of patients in psychotherapy are seen three or more times weekly. (This may be viewed as seen in psychoanalysis.) The data also indicate that a higher percentage of the users of psychotherapy (37%) come from the District of Columbia than from Ohio (4%) or California (6%). Also that the percentage of those incurring charges over $10,000 was 65% from the District, 4% from Ohio, 6% from California. Four percent of all members were from Ohio (notice that their utilization of psychotherapy and of three or more times per week treatment is the same); identical figures hold for California; 21% of all members come from the District. The District furnished 37% of all the users of the benefit and 65% of those paying over $10,000 in charges. The District has the youngest age group of employees plus the ones with the most education. It also has the most analysts per capita of these areas. Buried in these figures is the number of people in treatment for training purposes. And with all this only 1% of users over all are being seen three or more times weekly. It is difficult to draw implications from this study. But the 1% figure confirms previous studies. Does it mean that only 1% who seek help can use psychoanalysis? Or does it mean that, like the rest of our culture, potential users of psychotherapy are in a hurry and do not want to spend so much of their time on self-reflection?

What about the fewer times a week? Will it interfere with results? There is no time to go into the significance of this factor. But I wish to make one point—it requires greater skill and experience to achieve results on fewer times a week. In order to practice psychotherapy in a meaningful way, it is necessary for the therapist to be as fully trained as possible, including psychoanalytic training.

Time for reflection then may be an issue in determining frequency of sessions. In addition, individualism and autonomy are not such cherished ideals as they once were; horizontal collaborative decision-making is being emphasized now. This introduces a factor influencing the future of practice. Also, the growth in popularity of orthodox religions has to be considered as a negative influence. The rise of ethnicity has to be considered as another trend impacting upon psychoanalytic practice; assimilation into the mainstream is no longer the predominant goal it was. As a result there are subcultures obedient to other authority. There is a concomitant increase in fixed prejudices and stereotypes. Once these are clarified, therapeutic work can be done. But one has to clarify these issues—transcultural issues, if you will. They are not to be treated as resistance; they must be clarified, then issues of tranference can be worked on.

Practice has become more varied than it was. People from different phases of life are in treatment; for example, in the last six months I have seen one 66-year-old academician, one 64-year-old investment banker, and one 56-year-old housewife who are seeking treatment for the first time in their lives. They are working well in analytic therapy. More occupations, more life styles are represented in today's patient population. The ethnic origins have also varied. Among my last ten consultations there were two Orientals, one Irish Roman Catholic, and one East Indian—and none of these was in a profession remotely connected with mental health. The cycle of female patients demanding female therapists also seems to be diminishing. Thus, as the indications for treatment by a psychoanalyst have broadened so has the patient base. I take patients as they come if I have time, and this may account for my experience. But as I discuss this with colleagues—senior, peer, and junior—I find this to be true of their practices as well. I suspect this will be a continuing trend. More self-awareness on the part of the analyst is required for this kind of phenomenon than is usually emphasized in the stereotypes.

Coupling the inroads of inflation with the increased mateiral expectation of professions, no one can promise an analyst the income of, say, psychiatrists or other medical specialists. On the other hand, I know of no analyst who is starving. But for anyone who believes knowledge is better than ignorance, that conscious experience is preferable to unconscious compulsion, I know of no better way to earn a living. I suspect it will continue to exist as a profession.

REFERENCES

1. Arieti, S., *The Intrapsychic Self.* New York: Basic Books, 1967.
2. Chrzanowski, G., Implications of Interpersonal Theory. In: E. Witenberg, Ed., *Interpersonal Explorations in Psychoanalysis.* New York: Basic Books, 1973.
3. Edelson, M., *Language and Interpretation of Psychoanalysis.* New Haven: Yale University Press, 1975.
4. Fromm-Reichmann, F., *Principles of Intensive Psychotherapy.* Chicago: University of Chicago Press, 1950.
5. Hartmann, H.: *The Ego and the Problem of Adaptation.* New York: International Universities Press, 1958 (1939).
6. Horney, K., *The Neurotic Personality of Our Time.* New York: W. W. Norton, 1937.
7. Kris, E., Ego Psychology and Interpretation in Psychoanalytic Therapy. *Psychoanalytic Quarterly,* 1951, 20, 15-30.
8. Lacan, J., *The Language of the Self.* Baltimore: Johns Hopkins University Press, 1968 (1956).
9. Levenson, E., *The Fallacy of Understanding.* New York: Basic Books, 1972.
10. Lowenstein, R., The Problem of Interpretation. *Psychoanalytic Quarterly,* 1951, 20, 1-14.
11. Moulton, R., Women with Double Lives. *Contemporary Psychoanalysis,* 1977, 13, 64-84.
12. Rapaport, D., *The Structure of Psychoanalytic Theory.* New York: International Universities Press, 1959.
13. Schafer, R., *A New Language for Psychoanalysis.* New Haven: Yale University Press, 1976.
14. Schecter, D., On the Emergence of Human Relatedness. In: E. Witenberg, Ed., *Interpersonal Explorations in Psychoanalysis.* New York: Basic Books, 1973.
15. Schimel, J. L., Dilemmas of the Gifted Adolescent. In: E. Witenberg, Ed., *Interpersonal Explorations in Psychoanalysis.* New York: Basic Books, 1973.
16. Sharfstein, S., American Orthopsychiatric Association, New York, 1977.
17. Singer, E., *Key Concepts in Psychotherapy.* New York: Random House, 1965.
18. Singer, J. L., The Use of Imagery in Psychotherapy. In: E. Witenberg, Ed., *Interpersonal Psychoanalysis: New Directions.* New York: Gardner Press, 1978.
19. Spiegel, R., Psychoanalysis—For an Elite? *Contemporary Psychoanalysis,* 1970, 7, 48-63.
20. Sullivan, H., *Conceptions of Modern Psychiatry.* Washington, D. C.: W. A. White Foundation, 1946.
21. Tauber, E., Exploring the Therapeutic Use of Countertransference Data. *Psychiatry,* 1954, 17, 331-336.
22. Thompson, C., *Psychoanalysis.* New York: Hermitage, 1950.
23. Wolstein, B., *Transference.* New York: Grune & Stratton, 1954.

CHAPTER 12

Psychoanalysis and Future Growth

Arnold M. Cooper, M.D. and
Robert Michels, M.D.

THE FUTURE OF PSYCHOANALYSIS is a topic of perennial interest. The numerous articles on the subject over many decades (3, 6, 8, 9, 14, 17, 19, 23, 25, 30, 37, 39, 40, 47, 56 59, 60, 66) are an indication of the complex and, in many ways, ambiguous position which psychoanalysis occupies in the western world. Psychoanalysis is, as Freud indicated many years ago, three different thought related things: a theory of the mind, a method of psychological inquiry, and a form of psychotherapy. Today we add two others; psychoanalysis has become a powerful movement of thought within society, and it is also an organized profession of students and practitioners. The future of psychoanalysis is the future of each of these, and in many respects their futures may be quite different.

Psychoanalysis is now a part of our culture, a way of viewing the world, which has profoundly shaped the kind of people we are. To the degree that this is true, the future of psychoanalysis is no more foreseeable than the future of any other cultural movement; it may flourish or die depending upon political, social, and economic issues that are external to psychoanalysis itself. Even the scientific and technical aspects

Presented March 17, 1977. Arnold M. Cooper is Professor of Psychiatry, Cornell University Medical College, New York, New York. Robert Michels is Barklie McKee Henry Professor of Psychiatry, Cornell University Medical College, New York, New York. This paper is reprinted with permission of the publishers of J. P. Brady and H. K. H. Brodie, Eds., *Controversy in Psychiatry.* Philadelphia: W. B. Saunders Co., 1978.

of psychoanalysis depend upon this cultural background. Psychoanalysis is not value-free and would not survive in a society that did not place a high value on the individual. Psychoanalytic technique, research, and training will all be affected by the view of the individual that emerges from the present period of instability in the relationships of classes, governments, nations, and technologies. Discussion of the future, therefore, is predicated on the relatively unlikely assumption that society will continue unchanged in its essentials, following in an evolutionary way trends which are already visible to us.

In recent years, there have been repeated announcements that psychoanalysis is dead—a curious cultural phenomenon which had its moment, a religious belief which is no longer valued, or a brief aberration of a small group of Victorian Europeans. There are many indications, however, that despite the numerous obituaries the object of concern is still very much alive—studied, taught, practiced. There are even indications that psychoanalysis is entering a new period of growth. More candidates are applying to analytic institutions, new institutes are being formed, and there is an extraordinary burgeoning of theoretical ideas. It may be only now, more than a century after Freud's birth, that psychoanalysis is shifting from a reverence for his words to a true identification with his spirit of free, independent inquiry. The many schisms that characterized the growth of psychoanalysis and lent credence to the idea that the "movement" was more a religion than a science are less apparent now. Psychoanalysis may have required a period of orthodoxy in order to consolidate points of view that otherwise would have suffered from premature dilution. The influx of European refugee psychoanalysts to the United States provided a large and influential group who held strongly that Freud's heritage must be protected from heresy. At present, however, multiple points of view are being brought to bear in psychoanalysis and there is revival within the mainstream of psychoanalysis of ideas which previously were considered "deviant." The thinking of Sullivan, Klein, Adler, Horney, Rado, and others is being reexplored and, when appropriate, integrated into the dominant model of the field.

Thomas Mann (35), in his essay on Freud and the future, said, "The analytic revelation is a revolutionary force. With it a blithe scepticism has come into the world, a mistrust which unmasks all the schemes and subterfuges of our own souls. Once roused and on the alert, it cannot be put to sleep again. It infiltrates life, undermines its raw naivete, takes from it the strain of its own ignorance. . . ." Mann expressed the core of the psychoanalytic point of view as it affects culture. Psychoanalysis will likely remain alive and well as long as it continues to exert the force that Mann described.

PSYCHOANALYTIC THEORY

Psychoanalysis is a living science, and as such its theoretical structure is continually changing and evolving. Freud changed his theories many times, and in view of the present, more relaxed, investigative atmosphere of psychoanalysis, we can look to even greater changes in the future. Theories in psychoanalysis, as in any other discipline, attempt to organize data as well as to facilitate the generation of new data. In the physical sciences, technological advances lead to new experiences and new data that force theoretical change. In psychoanalysis, the impetus for new theory has come from new data generated by experiences with new patient populations (for example, severe character disorders, perversions, and psychoses), from the stimulation of theoretical developments and new findings in related disciplines, from experiments with technical modifications, and from studies of young children.

It would seem at present that the basic postulates of psychoanalytic theory are intact and continue to be productive (50). These include the concepts of dynamic, unconscious mental processes, a hierarchical, structural organization of the mind, the genetic point of view, and some version of psychic determinism. Many of the more special postulates of psychoanalysis, however, such as the economic point of view, libido theory, dual instinct theory, and perhaps even the nuclear role of the oedipus complex are increasingly brought into question. Psychoanalysis, of course, does not stand or fall on the basis of its special postulates, but it does do so on the basis of the basic theoretical propositions mentioned earlier.

While basic psychoanalytic propositions seem intact, there has been a gathering attack on traditional metapsychology, which constitutes one way of thinking about these propositions. The late George Klein (28), Gill (16), Holt (20), and others have expressed a desire to discard the baggage of metapsychology in favor of more phenomenologic, experience-close, descriptive terminology. They want to replace the mechanistic and reductionistic explanatory language of Freud with new modes of formulating analytic propositions. Similar attempts have been made by analytically trained psychologists, such as Schafer (53), by existentialist psychoanalysts, by the interpersonal school, by adaptational anlaysts, and others.

These are very different points of view, but they share a common goal of finding new ways to describe human psychological activity in appropriate human terminology. Where Freud attempted to explain the core of behavior by the nature of the biologically rooted drives and energies which the mind disposes, these other points of view accept the same clinical data, but seek the core of behavior in the meanings which the mind creates and expresses. Paul Ricoeur (51) has described psychoanalysis as a "hermeneutic" science—concerned with the study of meanings. In these terms, the goal of psychoanalytic inquiry is not to understand the nature of the drives, but to understand the nature of symbolic meanings and how the mind constructs them. A corollary of this view is the growing interest of psychoanalytic theorists in the science of language. If psychoanalysis is to be understood not as the study of the maturation of the organism's biological drives but rather as the exploration of symbols and meanings, then its basic science boundaries will be closer to linguistics than to neurobiology (32).

Closely related to these developments is the powerful and persistent attempt to find an appropriate place in psychoanalytic theory for some concept of self or identity. Sullivan (61), Horney (22), Rado (49), Erickson (11), Jacobson (24), Mahler (34), and Kohut (29), are some of the significant names in this movement. While the differences among them are huge, they share the view that the self should be in the center of analytic theory. The self in these views functions as an organizer, a regulator, a unified source of action. Attempts at an adequate definition of self or identity have so far been highly unsatisfactory, and some have criticized the concept as being basically nonanalytic, that is, conscious, global, and not amenable to understanding in terms of dynamic propositions. For example, the laborious efforts of Kohut (29) to construct a self theory congruent with classical drive theory seem an elegantly elaborate, yet basically clumsy, device for avoiding the central theoretical problems raised by the concept of self and its fundamental incompatibility with certain older metapsychological propositions. Despite these problems in theoretical construction, the many researches in narcissism in recent years have provided a great deal of data concerning the nature of self representations, the mode and circumstances of their internalization, and their significant role in self-esteem regulation.

The huge explosion of scientific activity in ethology (18), information theory (46), and child development (33) has had an impact on psychoanalytic theory, particularly through the increasing prominence of developmental and object relations points of view. Psychoanalysts are increasingly sophisticated in conceptualizing about the interaction of environmental and maturational events. Human beings are certainly not as plastic as some culturalists once envisioned, but there is also no question that drive and cognitive organization are far more culture bound than most early psychoanalysts believed only a few decades ago. We will discuss later the important role that these theoretical developments play in the social function of psychoanalysis.

We envision, then, a continuing sophistication of psychoanalytic theory in terms of systems theory and in conceptualizing about the hierarchical structures of wishes, feelings, and meanings. It seems likely that the theory will be increasingly psychological in language, linguistically informed, influenced by information theory, and will draw heavily from its boundaries with psychophysiology and ethology.

The scientific status of psychoanalysis has always seemed insecure. Positivists and philosophers of science such as Nagel (42) and Popper have claimed that science is strictly defined by the degree to which its propositions are subject to direct disproof by experimentation. Psychoanalysis has found it difficult to cast its propositions in such a form. Equally, the traditional role of the natural (and particularly the physical) sciences as the model for all science, with measurement, precision, and quantification as defining characteristics, leaves psychoanalysis handicapped by its conspicuous inability to cast significant propositions in quantifiable form.

However, this view of science is increasingly viewed as outmoded by both biologists, exemplified by George Gaylord Simpson (55), and philosophers, exemplified by Paul Ricoeur (51). Simpson, for example, states that an historical, adaptational, and scientifically teleologic view is essential in the study of living systems.

> "How?" is the typical question in the physical sciences. There it is often the only meaningful or allowable one. . . . But biology can go on from there. Here, "What for?"—the dreadful teleological question—not only is legitimate but also must eventually be asked about every vital phenomenon. In organisms, but not (in the same sense) in any non-living matter, adaptation *does* occur. Heredity and muscle contraction do serve functions that are *useful* to organisms. They are not explained, in this aspect, by such answers to "How?" as that heredity is transmitted by DNA, or that energy is released in the Krebs cycle. . . . Insistence that the study of organisms requires principles additional to those of the physical sciences does not imply

a dualistic or vitalistic view of nature. Life, or the particular manifestation of it that we call mind, is not thereby necessarily considered as nonphysical or nonmaterial. It is just that living things have been affected by upwards of two billion years of historical processes that are in themselves completely material but that do not affect nonliving matter, or at least do not affect it in the same way. Matter that was affected by these processes became, for that reason, living, and matter not so affected remained nonliving. The results of those processes are systems different in kind from any nonliving systems and almost incomparably more complicated. They are not for that reason necessarily any less material or less physical in nature. The point is that *all* known material processes and explanatory principles apply to organisms, while only a limited number of them apply to nonliving systems.

This view of science clearly places psychoanalysis, with its historical and goal oriented bases, at the center of modern scientific methodology. In his Herbert Spencer lecture, Professor Jerome Bruner (5) points out that the failure of academic psychology to come to grips with significant psychological problems was a consequence of its attempt to copy the natural sciences. Bruner pays tribute to Freud's genius in recognizing from the start that the important subject matter of psychology is the ordinary— the behavior of everyday life—and that it was Freud who found the human dramas which lurked behind the everyday. Bruner goes on to state:

> The ordinary, in a word, was to be understood as explicable in terms of its symbolic, coded value; coded values were to be understood in terms of the way in which the world was organized in secret thought below the surface; the response of society and of the self— whether indignation or anxiety or guilt—ought to be understood in terms of the sharing of these codes. Memory, perception, action, motivation were all to be seen as structure-sensitive constituents of this overall operation. The system may have been plainly wrong in content and detail, may indeed (as we know from a decade or two of principally American experimental research to tame it) have been totally unamenable to tests by controlled experiment of the kind representing the older positivism. But surely it represented a modern ideal and, in an abstract way, constituted the kind of explanation that we speak of as structurally systematic. Various writers have pointed out its similarities in this abstract sense to the theoretical programmes of Chomsky, de Saussure, and Piaget—all of them based on the analysis of surface phenomena derived from underlying structures through the interposition of transformation rules—

in Freud's case, dream work and the distortions of ego defense mechanisms were the principal transformations. Perhaps, as intellectual historians, we should take seriously the fact that this type of formulation has had so powerful an impact on common sense, on interpretations of the ordinary. The details of the Freudian drama have by now receded, but the approach in its formal character has become part of the educated common sense.

Professor Bruner has, it seems to us, expressed forcefully the central and continuing scientific validity of Freud's point of view.

PSYCHOANALYTIC TREATMENT

Psychoanalysis began as a treatment for patients with symptomatic neuroses, conducted by encouraging them to discuss their thoughts and feelings. Since that time the treatment has changed, both in regard to the patients for whom it is considered appropriate and by modifications of technique in conducting it (13, 54). The original population of patients with symptomatic neuroses has been expanded to include those with personality or character disorders, sexual disturbances, antisocial and impulse disorders, depression, some psychotic disturbance, psychophysiologic diseases, and children with developmental difficulties (58). There are relatively few categories of psychopathology for which psychopathology for which psychoanalysis has not been suggested, although in recent years there has been some diminution of enthusiasm in its application to schizophrenic disturbances, addictions, psychophysiologic disturbances, and serious impulse disorders. However, this does not mean that the "widening scope" of psychoanalysis has reached its natural horizons. Rather, the growth of psychoanalytic thinking and technique has led to a redefinition of the universe of psychopathology, and an expansion of therapeutic efforts to the treatment of individuals who have no presenting psychiatric symptomatology and whose character structure would not strike the casual, untrained observer as pathologic. These patients enter treatment with vague complaints of unhappiness and dissatisfaction and then reveal their distress and maladaptive personality organization most vividly as the process of treatment unfolds. This expansion of therapeutic effort may well reflect the general tendency in medicine for new methods of treatment to lead to redefinitions of health and illness—optical lenses, orthodontia, treatment for sexual dysfunction, and cosmetic surgery are all examples. In other words, a possible development in the future of psychoanalysis is the treatment of conditions not now considered psychopathologic—prophylactic intervention in children or adults in crisis who are predisposed to develop pathologic responses (those who experienced parental loss or are victims of physical abuse), or individuals with specific traits or characteristics that require special adaptive skills, physical disabilities, learning disorders, unusual family constellations, etc.

The technique, as well as the indications for, psychoanalysis has changed over the years. Freud's original interest in hypnosis rapidly shifted to the use of free association. The early interest in overcoming the patient's resistance to the free associative method was replaced by the recognition that the exploration and understanding of resistance was more important than its eradication. At the same time, analytic interest broadened from its initial focus on the content of unconscious, infantile, sexual fantasies to a simultaneous concern with the defenses and countermotivations arrayed against them (12). Similarly, the themes of the patient's unconscious fantasy life expressed in his relationship with the analyst, the transference, gradually came to be seen as more than a facilitator or obstacle to the psychoanalytic process and are now regarded as the major field of inquiry for exploring the patients' mental life.

Kohut (30) has written about the likely change of psychoanalytic technique from formal correctness towards empathic contact. There has long been a struggle within psychoanalysis between those who view it as a formal procedure with the analyst as a largely neutral figure, and those who view it as one of the healing arts, with the analyst as an empathic healer. Increasingly, as the role of the therapeutic alliance has been understood and expanded, the treatment situation has changed. Balint (4), Khan (27), Winnicott (67), and others emphasize that the analyst is a real figure participating in interactions in which both parties are fully involved. Existential psychoanalysis (38) has emphasized the crucial nature of the encounter as a therapeutic event and, while more "mainstream" analysts have not adopted this point of view, there seems a clear tendency towards an interactive view of the analytic situation and a deemphasis of analytic neutrality. Not everyone welcomes these changes and some feel they represent a loss of rigor in analytic technique. Nonetheless, it seems clear that many "analyses" that are being conducted today are in some way modified, and we believe this trend will continue in the future.

Psychoanalytic treatments may be conducted with lowered frequencies, in combination with medication or behavior therapies, or, at times, sitting up. These modifications or "parameters" have been viewed with suspicion by most psychoanalysts, their use often signifying a misunderstanding or misuse of the core principles of psychoanalytic theory and technique. We believe, however, that they will be handled with increasing skill, which should permit the analysis of transference and resistance and the reconstruction and recovery of past memories to occur. The integration of nonanalytic treatment methods with psychoanalysis, without destroying the essence of the psychoanalytic process, will be a challenge to the skill of analysts in the future.

Everyone agrees that shorter, more efficient forms of treatment are desirable. We do not share the concern of some that the treatment of a phobia with medication that diminishes anxiety and permits action in areas of previous inhibition, even though the reasons for the inhibition have not been understood, is incomplete and unsatisfactory. Functional competence is likely to lead to new adaptive capacities and these may be quite sufficient for the achievement of satisfaction, even without insight. It seems equally clear, however, that the majority of treatments, pharmacological or otherwise, will continue to occur in the context of interpersonal relationships. The management of these relationships, particularly if they are brief, will be more effective if it is based upon knowledge of psychic functionings and the operations of transference—that is, psychoanalytic knowledge. The greater the depth and precision of analytic theory, the better the chance that brief therapies will be conducted with scientific rationale. Psychoanalysis may become to psychotherapy what the study of immunology is to the treatment of infectious disease.

What of the future of psychoanalytic practice? If we make the assumption of relative cultural stability, we see few indications that analytic practice will change substantially. Economic pressures and concerns with just distribution of health care will probably lead to a reduction in the number of patients seen four or five times per week, but surveys have shown that most analysts already devote a significant portion of their time to briefer treatment. However, even if it does not receive wide public support as a routine form of psychiatric treatment, the practice of psychoanalysis will by no means disappear. There will always be a group of people who have failed to benefit sufficiently from other treatment modalities, for whom analysis is the appropriate next attempt or only hope. Some of these individuals will be willing to pay their own way and it seems likely that society will continue to support psychoanalysis along with other "treatments of last resort." Further, the development of self-knowledge and self-potential is a value held dearly by a significant sub-group within the culture. Some of these people will pursue psychoanalysis for the purpose of enhancing self-awareness, even at considerable personal difficulty. Finally, psychoanalysts and other psychotherapists in training, as well as those who wish to use psychoanalytic techniques in other forms of inquiry, will continue to seek personal analysis.

PSYCHOANALYTIC RESEARCH

The psychoanalytic situation is a method of scientific inquiry as well as a technique of psychotherapy. Indeed Freud, and many of his followers, recognizing the social and economic barriers to the widespread clinical application of psychoanalysis as a treatment, believed that its major role was a method for the study of human behavior, a method that could inform other types of therapy and could also lead to knowledge that would have an impact on law, education, morality, child rearing, philosophy, anthropology, aesthetics, and every other field related to an understanding of man.

Shifts in the technique of treatment, discussed above, are at the same time shifts in the method of inquiry, since these are but two facets of the same process. However, there have been shifts in our technique and, even more, in our thinking about technique that have a specific relation to psychoanalysis as a method of inquiry that can be projected into the future.

The original psychoanalytic focus on the patient's unconscious fantasies shifted to a concern with resistances as obstacles to the uncovering of these fantasies and then to the treatment relationship as a field for exploring the patient's mode of structuring his experience in general, and the specific pathologic impact of dominant, unconscious fantasies on that structuring process in particular. This shift has been described as a shift from an id psychology to an ego psychology, and we would add, a further shift from a psychology of ego defense to a psychology of ego adaptation. One consequence of this shift is that psychoanalytic treatment has been employed in many conditions far removed from the symptomatic neuroses stemming from repressed, sexual impulses on which it was first employed. Further, the findings of psychoanalysis have relevance for an even broader range of related fields of knowledge.

The early concern with the unconscious, infantile, sexual fantasies of patients, and then with unconscious fantasies in general, their formal characteristics, and problems of defensive operations stimulated by them has been joined by an exacting scrutiny of the psychoanalytic situation and its various components. Psychoanalysis is increasingly a setting for the study of interpersonal experiences, communication—both verbal and nonverbal—language, metaphor, meaning and interpretation, genetic reconstruction, structure, and other concepts relating to the process of psychoanalysis. Psychoanalysis has from its beginnings been a setting for inquiry into the psychodynamics of human behavior; increasingly this inquiry has recognized the analytic situation itself as paradigmatic for all human interactions (64).

Current patterns of research in psychoanalysis suggest the major outlines of future directions. It is increasingly apparent that one still relatively unpopular area of investigation, outcome research, cannot be delayed indefinitely and that it is methodologically feasible today (21). In the words of a friendly critic (60):

> How is it possible that in a field like modern psychotherapy, which will soon reach its first centennial, questions continue to be raised whether it has any therapeutic utility? How is it possible for controversy to persist on what constitutes a satisfactory outcome, the relative usefulness of one set of techniques over another, the relative importance of the therapist's personality in comparison to the techniques he employs, the selection of suitable patients for a particular form of therapy, the conditions that impede or alternatively potentiate the success of a given form of treatment, the factors responsible for the absence of therapeutic change or the occurrence of deterioration? Questions and doubts are being raised not only by an uninformed public—who might be forgiven for its ignorance—but by experts within the field. . . .
>
> The answer to these questions is that psychotherapy has not done its homework, or in Engel's (10) blunt phrase, psychoanalysts "haven't delivered the goods." But what is it that we have not done? What have we failed to deliver? We must be more specific. Put simply, if psychotherapy of whatever variety is a treatment modality, that is, if it is to ameliorate a problem in living or psychopathology however defined, it is incumbent upon those who advance such claims to specify: 1) the nature of the problem or problems it is supposed to help; 2) the conditions under which it is helpful; 3) the kinds of changes or improvements that may reasonably be expected;

4) the operations necessary to bring about the change; and 5)—perhaps further down the road—the advancement of reasonable theoretical formulations to explain its modus operandi. Each of these requirements entails careful definition of variables, the description of measurement or assessment operations, and the ruling out of alternatives, e.g., the possibility that the observed changes are "spontaneous," that is, due to extraneous factors unrelated to the treatment under investigation. Toward the end of his career, Freud said in cavalier fashion that the problem of therapeutic action in psychoanalysis was well understood, and he added that he was not in need of "statistics" to demonstrate what, to him, were established facts. Many clinicians continue to subscribe to this comforting belief, and any one of us who has practiced psychotherapy has certainly witnessed therapeutic change in a fair number of our patients. However, we have failed to convince the larger scientific community, legislators who hold the purse strings, as well as the general public, of the uniqueness of our contribution or the efficacy of our treatment efforts.

The pressure for psychoanalysis to demonstrate therapeutic efficacy is clearly related to the general concern with cost effectiveness in the delivery of health services, and the desire of psychoanalysts to remain part of the health professions, protecting their personal interests and the viability of their scientific institutions. This type of research will require greater openness on the part of individual practitioners, and this trend towards sharing of information has already begun. However, one must recognize that whatever the results of those outcome studies, they are not conclusive for the future of psychoanalysis. There will always be individuals who want to undertake personal analysis in order to expand self-awareness, even if studies show it not to have significant therapeutic effect.

Apart from investigations concerning the efficacy of psychoanalysis as a treatment, major research will continue to focus on psychological maturation and development and the functioning of the internal psychological world. As psychoanalytic techniques change and improve, there is a continuing supply of new data from the psychoanalytic situation. Much of the recent work on narcissism has stemmed from the study of new patients or the use of new clinical techniques (26). Each time a new method of handling transference or resistance is attempted, there is a potential for new psychological data. However, the mode by which psychoanalytic research is conducted has been changing in recent years. Direct clinical observation, "couch research," while not supplanted, is being increasingly supplemented by other methodologies. The data of direct child observation, extrapolations from ethological data, the nonanalytic study of psychotic and borderline patients, the developmental study of "experiments of nature" such as blind or deaf children, or children separated from parents, studies of cognition, perception, and other autonomous ego functions, the work of Piaget and the genetic epistemologists, psychophysiologic research, as in the study of sleep and dreams, are examples of rich lodes that have contributed to psychoanalsyis (2, 57). Psychoanalytic interviewing techniques applied to groups of special interest—members of minorities, sexual deviants, suicide attemptors, individuals from different cultures, etc.—have also yielded important data not available by other means. While there are theoretical problems in the integration of analytic and nonanalytic sources of data, there is little doubt that these data are valued and probably essential. Developmental researches based upon child observation, for example, have made an essential contribution to our knowledge of the stages of self and object representation (34).

Two other areas of psychoanalytic research deserve mention. The studies of severe character disorders conducted in the past decade, the so-called borderline and narcissistic characters, have led to the early stages of what may be sweeping revisions in analytic theoretical points of view (26, 36). The emphasis on the critical nature of pre-oedipal aspects of development, the evidence for the very early role of psychic mechanisms such as splitting, projection, and projective identification (concepts related to the theories of Melanie Klein) have not only made possible new insights into the psychology and treatment possibilities in these disorders, but have also provided new ways of understanding development. They have focused attention on the theory of self and object relations, and away from drive and economic concepts. We believe that these trends will continue and that as a result analytic theory of the future will be quite different from the metapsychology so familiar to us now.

A second area of research involves the understanding of group behavior. Although this topic was of interest to Freud, later psychoanalysts have lagged in these investigations. More recently, spurred considerably by Wilfred Bion and his effect upon the A. K. Rice Institute as well as by the huge explosion of the group therapy movement, psychoanalysis has begun to take a more serious interest in group process. The fact that human beings behave in ways incompatible with their individual character when they are in groups requires analytic explanation. The need for an understanding of group behavior in hospital milieux, in administrative groups, in group dynamics, in investigative settings, as well as in the now traditional psychotherapy groups increasingly engages psychoanalysts in attempting to understand the nature of transference, resistance, regression, and defense mechanisms under the special conditions of group process. These researches clearly have important implications for social and political life.

The firmer grounding of psychoanalytic theory has led to a new surge of interest in so-called "applied analysis" (1, 31, 41, 45, 48, 52, 62, 63). Art, literature, biography, history, political science, and philosophy are all areas in which the application of psychoanalytic knowledge of the dynamic unconscious and the organization of intrapsychic processes should permit continued discoveries. Although many past analytic studies in these areas have yielded mundane and reductionist results, modern psychoanalytic theory permits more sophisticated efforts. Similarly, our greater knowledge concerning the nature of early psychic development and the genetic point of view provide increased opportunities for applied research into education, child rearing, and cultural anthropology. The expansion of our concepts of the superego invite analytic contributions to the investigation of the relationship of the individual to authority, justice, and punishment, and psychoanalysis may, therefore, be able to make further contributions to ethics and law.

The application of the psychoanalytic point of view into these areas of knowledge has been both applauded and deplored, but it is the nature of psychoanalysis that it should touch upon every aspect of human activity, and interdisciplinary collaboration would seem essential for this work to go forth. Many such efforts have begun at universities and research institutes around the country, and we look forward to an increased yield in the future.

THE PROFESSION OF PSYCHOANALYSIS

The practice of psychoanalysis is organized as a profession; that is, psychoanalysts have formed social institutions that are concerned with sharing and advancing knowledge, defining appropriate clinical practice, developing educational programs, promulgating and maintaining standards, and generally promoting the interests of psychoanalysis and psychoanalysts.

A central, and still unresolved, professional concern of psychoanalysis is its appropriate relation to medicine. Although himself a physician,

Freud felt that psychoanalysis could be learned and practiced by non-physicians, and he argued strenuously for this position. In spite of this, and in spite of the existence of highly regarded non-physician psychoanalysts from its earliest years to the present, psychoanalysis today is predominantly organized as a branch of psychiatry, itself a branch of medicine. The medicalization of psychoanalysis reached its height in the United States in the years following World War II, responding to the prominence of psychoanalytic psychiatrists in American military psychiatry and the impact of their approach on post-World War II American medicine, the popularity of "psychosomatic" approaches, and the influence of Central European psychoanalysts who had come to the United States in large numbers just before and just after the war.

In the last decade, there seems to have been some diminution of the status of psychoanalysis in psychiatry, of psychiatry in medicine, and of the conviction that psychoanalysts must be physicians. The success of modified psychoanalytic approaches in treating the acute psychiatric crises of the military led to high hopes for their application to the more chronic and often more pathologic disturbances of civilian life. These hopes were often disappointed, with a resultant backlash. At the same time new approaches, pharmacologic and social-environmental, became popular and had obvious appeal from a public health point of view. Finally, the growing interest in the distribution of health care and its equitable availability to those in need raised obvious concerns about psychoanalysis as a solution to the psychiatric problems of the nation. During the last few years, there has been a general desire to change the medical profession from one of highly specialized experts to a profession largely composed of primary caretakers. The psychoanalytic psychiatrist, who had made an important impact by arguing that the physician of the fifties should attend to the whole patient, now found that he himself was considered a narrow specialist in contrast to the family practitioner.

The position of psychoanalysis as a specialty of psychiatry, itself a specialty of medicine, has led to a complex relationship between psychoanalysis and its parent disciplines (43, 44). The selection and recruitment of candidates for psychoanalytic training are limited by the criteria for selection of medical students and psychiatric residents, and the pre-analytic curricula of the candidates is determined by medical schools and departments of psychiatry. In recent years, there were approximately 14,000 graduates of American medical schools each year, approximately 1,500 psychiatric residents completing training each year, and approximately 250 candidates graduating training programs approved by the American Psychoanalytic Association each year. (It should be noted that these figures are not strictly comparable. Each represents a portion of a different historical cohort, and the size of medical student classes was steadily increasing in the years in question.)

Psychoanalysis has not only been influenced by medicine and psychiatry; it has also influenced them. Psychoanalysts are prominent in medical education and have served as deans of some of the most prestigious medical schools. They have also been prominent in academic psychiatry, particularly in the planning and conduct of educational programs for medical students and residents. A recent report of the National Institute of Mental Health (7) suggests that residency training programs ranking highest tended to be those with a strong emphasis on dynamic psychiatry.

Like other branches of medicine and psychiatry, psychoanalysis has been concerned with accountability and with the establishment and maintenance of professional standards. Certification in psychoanalysis, which has been discussed by the American Psychoanalytic Association several times over the past fifteen years, has now been approved, and is likely to involve the American Psychoanalytic Association in increasingly close contact with the Academy of Psychoanalysis. The social demand for an agreed-upon definition of psychoanalytic practice and standards would dictate this cooperation. However, collaboration of this type can have unpredictable effects. It is possible that there will be renewed splintering, as some groups try to protect their version of psychoanalysis from contamination. However, it is also possible that there will be collaboration in a freer intellectual atmosphere.

For many years, the only "official" (i.e., approved by the American Psychoanalytic Association) training of non-physician psychoanalytic candidates in the United States has been of scholars in related fields interested in psychoanalysis as a research tool. Recently, a number of groups have attempted to broaden the opportunities for clinical psychoanalytic training for non-physicians. The Chicago Institute for Psychoanalysis in 1974 proposed to the Board on Professional Standards of the American Psychoanalytic Association an experiment in the training of non-physicians for clinical practice. The proposal was defeated, but it engendered a dialogue that seems to be leading to the institutionalization of non-medical training in the official circles of psychoanalysis. Without awaiting this event, however, the burgeoning of "unofficial" analytic institutes in major urban centers, New York in particular, indicates the pressure on the part of many persons for analytic training. "Lay" analysis already exists outside of organized psychoanalysis, and it seems clear that there are irresistible pressures toward an appropriate integration with the "official" profession.

PSYCHOANALYTIC EDUCATION

One can imagine under optimal circumstances an organizational structure for psychoanalytic education vastly different from the present mode of the independent institute—psychoanalysis as a true division of a university. Under such conditions, there would be a number of different kinds of analytic education for people with different backgrounds. The undergraduate college of the university would utilize psychoanalytically trained persons in the interdisciplinary teaching of selected courses in English, history, sociology, psychology, sex, etc. University programs in the humanities, notably at Buffalo and at Columbia, have already made psychoanalysis an integral part of their study programs and significant numbers of persons have begun to pursue analytic study in conjunction with their primary scholarly discipline. Psychoanalysts who are specially trained psychologically would be members of departments of psychology, bringing to bear the concepts of psychoanalysis on ongoing research in social behavior, child development, cognition, learning, perception, etc. The psychoanalytic training institute attached to the university would have strong connections with the medical school and its Department of Psychiatry, as well as with the graduate and undergraduate faculties. This psychoanalytic institute would be responsible for training psychiatrists who would become psychoanalysts, as well as those who would work in branches of psychiatry where the psychodynamic point of view would seem to be essential, including the various psychotherapies, liaison psychiatry, group and family therapy, community psychiatry, etc. The analytic training institute would also reach out to the graduate faculties to train the appropriate researchers from other fields and to bring their points of view to bear in the training of the practicing analyst. The proportion of candidates who would go on to be analytic practitioners would be determined to a considerable degree by social and economic factors beyond the control of the institute. In any event, psychoanalysis would continue to play a vital role in the health of psychiatry and the behavioral sciences, and they in turn would continue to nourish the analytic training institute.

PSYCHOANALYSIS AND SOCIETY

As long as man maintains an interest in understanding his own nature, psychoanalysis will have a future. No other theory or investigative method provides as much depth or richness to our understanding of the mind. No other theory speaks to the special human concerns which psychoanalysis addresses—the logic of and the reasons for both our extraordinary and our ordinary behaviors. Advances in the neurosciences will add new dimensions, refinements, and limiting circumstances to psychoanalytic explanations, but they can never replace understanding in terms of human intention, meaning, and relationship. Human existence will always be experienced in terms of desire, feeling, and personal history—the stuff out of which we create the meaning of our lives—and psychoanalysis is the path to understanding those meanings.

This kind of inquiry is invaluable, not only for individual self-knowledge, but also because knowledge in depth of human behavior is essential for the understanding of ourselves in society. We must know better how to rear our children, punish or rehabilitate criminals, and prepare for uncertain futures. The disappointment engendered by the excessive optimism and naive misuse of psychoanalytic theory in the sphere of social action from the thirties through the fifties should not discourage the continued exploration of psychoanalytic contributions to the solution of social problems. Social engineering is an aspect of every advanced culture, and the more it is informed by an understanding of human experience, the more humanistic its effects. The construction of a new housing development, the recommendation that women join the work force and place their children in nurseries, community plans to combat crime, the increase in leisure time, the greater longevity past retirement age—all of these represent changes in the psycho-social web which have consequences that cannot be fully understood without a psychoanalytic point of view. There is no longer any doubt that man is one of the socially cooperative species, definable only through his social interactions (15). Psychoanalysis has only recently shifted its emphasis from the study of the individual in conflict with society to the study of the individual within society. Societies are increasingly concerned with planning for the proper relation of the individual and the group. Psychoanalysts can make a contribution to such planning, particularly if they recognize the nature of psychoanalytic knowledge and prediction. The subject matter is so complex that conclusions are often suggestive but rarely definitive.

Society will never and should never relinquish to psychoanalysis the task of defining the kind of human being it wishes to foster. Psychoanalysis is not value-free and psychoanalysts should be aware that the human being they favor—loving, questioning, peaceful—may not always be the human being society wishes. Patriotism, group cohesion, self-sacrifice for the good of the state may be higher social goods at some points in history. Psychoanalysis can, however, contribute to an understanding of the expectable behaviors of people who have had differing developmental experiences and who live under conditions of different demand and anticipation. It can help to make a good society better!

REFERENCES

1. Agosta, L., Intersecting languages in psychoanalysis and philosophy. *Int. J. Psychoanal. Psychother.*, 1976, 5, 507-534.

2. Anthony, E. J., Freud, Piaget, and human knowledge: Some comparisons and contrasts. *Ann. of Psychoanal.*, 1976, 4, 253-277.

3. Astley, M. R. C., Psychoanalysis—the future. *J. Am. Psychoanal. Assoc.*, 1974, 22, 83-96.

4. Balint, M., *The Basic Fault: Therapeutic Aspects of Regression.* London: Tavistock, 1968.

5. Bruner, J., Psychology and the image of man. *Times Literary Supplement,* 1976, 1591. (In press, Oxford University Press.)

6. Coriat, I., The future of psychoanalysis. *Psychoanal. Rev.,* 1917, 4, 382-387.

7. Daniells, R. S. et al., Characteristics of psychiatric residency programs and quality of education. *Am. J. Psychiatry: Supplement. American Psychiatric Education: A Review,* 1977, 134, 7-10.

8. Eissler, K. R., *Medical Orthodoxy and the Future of Psychoanalysis.* N. Y.: International Universities Press, 1965.

9. Eissler, K., Irreverent remarks about the present and future of psychoanalysis. *Int. J. Psychoanal.,* 1969, 50, 461-471.

10. Engel, G. L., Some obstacles to the development of research in psychoanalysis. *J. Am. Psychonal. Assoc.,* 1968, 16, 195-204.

11. Erikson, E., *Identity: Youth and Crisis.* New York: W. W. Norton, 1968.

12. Freud, A., *The Ego and the Mechanisms of Defense.* Rev. ed., New York: International Universities Press, 1966.

13. Freud, A., Changes in psychoanalytic practice and experience. *Int. J. Psychoanal.,* 1976, 57, 257-260.

14. Freud, S., The future prospects of psycho-analytic therapy. *The Standard Edition of the Complete Psychological Works of Sigmund Freud,* 1910, 11, 141-151.

15. Gaylin, W., *Caring.* New York: Knopf, 1976.

16. Gill, M., Metapsychology is not psychology. 71-105. In: *Psychology versus Metapsychology (Psychol. Issues,* 9:4 mon. 36), N. Y.: International Universities Press, 1976.

17. Glover, E., The future development of psychoanalysis. In: *On the Early Development of the Mind.* New York: International Universities Press, 1956.

18. Harlow, H., Primary affectional patterns in primates. *Am. J. Orthopsychiatry*, 1960, 30, 676-684.

19. Hildebrand, H. P., Reflexions on the future of psychoanalysis. *Int. Rev. Psychoanal.*, 1976, 3, 323-330.

20. Holt, R., Drive or wish? A reconsideration of the psychoanalytic theory of motivation, 158-197. In: *Psychology versus Metapsychology*. (*Psychol. Issues*, 9:4 mon. 36). New York: International Universities Press, 1976.

21. Holzman, P. S., The future of psychoanalysis and its institutes. *Psychoanal. Q.*, 1976, 45, 250-273.

22. Horney, K., *New Ways in Psychoanalysis*. New York: W. W. Norton, 1939.

23. Horney, K., The future of psychoanalysis. *Am. J. Psychoanal.*, 1946, 6, 66-67.

24. Jacobson, E., *The Self and Object World*. New York: International Universities Press, 1964.

25. Jones, E., The future of psycho-analysis. *Int. J. Psychoanal.*, 1936, 17, 269-277.

26. Kernberg, O., *Borderline Conditions and Pathological Narcissism*. New York: Aronson, 1975.

27. Khan, Masud R., *The Privacy of the Self*. New York: International Universities Press, 1974.

28. Klein, G., Freud's two theories of sexuality, 14-70. In: *Psychology versus Metapsychology*. (*Psychol. Issues*, 9:4. mon. 36), New York: Interantional Universities Press, 1976.

29. Kohut, H., *The Analysis of the Self*. New York: International Universities Press, 1971.

30. Kohut, H., The future of psychoanalysis. *Ann. Psychoanal.*, 1975, 3, 325-340.

31. Kohut, H., The psychoanalyst in the community of scholars. *Ann. Psychoanal.*, 1975, 3, 341-370.

32. Kubie, L., The language tools of psychoanalysis: A search for better tools drawn from better models. *Int. Rev. Psychoanal.*, 1975, 11-24.

33. Lipton, E., Psychoanalytic child development research and the practice of general psychiatry. *Int. J. Psychoanal.*, 1976, 57, 113-124.

34. Mahler, M., Pine, F., and Bergman, A., *The Psychological Birth of the Human Infant*. New York: Basic Books, 1975.

35. Mann, T., Freud and the future. (Lecture in honor of Freud's 80th birthday.) In: Mann, T.: *Freud, Goethe, Wagner*. New York: Knopf, 1937.

36. Masterson, J. F. and Rinsley, D. B., The borderline syndrome: The role of the mother in the genesis and psychic structure of the borderline personality. *Int. J. Psychoanal.*, 1975, 56, 163-177.

37. Marmor, J., The future of psychoanalytic therapy. *Am. J. Psychiatry*, 1973, 130, 1197-1202.

38. May, R., Contributions to existential psychotherapy. In: *Existence: A New Dimension in Psychiatry and Psychology*, ed. by R. May et al. New York: Basic Books, 1958.

39. Miller, I., Reporter: A critical assessment of the future of psychoanlaysis: A view from within. *J. Am. Psychoanal. Assoc.*, 1975, 23, 139-153.

40. Miller, I. (Reporter), A Critical assessment of the future of psychoanalysis: A view from the outside. Panel report. *J. Am. Psychoanal. Assoc.*, 1975, 23, 587-602.

41. Mitscherlich, A., Lorenzer, A., Horn, K., Dahmer, H., Schwanenberg, E., Brede, K., and Berndt, H., On psychoanalysis and sociology. *Int. J. Psychoanal.*, 1970, 51, 33-48.

42. Nagel, E., Methodological issues in psychoanalytic theory. In: *Psychoanalysis Scientific Method and Philosophy*, ed. by S. Hook. New York: New York University Press, 1959.

43. Ornstein, P. H. and Goldberg, A., Psychoanalysis and medicine. 1. Contributions to psychiatry, psychosomatic medicine and medical psychology. *Dis. Nerv. Syst.*, 1973, 34, 143-147.

44. Ornstein, P. H. and Goldberg, A., Psychoanalysis and medicine. 2. Contributions to the psychology of medical practice. *Dis. Nerv. Syst.*, 1973, 34, 277-283.

45. Parin, P., Is psychoanalysis a social science? With discussion by R. LeVine and L. Friedman. *Ann. Psychoanal.*, 1975, 3, 371-393.

46. Peterfreund, E., *Information, Systems and Psychoanalysis. An Evolutionary Biological Approach to Psychoanalytic Theory (Psychol. Issues, 7:1/2.* mon. 25/26), New York: International Universities Press, 1971.

47. Pollock, G. H., What do we face and where can we go? Questions about future directions. *J. Am. Psychoanal. Assoc.*, 1972, 20, 574-590.

48. Prelinger, E., Does psychoanalysis have a future in American psychology? *Psychoanal. Q.*, 1972, 41, 90-103.

49. Rado, S., *The Psychoanalysis of Behavior*, vol. 1. New York: Grune and Stratton, 1956.

50. Rapaport, D., *The Structure of Psychoanalytic Theory. A Systematizing Attempt. (Psychol. Issues, 2:2.* mon. 6), New York: International Universities Press, 1960.

51. Ricoeur, P., *Freud and Philosophy*. New Haven: Yale University Press, 1970.

52. Ross, N., Methodology in the application of psychoanalysis to philosophy. *Am. Imago.*, 1972, 29, 278-291.

53. Schafer, R., *A New Language for Psychoanalysis*. New Haven: Yale University Press, 1976.

54. Shengold, L. and McLaughlin, J. (Reporters), Plenary session on changes in psychoanalytic practice and experience: Theoretical and social implications. *Int. J. Psychoanal.*, 1976, 57, 261-274.

55. Simpson, G., Biology and the nature of science. *Science*, 1963, 139, 81-88.

56. Stekel, W., The future of psychoanalysis. *Psychoanal. Rev.*, 1933, 20, 327-333.

57. Stoller, R., Overview: The impact of new advances in sex research on psychoanalytic theory. *Am. J. Psychiatry*, 1973, 130, 241-251.

58. Stone, L., The widening scope of indications for psychoanalysis. *J. Am. Psychoanal. Assoc.*, 1954, 2, 567-594.

59. Stone, L., Some problems and potentialities of present-day psychoanalysis. *Psychoanal. Q.*, 1975, 44, 331-370.

60. Strupp, H., Some critical comments on the future of psychoanalytic therapy. *Bull. Menninger Clin.*, 1976, 40, 238-254.

61. Sullivan, H., *The Interpersonal Theory of Psychiatry*. New York: W. W. Norton, 1953.

62. Waelder, R., Psychoanalysis, scientific method and philosophy. *J. Am. Psychoanal. Assoc.*, 1962, 10, 617-637.

63. Wallerstein, R. and Smelser, J., Psychoanalysis and sociology: Articulations and applications. *Int. J. Psychoanal.*, 1969, 50, 693-710.

64. Wallerstein, R. and Sampson, H.: Issues in research in the psychoanalytic process. *Int. J. Psychoanal.*, 1971, 52, 11-50.

65. Wallerstein, R., The futures of psychoanalytic education. *J. Am. Psychoanal. Assoc.*, 1972, 20, 591-606.

66. Wallerstein, R., *Psychoanalysis as a Science: Its Present Status and Its Future Tasks*. 198-228. *(Psychol. Issues, 9:4,* mon. 36), New York: International Universities Press, 1976.

67. Winnicott, D. W., *The Maturational Processes and the Facilitating Environment*. New York: International Universities Press, 1965.

Index

211